A PLUME BOOK

THE SECRET PSYCHOLOGY OF HOW WE FALL IN LOVE

PAUL DOBRANSKY, M.D., is a board-certified psychiatrist, a former associate professor of psychiatry at the University of Colorado, a national speaker, and a business consultant. He has appeared on broadcast and cable television numerous times and in a wide variety of print publications, including *USA Today*, *Marie Claire*, *Maxim*, and *First for Women*. This is his first book.

Visit his website: www.DrPaulDobransky.com

The
Secret Psychology
of How We Fall in
Love

∽

Paul Dobransky, M.D.
with L. A. Stamford

A PLUME BOOK

PLUME
Published by Penguin Group
Penguin Group (USA) Inc., 375 Hudson Street, New York, New York 10014, U.S.A. •
Penguin Group (Canada), 90 Eglinton Avenue East, Suite 700, Toronto, Ontario, •
Canada M4P 2Y3 (a division of Pearson Penguin Canada Inc.) • Penguin Books Ltd.,
80 Strand, London WC2R 0RL, England • Penguin Ireland, 25 St. Stephen's Green,
Dublin 2, Ireland (a division of Penguin Books Ltd.) • Penguin Group (Australia),
250 Camberwell Road, Camberwell, Victoria 3124, Australia (a division of Pearson
Australia Group Pty. Ltd.) • Penguin Books India Pvt. Ltd., 11 Community Centre,
Panchsheel Park, • New Delhi – 110 017, India • Penguin Group (NZ), 67 Apollo
Drive, Mairangi Bay, Auckland 1311, New Zealand (a division of Pearson New
Zealand Ltd.) • Penguin Books (South Africa) (Pty.) Ltd., 24 Sturdee Avenue,
Rosebank, Johannesburg 2196, South Africa

Penguin Books Ltd., Registered Offices: 80 Strand, London WC2R 0RL, England

First published by Plume, a member of Penguin Group (USA) Inc.

First Printing, June 2007
10   9   8   7   6   5   4   3   2   1

LIBRARY OF CONGRESS CATALOGING-IN-PUBLICATION DATA

Dobransky, Paul.
    The secret psychology of how we fall in love / Paul Dobransky with L.A. Stamford.
    p. cm.
    ISBN 978-0-452-28818-8
    1.   Mate selection—Psychological aspects. 2.   Man-woman relationships—
Psychological aspects. 3.   Men—Psychology. 4.   Love.   I. Stamford, L. A. II. Title.
    HQ801.D62 2007
    646.7'7—dc22

                                                                    2006034408

Printed in the United States of America
Set in Sabon

Dedication

This is, first, for my sister, Laurie, my only sister, who, through stories of loves won and lost, taught me far more of the real experience of today's single woman than I could teach her back in cutting-edge science.

Especially for you, Angela. And Geraldine, Cheryl, Randi, Janine, Stacy, and all those who have loved me and have been loved, or not loved me but taught me the lessons of a lifetime.

For women everywhere who have the faith and spirit to believe in love at all costs—even when our leaders, spiritual mentors, and very cultures we live in fail to show the way, even as divorce rates climb and "good men" fall from what you'd hoped they'd be. You will find love in spite of the past or what desolate experiences you have had or now have.

And finally, but not least, for men everywhere with no voices but strong hearts. Men who want to give women all they have without losing who they are, who are right now, looking for you, their soul mates, but are silently as lost at times as you.

If only you knew, whether married in the next room or single an ocean away: The one man for you wants to understand you, know you, and be known.

All we ever needed was a common language.

Acknowledgments

Thanks to Peter Miller, my literary manager—a lion of a man, and a man's man—who after ten years of this technology waiting to be given to people, made it possible to help far more than I could ever see alone in an office.

I have been trying to reach them for a very long time.

Thanks to Lou A. Stamford, who with graceful criticism, advice, and, above all, friendship, helped me turn to words on a page, in a brief time, the diagrams that had been in my head for more than a decade. He is the patient, caring chef with words that he is with cuisine.

Thanks to Brett Kelly, my brief but cool editor, and Ali Bothwell Mancini, my new cool editor for the future, who has an easy smile, spreads peace to those around her, and is a hero of equanimity under stress. To Trena Keating—my publisher who is razor sharp, and "gets it" immediately—and to Plume and Penguin for believing in me and the ideas I dearly hope will help many.

To the thousands of scientists of the past century who were not very good marketers, but are what matter most—innovative seekers of the truth in what makes us tick, whose contributions to psychoanalysis, psychodynamics, object relations, ego psychology, self psychology, Jungian psychology, cognitive-behavioral therapy, systems theory, intersubjectivity theory, game theory, positive psychology, and evolutionary psychology form the ground material for the original synthesis and unification theory of psychology I developed, called MindOS™, which is the theoretical basis of this book.

And to my colleagues Art Staats, Marty Seligman, and Dan Goleman, who opened the doors to psychology as more than just the treatment of disease, but, rather, as help in growing our potential as people. That what was recently called "self-help"—devised as only clever slogans at someone's kitchen table—could evolve into a field more appropriately called "self-science." The new ideas of our field have more substance for everyday people, and translate the complex beauty of the mind into simple language we all understand—the definition of elegance. Peter, Lou, Brett, Ali, Trena, Art, Marty, Dan— you are all elegant.

Contents

Introduction

∽

*The future of the world will not be determined by
nations, but rather in the relations between men and
women.* —D. H. LAWRENCE

AMANDA WAS A BEAUTIFUL petite Jewish girl from a suburb of
New York City. An epidemiologist responsible for analyzing dangers
to public safety and educating the masses about disease, she felt
complete and happy in her career. She was funny and wildly intelligent, both in classical education and in art.

Adam was a star salesman at his corporation. Known as the
youngest and most successful at his firm, he worked hard at what he
did. Tall and muscular, with a winning smile, he was physically attractive to the women at the office, and they wanted him even more
for his creative mind. When Amanda met Adam at a gallery opening,
she was quickly smitten with him.

Amanda and Adam truly hit it off and got into a sexual relationship quickly. There was always good emotion when they were together,
either alone or with their many friends and associates. They rapidly
committed to an exclusive relationship. They were best friends bonding over art, literature, and a shared love of urban living—it was perfect. The relationship moved forward at a dizzying pace. Amanda
believed that Adam was her "Mr. Right." After all, even though they
were moving very fast, she could see that he was a lover and friend all
in one.

Then Adam's company offered to transfer him to its office out
west. He quickly jumped at the chance—and stunningly did not ask

Amanda to come along. Their whirlwind romance came crashing to the ground.

⌒

Carl and Cathy were mature people who worked for the same accounting firm. They were attractive physically and liked many of the same outdoor activities in California. When they started dating, everything was great for the first three months. It was a fun time, filled with sexual attraction and mature handling of the stresses that could otherwise kill a relationship.

Things were so good that Carl and Cathy decided to move in together. That's when the problems started. They discovered they couldn't work at this as a team because they were too identical in psychological skill. Both were analytical accountants, so when they searched for a place to live, it had to be of such a perfect fit for the both of them that they couldn't agree to sign the lease.

After looking for six months, Carl and Cathy did agree on a place, but once they moved in, neither could decide how to best decorate it. Everything became a competition. Each approached every disagreement analytically and couldn't find a way to lighten up and reach a common ground.

After nine months, Carl and Cathy broke up. They were mature enough to see that what was fun and exciting for the short term could not possibly last for a lifetime if every major decision led to a conflict. Their personalities were so similar that they couldn't act as a team.

⌒

Penelope was a French national on a temporary visa, working in Chicago for an international entertainment company. She was thirty-one years old, with light blond hair like her Dutch mother and deep blue eyes like her powerful father. She had a sparkling and highly social personality, she developed dozens of friendships in the two short years she had been stationed in the States, and she was a direct descendent of French royalty.

Ted, a surgery resident at a local hospital, was very attractive, ambitious, and intelligent. This much Penelope knew. What she *didn't* know was that when they first met at a jazz club, Ted was more sexually attracted to Rose, Penelope's friend who already had a boyfriend. Penelope had an attractive face, but she was also more than twenty pounds over her ideal weight. Rose, on the other hand, looked like a supermodel.

In spite of his stronger attraction to Rose (or perhaps because Rose was unavailable), Ted started dating Penelope. They became good friends, did many fun things together, and stayed with each other for two years. The sexual spark between them, however, was never terribly strong. When Penelope's visa ran out, they parted and she returned to France. Secretly, Penelope hoped Ted would marry her and allow her to become an American citizen, but he simply let her go.

Do you have a story similar to Amanda's, Cathy's, or Penelope's? Do you have *several* stories similar to theirs? Perhaps you have a different but equally perplexing story (or three or twelve). Perhaps you thought you found Mr. Right and learned the hard way that you were wrong. Perhaps you've settled for a number of Mr. Wrongs in the hopes that one might magically transform from frog to prince through no more than your earnest kiss. Perhaps you've never even come close to finding Mr. Right and aren't sure you'd know who he was if he literally showed up on your doorstep.

There's a reason for this: You've been going about things the wrong way. The good news, however, is that the *right* way—the time-tested, clinically proven, scientifically supported way—is in this book. There is a system for understanding and mastering the world of men, dating, and romance. If you're truly looking for Mr. Right, get ready to find him.

Throughout my professional life, I've been an avid student of character and developed innovative ways of treating identity and personality problems for my clients. One thing that always fascinated me about character was that all men and women are unique individuals, yet they share distinct commonalities with their genders.

An ambitious, hard-driving female lawyer or surgeon can also be feminine. A soft, kind male nurse can also be very masculine.

With this in mind, I looked at the romantic relationships of my patients and found consistent stories about how "the spark died," "something was missing," "we ran out of gas," "we weren't friends anymore," or "he just couldn't commit." These common problems had to relate in some way to what I knew about character.

At the same time, I knew of numerous people who were in happy, durable marriages. When I asked these people their secret, how they knew they had found their perfect partner, I heard the same answer repeatedly: "We just knew."

This frustrated me over the years, because I have always been a systematic thinker. Humans behave in specific ways for specific reasons, and I was intent on finding the reasons for failure and success in sex, dating, and relationships. I spun my wheels on this for years until I encountered a film that critics considered awful and panned brutally.

The 2001 movie *Serendipity* changed my thinking about relationships and sexuality as well as their connection to character and personality. It told the story of a blooming romance between characters played by John Cusack and Kate Beckinsale with perfect timing and pace. In addition, it showed something that no psychiatric text had ever shown me—that some people are *not* meant for us no matter how good the match seems, while others are true soul mates. There were rare junctures between men and women that were possible to notice if only we had our eyes opened—the rare moments when the story of a man's life crosses the story of a woman's life for seconds or minutes, and then is lost again forever—unless we act.

It then struck me that each of the three major parts of the brain (more on this in a bit) has a different role in relationships. A successful relationship has three roles (being lovers, being friends, and being committed partners), and each role has a particular "brain" that guides it to fruition. These three roles are three mysteries that every woman must solve if she is to find her one true love. Three secrets must be discovered—those of sexual, emotional, and intellectual attraction—if a woman is to truly merge her story with Mr. Right's.

All of this—the movie, the "three brains," the observations of both failed and blissful relationships—combined to lead me to a system that would help men and women diagnose and solve dating and relationship issues with precision and perfection. I've spent years working as a symbologist for you, an adventure that has at times left me feeling like Dan Brown's *Da Vinci Code* protagonist Robert Langdon. I have fit together pieces of the grand puzzle of dating and relationships and the image the puzzle creates is not always one that women want to see. It has, however, gotten thousands of women exactly what they really want in a man.

It turned out that every time a woman told me about something wrong with a man, she related one or two things missing in him. He was a good lover and friend, but couldn't commit. He was a nice, friendly, committed man who was very lacking in bed. He was a great lover and loyal partner, but didn't share her interest or didn't provide the comfort of her best friends. A lover alone, a friend alone, or a partner alone was always Mr. Wrong. However, the man who could somehow be all three was exactly what she always wanted. After hearing this hundreds of times, I came to my "aha" moment, and I'm going to share what followed from that moment with you in this book. If you follow my advice carefully, it can prevent you from heading down a path—before you've even savored your first kiss together—that leads to breakup or divorce.

I want you to learn to prevent divorce and eternal singledom before their seeds are planted by using this system to make your eventual relationship completely durable. Most marriages fail within the first five years because this is the maximum length of time you can hold on to a situation that does not have all three of your brains gelling well with those of Mr. Right.

I often tell women to "choose well in the first thirty minutes." When they do, with my system, things rarely go wrong later. Our

Divorce Rate by Length of Marriage (2002)

culture is rife with divorce, and as you will see, the length you are together is a direct marker of how well your three brains click with the three brains of Mr. Right. If you plan ahead, as early as the first date, you won't get into this five-year failure category in the first place.

This system has the ability to revolutionize your life. Before we go any further, though, you need to understand and accept a few things:

- In order for this system to help you, you need to agree that you are willing to avoid making mistakes before you even start. Mr. Wrongs can be very tempting. If you don't think you can avoid that temptation, don't start this program. You need to commit to choosing well in the first thirty minutes, screening out Mr. Wrongs before they get anywhere near you.

- You need to be willing to follow the system in sequential steps. Again, this means avoiding the temptation to jump ahead or do things in a different order.

- You need to be willing to work. Nothing this wonderful and life-changing comes without some work. Think of it this way, though: If you master my system, you'll only need to go through the process once. After that, you can dedicate your life to your future with Mr. Right.

- You need to accept that to get, you have to give. This means speaking *his* language and taking actions that matter to *him*.

- You need to acknowledge that it is only okay to be yourself as long as you are being your *best* self, willing to grow, and willing to see if that growth is toward what he wants, or, if not, toward accepting the end of the budding relationship.

- You need to realize that relationships are voluntary. We don't owe them to each other—ever. Even after we commit, our relationship is a gift, not an agreement to employment or slavery.

- You need to understand that men will always dangle the carrot of commitment in an attempt to get sex, and women will always dangle the carrot of sex in an attempt to get commitment.

At the core of my system is a scientific fact: The human brain has three general parts that essentially work independently of one another. Practically speaking, each of us has not one, but *three* separately functioning "brains" in our head: Every human being has a *reptilian brain* (the brain stem and hypothalamus), a *mammalian brain* (the midbrain and cerebellum), and a *higher brain* (the cortex). The reptilian brain focuses on instincts, the uncontrollable impulses and drives that are responsible for survival. This is the seat of sexual attraction or lust. The mammalian brain focuses on emotional attraction. This is the brain responsible for forming friendships, placing value on ideas and even people, and the exclusive location of what we call love. Unlike sexual, or lust instincts, you *do* control this. The higher brain is responsible for intellectual attraction: communication of ideas and respect of rights, expectations, beliefs, values, goals, and preferences. Most important, it is the center of your Personal Boundary—the home of your rights, your ideas, and your free will to act in the world with a unique identity. Without a strong boundary, it is impossible to have a true commitment or partnership with another person.

The three brains govern every romantic relationship. The secret to successful relationships, however, is satisfying the needs of each brain through *the right stages* and in *the right order*.

The "3-Brain Dating Method"

My system involves a phase (divided into three steps) dedicated to each of the brains: Attraction (reptilian), Bonding in Friendship (mammalian), and Commitment (higher). These are the ABC's of courtship, and you need to move successfully through each phase *in the right order* to have a permanent romance. You don't want a man who is only capable of sex with you. You also don't want a man who is only capable of being your friend. And you never want a man who only commits to you but will never truly desire you or be your best friend in the world. Only a man who can be a lover, friend, *and* lifelong partner is one befitting the title "Mr. Right."

You can find him (and equally importantly reject all of the pretenders) if you take the time to understand each phase and make the commitment to apply them in the right sequence.

If you go through all nine of these steps in order, you are well on your way to capturing Mr. Right:

Phase I: The Attraction Phase (Sexual Attraction).   This is the instinct-based (reptilian) set of moves that captures a man's sexual attraction.

- *Step One:* Displaying beauty.
- *Step Two:* Demonstrating ability to elevate the man's alpha-male status in terms of rank, territory, or power.
- *Step Three:* Creating a contest or competition for the man to win your attention.

Phase II: The Bonding in Friendship Phase (Emotional Attraction).   This is the emotion-based (mammalian) set of moves that captures a man's emotional attraction.

- *Step One:* Demonstrating mastery of anger and converting this into good emotion.
- *Step Two:* Demonstrating mastery of anxiety and converting this into good emotion.
- *Step Three:* Demonstrating teamwork and complementary personality by working on a project together and sharing the process of creating something.

Phase III: The Commitment Phase (Intellectual Attraction). This is the intellectual- and maturity-based (higher brain) set of moves that captures a man's intellectual attraction.

- *Step One:* Demonstrating mastery of the Personal Boundary, communication, and shared beliefs.

- *Step Two:* Demonstrating mastery of achieving joint life goals.
- *Step Three:* Demonstrating mastery of constructive decision-making and deciding officially to commit.

Mastering the nine steps is the biggest job ahead of you. After you do this, though, there is still one more thing to address. Every great relationship has a *story* attached to it. This is the completely individual tale of your romance with Mr. Right, and if you are aware of it, it will guide you, inspire you, and keep you from making terrible mistakes. When couples say they "just knew" that they would be together forever, what they're really saying is that they had a unique story in getting together and staying together, one that came to the same conclusion (a forever relationship), but in their specific way. Every woman must locate a set of story plot points if she is to build her unique romantic drama and follow it to a happy ending. These plot points are the same for every woman ever born who finds love, but the details are decidedly individual, and you can savor them as your very own. This book will teach you how to keep your eyes open for your story and what to do with it once you find it.

The odds are that you picked up this book because you've had a number of relationships fail for reasons you don't entirely understand. Once you absorb the material in this book, you'll never be confused about this again. You'll begin to know within the first few minutes of meeting a man if you have any chance of a satisfying future with him—and you'll get the rejects out of the way quickly.

Most important, though, you'll know how to spot a potential Mr. Right when he comes along, and you'll know what to do to take that relationship as far as you want it to go. Many women I have known say that they are sick and tired of games that men play or are tired of being told by their friends that love is a game they must learn to play. They want to just be heard and understood and yet are just as easily bored by reliable but predictable men who don't play games. It seems that in word, women want a man who can commit, yet in action—in their fiery passions of the heart, in their yearning impulses of the loins—women crave nothing less than a mystery man.

Ideas like this drive both men and women crazy. How can a woman want a man to be mysterious and yet so similar to her that he can know her as well as she knows herself? How can a man want a woman to be desirable, a prize to be won as if love really were a game, and yet be reliable and loyal? You'll find out in this book, and some of the reasons will be surprising. You'll probably feel the same way about the answers to these questions:

- Why doesn't he listen to me?
- Why does he spend less time with me than when we first met?
- Why is there less sex?
- What is our future going to be like if we stay together?
- Why do we fight?
- Why do I feel fear about "us" working out?
- Did I make a mistake in staying with him or in being with him in the first place?
- We seem so different. Is there something wrong with us?
- We're so much alike. Why do I not "feel it" for him?

The answers rest not in a mere tug of the heart or urge in the loins, but in the three brains of Mr. Right and the story you will live together.

Throughout this book, you will find riddles of men's behavior to solve, codes of men's communication to break, and mysteries of men's minds to satisfy every dilemma you have ever had with them. I will be your erstwhile symbologist and guide, showing you, through ancient stories, modern films, and timeless symbols, exactly how to find "the One." You've spent too much time with Mr. Wrong. Mr. Right is waiting for you with open arms, a perfect fit in three roles those others could never fill: the lover, the friend, and the loyal partner.

The
Secret Psychology
of How We Fall in
Love

~⌒~

The Three Brains of Mr. Right

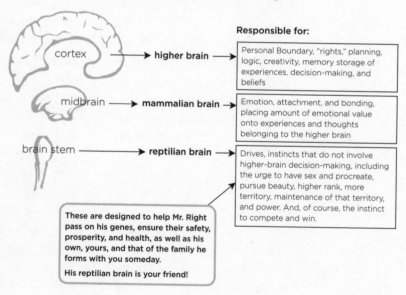

Responsible for:

cortex → **higher brain** →
Personal Boundary, "rights," planning, logic, creativity, memory storage of experiences, decision-making, and beliefs

midbrain → **mammalian brain** →
Emotion, attachment, and bonding, placing amount of emotional value onto experiences and thoughts belonging to the higher brain

brain stem → **reptilian brain** →
Drives, instincts that do not involve higher-brain decision-making, including the urge to have sex and procreate, pursue beauty, higher rank, more territory, maintenance of that territory, and power. And, of course, the instinct to compete and win.

These are designed to help Mr. Right pass on his genes, ensure their safety, prosperity, and health, as well as his own, yours, and that of the family he forms with you someday.

His reptilian brain is your friend!

Chapter One

∽

Connecting with Mr. Right Through His Three Brains

Never trust a husband too far, nor a bachelor too near.
—HELEN ROWLAND

MEN AND WOMEN are equal in value, of course, but different in nature. It almost seems to me at times as if we are two unrelated species. Yet as much as we tend to criticize each other for those differences, deep down we are wildly attracted to each other because of them. Anatomically both men and women have "three brains": a brain stem, which sets our sexual instincts on fire; a midbrain, full of emotional fuel for that fire; and a cerebral cortex, which keeps the others in check, the civilizing force of all things right, proper, and honest—the only part of the brain capable of making a commitment.

What most women don't know is that the reptilian brain, or center of unconscious sexual instincts, is subtly different for men and women even though our other two brains are very similar. Of course, our reptilian brains communicate with and influence our other two brains. At times, it even manages a hostile takeover of the other two brains, though it is usually harnessed and tamed by them. This gives the illusion that the *entire* brain of a man behaves differently from a woman's when it is really only one part of that brain.

Because of the walnut-sized reptilian brain, men and women have profound differences in communicating, learning, and loving. This subtlety of brain function is the source of all the confusion in any gender war. It creates obstacles to our joining each other in love and at the same time the very difference that causes us to be attracted to each other in the first place.

We are all individuals by virtue of our unique choices, personal identity, beliefs, emotional experiences, and the stories of our lives stored in the mammalian and higher brains, even though those upper brains behave similarly between the genders. Men are like men and women are like women in our reptilian brain *instincts*, yet we are different from every other person on earth in the *personality* of those upper two brains.

This is a critical point to acknowledge because it is a key to understanding how to master your romantic life. You will not progress in your quest for Mr. Right unless you accept this fact: To capture us, you need to speak our three different "brain languages" fluently, even while respecting and honoring your own unique identity as a feminine woman.

Let's look a little closer at those three brains.

The *reptilian brain* (brain stem) is responsible for primitive instincts—territoriality and the three F's: food, fighting, and, well . . . sex. The brain stem is all about instincts and impulses that have no logic, though the emotional energy from the mammalian brain can certainly take these instincts for a wild ride. Your higher brain cortex is all about logic and rational decision making. Your reptilian brain is not; it has a mind of its own. This is the reason that sexual attraction to others is not a logical choice; it's an unconscious instinct. Like a reptile, the brain stem is quick, impatient, and not characterized by wisdom other than the biological "wisdom" of survival and procreation of the species. The reptilian brain controls the animal side of us.

The reptilian brains of men and women are programmed differently because of biology. Men want sex in the short term and the long term because they were built with billions of sperm to spread around indiscriminately in an effort to assure the continuance of the species. We men have an adolescent desire to spread the seed in an effort to get the best genes into our offspring, regardless of our higher brain's morality, respect for others, and civility. Women want sex in the short term but *commitment* in the long term because they only have some two hundred to three hundred eggs available for the entirety of their lives, and they lose one every month. Women can't guarantee great genes in their offspring through sheer numbers of mates alone, because they have only those hundreds of chances to choose a man well. Therefore, they unconsciously screen men for the ability to commit and to provide well for their offspring.

This means that from the very start, men and women have different agendas. These agendas are not mutually exclusive, but they need to be addressed, negotiated, and navigated with the help of the higher brains. One thing is certain: If you master your understanding of a man's reptilian brain, you will absolutely master sexual attraction.

The *mammalian brain* (midbrain) is responsible for all things emotional. Here we deal with our reactions to local or personal events that don't specifically have to do with primitive needs such as survival or procreation. The mammalian brain deals with socially important human situations such as friendship, and has the role of assigning emotional value to events, information, and symbols. This brain causes us to value another person as more than just an acquaintance or stranger. Our mammalian brain doesn't "think"—it feels and bonds with another person, making a relationship more durable than a one-night stand (romantic friends rather than just lovers) but less durable than a marriage.

The mammalian brain has an incredibly important role in romantic relationships. Why? Because of the very definition of human friendship. While many men think of people as either "friend" or "not a friend," women have "casual friends," "shopping friends," "dinner friends," "lunch friends," "best friends," "romantic friends," and various additional categories of friends. What unites all friendships is this: They are comprised of consistently shared, mutual positive emotion between two people. This is equally true whether you see a friend daily or infrequently—when you see her or him, the emotion between you makes you feel good most of the time.

Since the mammalian brain is the emotional center of a person, it is entirely responsible for the quality of friendship you have with a man, whether he is a casual acquaintance or Mr. Right himself. Master your mammalian brain and you will master emotional attraction. Master *both* the reptilian brain and the mammalian brain, and you are well on your way to having a romantic friendship full of spark and fire.

The *higher brain* (cerebral cortex) is responsible for logic, creativity, decision making, ethics, identity, and interacting with others with diplomacy and civility. It also activates your Personal Boundary (I will describe this in detail later—it is one of your greatest powers). Your higher brain is your civilizing force and responsible for all structure, organization, rights, laws, customs, stories, and creativity. Unlike the reptilian and mammalian brains, the higher brain *does* think. It allows people to learn and grow together. It is the center of maturity and intellectual attraction, and allows us the ability to commit to one another. The higher brain pulls together the powers of all three brains to allow us to be lovers, friends, and partners with one special person.

The higher brain works with the midbrain to assign emotional value to the information it stores. We know these as beliefs and they form the basis of both your identity and worldview. The mammalian and higher brains work together to create our personalities, which is the very expression of identity that makes every man and woman unique. The reptilian brain does not influence the uniqueness of our conscious personality, only the general unconscious instincts all those in the same gender share, so in a sense all men are the same only in this reptilian part of ourselves. If you believe the notion that all men want is sex, this is true to some degree. That is certainly the agenda of our reptilian brains—and there's nothing for men to be ashamed about regarding this.

Since I'm taking you into a man's world, I'd like to use an anal-

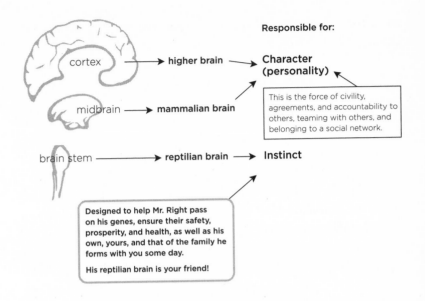

Responsible for:

cortex → **higher brain** → **Character (personality)**

midbrain → **mammalian brain**

> This is the force of civility, agreements, and accountability to others, teaming with others, and belonging to a social network.

brain stem → **reptilian brain** → **Instinct**

> Designed to help Mr. Right pass on his genes, ensure their safety, prosperity, and health, as well as his own, yours, and that of the family he forms with you some day.
>
> His reptilian brain is your friend!

The mammalian and higher brains work together to create personality.

ogy featuring a topic near and dear to men (no, not sex)—cars. Our three brains work like a car's engine designed to propel relationships. The reptilian brain is the spark plug, using the flash of attraction to get the relationship started. The mammalian brain is like the gas tank, storing the emotional energy that fuels these relationships. The higher brain is the engine itself, the container that houses the tools necessary to make a relationship run.

Just as a car won't operate without all three of these components in working order, your relationship won't operate (at least not for very long) unless your engine is in top shape. If your spark plug is faulty, your relationship will lack sexual chemistry. If you run out of gasoline, you won't have the fuel necessary to keep the relationship going. If the engine itself isn't there, the spark and the fuel mean nothing because you don't have anywhere to keep these things and build a life together.

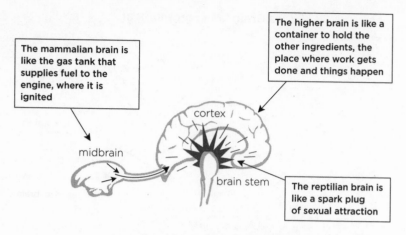

The three brains of Mr. Right work like an
engine designed to run relationships.

How We Communicate with "Crossed Brains"

Communication is a huge issue in any relationship, and communication problems can snuff the life out of a romance. At any given moment, one of our three brains is the most active. The man with only sex on his mind is in his reptilian brain and is not necessarily being a good committed partner at that moment. The man with only anger about a bad day at the office is in his mammalian brain and makes a bad friend during that period. The man who is patient with you, working toward a shared budget with you, or is on bended knee proposing to you is in his higher brain at those times. When we fail to communicate effectively with our romantic partners, it's likely because each of us is using a different part of our brains at the time.

For instance, a woman might be in her higher brain, trying to speak logically to a man's sports-loving, career-competitive, territorial reptilian brain. Alternatively, a woman might be in her mammalian brain, getting emotional and imploring a man to feel the meaning of a passion she has, when the man is living in his higher brain telling her she is utterly illogical. Instead, a woman might be deeply into her rep-

"Cross Brain" Miscommunication

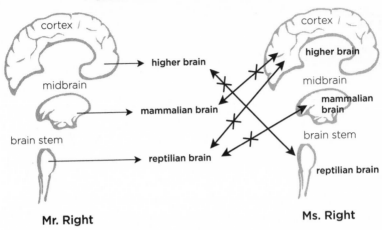

Mr. Right   **Ms. Right**

tilian brain, feeling that she needs to be cuddled, supported, or just heard—while her man sits on the computer doing taxes with his higher brain. Communication in any of these situations would be like trying to teach a frog to speak French—frustrating and more than a little pointless.

Here are some typical relationship one-liners spoken by men and women with "crossed brains":

- Man's reptilian brain instinct speaking to woman's higher brained logic: *"Come on. Why can't we just sleep together? I don't understand why you think it's too early."* Not very effective. Instincts aren't logical.

- Man's higher brain to woman's reptilian brain: *"Your constant need for companionship is totally illogical!"* That's right. Her instincts to seek "connection" to others aren't "logical" either, but they are quite valid and normal.

- Woman's reptilian brain to man's higher brain: *"Why don't you listen? I feel like you're always thinking about work."* Of course. Our ears perk up and listen most often if you talk about sex.

- Woman's higher brain to man's reptilian brain: *"Why is it that men only want one thing?"* Because we have a reptilian brain and it works just fine.

- Man's reptilian brain instincts to woman's mammalian-brained emotion: *"I can't always be there for you when you're afraid—I need my freedom sometimes and for you to stand on your own two feet."* Sometimes we men get a knee-jerk reflex in our reptilian brain that makes us feel threatened for calm, personal territory when you get (rightfully) emotional in your mammalian brain.

- Woman's reptilian brain to man's mammalian brain: *"But I need to cuddle! Why are you so afraid to hug me? You think someone might see us?"* Well, because he is so stressed emotionally that he can't get out of his mammalian brain to join you in the sexual reptilian brain.

- Man's higher brain to woman's mammalian brain: *"Your fears don't make sense—just go get it over with!"* The last thing you need to hear, right? It's because he's thinking in the higher brain rather than feeling in the mammalian brain.

- Woman's higher brain to man's mammalian brain: *"Why do you always have to yell?"* There is no reason why. "Reason" is a higher-brained intellectual thing, and emotions are not logical or "reasonable" at times. He needs to get more into the higher brain to "get" you.

Instead of this confusion, we all need to learn to speak to each other's brains with the same type of brain in ourselves. This way, each part of us is speaking the right language.

You may notice that as you follow along in our journey through the reptilian brain, mammalian brain, and higher brain that these

When the 3 Brains Communicate Well

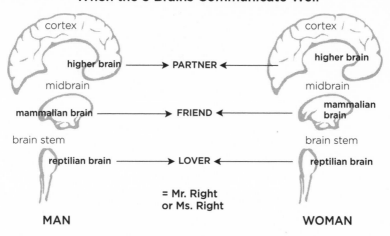

three parts of our mind actually represent the dominant brain skills of different levels of maturity. Each brain communicates to the opposite gender at the level of maturity that fits it.

You might see that adolescents spend most of their time mastering the reptilian brain: learning to understand the instincts of sexuality and lust, connection to others, conflict and competition, territory and belonging, among other instinctual, reptilian-brained skills. Our reptilian brains speak like an adolescent full of sexual and aggressive urges.

Young adults tend to work hard at mastering emotions and teamwork in friendships. They learn to turn their adolescent anger into getting real needs met, and they turn adolescent anxiety into real confidence to face risk, change, and loss in the real world. The mammalian brain that contains emotions, friendship, and teamwork is the perfect one to focus on as they make their way through higher education and into the workforce. Our mammalian brains speak like young adults full of the ups and downs of emotion in life.

Finally, fully mature adults have taken the instinctual adolescent skills of the reptilian brain, combined them with the emotional skills of young adulthood, and found mature ways to channel them into building a life through commitments to others, honesty, good boundaries that respect the rights, emotions, and opinions of others, wise decisions, and the patience to work toward long-term goals. Our higher brains speak like sensible, logical, mature adults. Yet in mature relationships, we bring our whole selves, our whole histories, and our whole lives to the table: the child, teen, and young adult versions of you that are still living within your full mature self.

What Happens If Your Relationship Doesn't Activate All Three Brains?

The three phases of courtship are analogous to the three levels of human maturity. Through these phases, your relationship will either mature at a pace that it can handle, or you will find out the man you are spending your time and energy on is just not capable of getting that far with you. In that case, he's Mr. Wrong.

Knowing about the three brains of Mr. Right gives you a unique advantage as a smart woman. It will let you practically predict the future with a man, based on his character maturity. What if you notice early on that he is all reptilian brain? He only thinks of sex, territory, competition, and power, and can't handle his own emotions well or isn't able to work with other guys as a part of a team. He won't make a very good friend to you at this point, let alone be capable of commitment. Mr. Wrong.

Likewise, what if you notice early on that he is all mammalian brain? He is great at using his emotions, working on a team, and doesn't lose his temper or get overly fearful of change around him. Yet you catch him puffing up his image to you, bragging, breaking his word to others, or even lying to them. In that event, he hasn't reached a full mature adult level with good higher-brained Personal Boundary skill. He won't be able to commit to you or be a good partner. Mr. Wrong.

Finally, he may be able to liven up fun emotions in others (a good friend), keeps his promises, doesn't lie, and has realistic goals that are similar to your own. Nice, but without long ago building skill in adolescence that could now arouse sexual attraction in you, he could be a committed friend, but the sex will soon be stale. Sexual attraction in you (for him) will die. There is something missing about him, and it is a glitch in his adolescence. Mr. Wrong.

The same goes for you, too. If you want an active, bonded, committed relationship, you *absolutely must* appeal to all three brains of Mr. Right. If not, the relationship is destined for failure. The chapters that follow will easily help you sort the Mr. Wrongs out of your life, but it falls upon you to make yourself ready for the one, true Mr. Right when he comes along.

A one-night stand is never the path to finding Mr. Right. Sleep with him in the first few hours of meeting (or even within the first month of dating) and you will end up being only acquaintances that satisfied an impulse. You will not even go on to being friends, and you certainly won't ever achieve true commitment. The reason is that quick sex appeals only to a man's reptilian brain. It short-circuits the patient, positive emotions necessary for him to value you emotionally through bonding with his mammalian brain. Yes, there are exceptions—some people fall into bed quickly and stay married for life—but those exceptions are nearly as rare as lottery winners are. What happens in these exceptional cases is that somehow all of the necessary switches are tripped at the same time. The odds of doing this are decidedly not in your favor.

Even if you do sleep with a man quickly and find a keeper that goes out with you for years, you have paralyzed the potential romantic story you could have lived together—one that requires his climactic and hard-won prize to be sex and yours to be a hard-won commitment. You will have stolen your own plot line and character development from the would-be, romantic bestseller that is your life (more on this later when we talk about stories). You will have denied both of you the whole reason for relationships—a chance to grow slowly through knowing another. You skipped over the middle and end of your own romantic novel to the last page.

On the other hand, if you don't first attract his reptilian brain and jump instead to bonding with his mammalian brain, you will be doomed to being friends who never share a true spark of sexual attraction. Have you ever resented being pegged as "only a friend" by a guy you desperately wanted? This is why it happened.

If the sexual attraction is strong between you but you skip over the connection with the mammalian brain and go right to commitment, you will one day realize that you made good lovers, never became friends, and forged a partnership on a shaky foundation. With few exceptions, this leads to an unhappy end. I don't know of any states that consider lack of friendship as legal grounds for divorce, but it is in fact one of the primary causes.

If you skip both the attraction and friendship phases and go right for pure intellectual commitment via the cortex, you'll have built a partnership (like a law firm) instead of a relationship. You'll have a very cordial arrangement—maybe even for life—but you won't have any of the fire that makes romantic relationships worthwhile. You'll wake up one day and realize that you are stuck with a person whom you are not attracted to, that you never really were, and that you will never even be good friends. This is a very sad scenario.

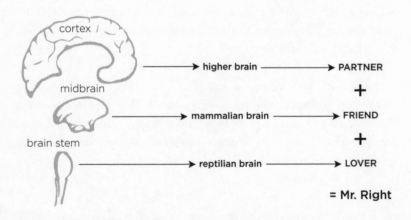

cortex

midbrain

brain stem

higher brain ──────▶ PARTNER

+

mammalian brain ──────▶ FRIEND

+

reptilian brain ──────▶ LOVER

= Mr. Right

Activating the Three Brains Is as Easy as ABC

If you take the time to do it right, however, the results are wonderful. The only way to find Mr. Right and enjoy a lasting love is through becoming lovers who don't give in too soon to the final reward of sex and commitment, then friends who come to value each other emotionally above all others, and then committed partners who join their lives together. The three phases of attraction, bonding, and commitment—in that order—ensure your success. This is the deep anatomy of human courtship, whatever cultural or religious background you come from: the "ABC's" of dating.

Attraction.   Assessing his ability and interest in you as a lover via sexually communicating to his reptilian brain—sexual attraction.

Bonding.   Developing a friendship via emotionally communicating to his mammalian brain—emotional attraction.

The Three Phases of Romance

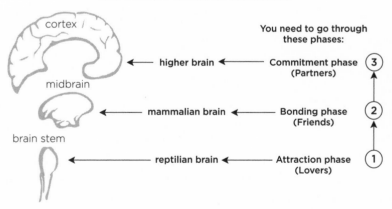

In finding, dating, and marrying Mr. Right, you need
to go through phases 1, 2, and 3 in order, while paying
attention to the other two brains, too.

Commitment.   Forming a partnership via intellectually communicating to his higher brain and its sense of rights, agreements, creativity, discipline, and maturity—intellectual attraction.

Every great romance story follows these same three phases. Think of the romantic comedies you love. Can you track their progression through these phases? If you can't yet, you'll certainly be able to do so by the time you finish this book.

Your Story Leads You to Meet the Right Guy at the Right Time

All human beings have an animal instinct in their reptilian brains. You must appeal to this instinct to attract a mate sexually, and this must happen in the first seconds to hours of meeting that person. First impressions are hugely important with regard to the animal instinct. If you don't appeal to a man in this way immediately, you likely never will. The reason for this is that in a true, lifelong romance, a man and woman will find a wonderful story together.

Myths are stories that speak to all people. Yet of all the thousands of modern stories we discover in novels, films, and by word of mouth, a handful speak to our individual hearts as no others do. Our individual stories of romance must speak to our individual hearts uniquely and privately.

A good story has timing, and regardless of whether you fit the laundry list of traits a particular man wants, your romance is going to fizzle if your timing is off. Have you ever seen a romantic comedy where there was no attraction between the two lead characters? If you were to watch them form a friendship or even dive into a marriage commitment with absolutely no sexual chemistry, you wouldn't buy it. The same is true in real life. The sexual chemistry called attraction in a man's reptilian brain must be stimulated first before anything deeper happens between you. A man can't successfully be a romantic friend and partner before he sees himself as a potential lover.

To move beyond sexual attraction, or lust, into those higher levels of romance we call friendship and committed partnership, one needs to appeal to the personality, that product of the mammalian and higher brains. Yes, you can have attraction and sex by appealing only to a man's brain stem (and several men out there would love more women to think this way). Yet if you aren't already making judgments about his other two brains, you may invest months or years of your life only to wake up next to Mr. Wrong someday.

You can also have friendship and commitment from a man if you connect with the midbrain and the cortex even if the sexual spark is missing. You may make a good-enough marriage for you both, one that makes your mother or your church happy (not you), is cuddly at times, stale at others, but always lacking passion.

You can't have it all, however, without learning to connect with all three brains in concert. This is necessary to create a durable, rich, exciting relationship that is also a story. On a certain level, the relationship is a beautiful story, and the story you share is the beautiful relationship.

The three brain phases of courtship are psychological and sequential, but the amount of time each phase lasts varies within a certain range. In general, the Attraction Phase begins even before hello and lasts up to one month as an initial process. The Bonding in Friendship Phase tends to begin at or just after the first date and tends to develop completely in three months. The Commitment Phase usually begins in small ways around the first month and under the best circumstances can continue for life.

There's some wiggle room here. You and the potential Mr. Right might begin bonding as friends right after you meet and even before your first date, or you may not start bonding until the second date if attraction is still growing and on the upswing. This is fine, and great relationships can come from this.

However, you'll start getting into trouble if your phases with each other jump around wildly—for example, bonding strongly before attraction grows, or going out of order and jumping to commitment before bonding. Likewise, it will be tough to make anything last if the timing of your phases varies too much from the norm.

At this point, you may be wondering, Well, how do "meeting," versus "casual dating," versus "exclusive dating" relate to these courtship stages? How does timing work as far as these "types of dating" go? "Meeting" is when sexual attraction is likely the only thing going on between you. When you start bonding together in friendship, "casual dating" is likely what you are doing, and "exclusive dating" is when the beginning of a commitment has formed. I feel that many women have an intuitive sense of timing in dating—far better than we men do—but you ladies may have never actually drawn it out to analyze. Now you can.

The Way All Women and Men Date

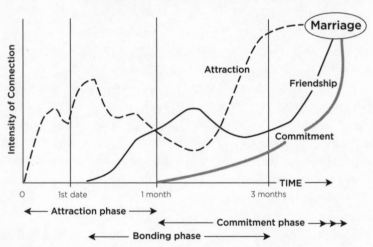

If you take a whole month just to build attraction, you may be already just friends in his brains. If you take a month to get to bonding in friendship, you might have simply been an interesting conquest he was attempting to arrange a one-night stand with. As I said, there's wiggle room here, but you can't go too far outside the norm, or there is a problem in the flow of the story you are creating together. Have you ever seen a romantic film that had scenes that droned on and on and on, to the point where you wanted to fall asleep? What about a romance that had those silly montage clips of the couple going through weeks of romance in two minutes of film? You thought it was contrived, right? Not believable. The same is true of your real-life story.

Choosing the right guy (and moving on from the wrong guy) is crucial to success in your dating and relationships. However, timing is just as critical. Romance is about being with the *right person at the right time*. If you're with the right person at the wrong time, or the wrong person at the right time, things won't work out, either. Understanding this dating method will allow you to choose the right guy for you, avoid wasting time and emotional energy on a relationship that simply can't work, and follow an order and pace of dating that helps that right guy grow with you in a story that only the two of you were ever meant to share. There's only one Mr. Right out there for you, and only one *story* you were meant to share with him. Why spend even a minute with Mr. Wrong? Now that you've begun to understand how the three brains work, that's no longer necessary.

Let's get into the first step of Phase One and closer to finding Mr. Right.

The Attraction Phase

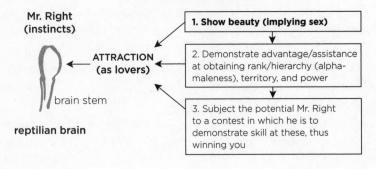

Chapter Two

"Beauty Is in the (Cool) Eye of the Beholder"

Phase I: The Attraction Phase
Step One: Displaying Beauty

The desire of a man for a woman is not directed at her because she is a human being, but because she is a woman. That she is a human being is of no concern to him.
—IMMANUEL KANT

THIS FIRST MOVE in attracting a man takes place in the reptilian brain, because you can't find Mr. Right until you first appeal to his animal instincts. However, you need to master one crucial higher brain skill before we start. If you lack it, it is impossible to grow, change, or deal with the random stresses that come our way in dating and relationships. I call this skill the "Cool Eye," well known to psychoanalysts by the term "observing ego."

Have you ever interacted with a man and some minutes, hours, or days later, slapped yourself on the forehead and said, "What was I thinking? Why did I say that?" (Or "Why *didn't* I say that?") Did you ever regret shouting at a man, disrespecting yourself with a man, or giving in to a man's control, demands, or manipulation? Did you ever wish you had followed your intuition, and then felt sorry months or years later that you didn't? If so, the reason you have regrets, doubts, resentments, and relationship pain is that you failed to use your Cool Eye.

How to Be a "Cool Girl," with a "Cool Eye"

Have you ever wondered what it means to be cool? "Cool" is the exact behavior that the Cool Eye allows. With it, you can stop breakups, divorce, conflict, and loss of sexual spark before they even have a chance to mess with your relationship. If you make the decision to move forward with a potential Mr. Right and avoid all the Mr. Wrongs as soon as you meet them, you will save yourself a lifetime of struggle. Cool girls dispense with Mr. Wrongs quickly in order to get to their one, solitary Mr. Right.

So many women spend so much time just trying to get a man who has Mr. Right potential. Overwhelmingly, they discover—months or years later—that this man wasn't Mr. Right at all. Cool girls don't waste their lives this way. They don't take just any man that comes their way and turn him into a pet project. They start with the guy who is right for them just as he is. Not only does the Cool Eye make a woman cool, but it also works like a sorting device, allowing you to quickly filter out which men are wrong for you. It also helps you to identify what is right for you, so you can act on an opportunity with a man in the right way, at the right time, before the momentary window of opportunity closes.

Imagine that you are at a party. You see a man who is striking to you. He has Brad Pitt looks. He seems charming, intelligent, and diplomatic. He's a sharp dresser, and his watch and grooming reveal that he has means. He could be Mr. Right. You walk near him and turn. He turns toward you and offers you a sidelong glance. He smiles. He says hello.

If your Cool Eye is fully activated, this is what will happen next: You'll imagine stepping outside your own body to *coach your own behavior*, even as you say hello back. As that version of you looks down at you, it instructs you on how you are doing—in real time—while you continue this encounter. Your Cool Eye will speak to you softly about your posture, your facial expression, your choice of words, tone of voice, and the energy you project. It will guide you and nudge you gently without putting undue pressure on you. It will be you, being your own best friend.

Perhaps for a moment, as you talk to the man, the smile drops from your face and then his smile drops as well. You glance away in fear of rejection. He begins looking at the other beautiful women in the vicinity. You lose eye contact and you begin to feel disappointed that you may have lost your window of opportunity—but your Cool Eye snatches it back for you. It tells you, *Hey, don't feel down! You're just not making very good eye contact. Do you see how he is looking away? Did you notice that you are not smiling anymore?*

Because you've taught yourself to make these observations, you can adjust in the moment rather than beat yourself up later for missing your chance. You consciously, purposely, smile again. He unwittingly smiles back completely unaware of the conversation you are having with yourself, because you are still talking to him at the same time. You purposely make better eye contact and even purposely decide to brush your hand on his arm because your Cool Eye tells you it is time to do so. You make even better eye contact. He does the same.

Now he is not looking around at the other women anymore. He is focused only on you. You look deep into his eyes and take a step back from him, because your Cool Eye tells you that it is time to do that as well. Doing so creates a physical vacuum of your presence that he unconsciously feels the need to fill up again. His body needs to pursue you because you have purposely triggered his reptilian brain to keep what was in his male territory just moments before.

He thinks you're cool. He asks for your number.

Why are you cool? Because you used your Cool Eye: the ability to step outside of yourself, coach yourself, and change your approach when it is the right time. The Cool Eye is like a little adviser sitting on your shoulder, watching and commenting as you interact with others. This is a very powerful tool, and it is easy to master once you are aware of it.

The best way to develop this Cool Eye, this skill at stepping outside yourself to look back and comment on your own behavior in the moment, is simply through practice. Keep a diary and meditate, because both of those things are experiences of you looking at you. As you go about your daily activities, ask yourself questions such as, *How am I doing?* and *Is this what I should be doing right now?* It isn't about getting overly analytical. It is about being aware of who you are and what you want to be in life, and checking in on yourself to make sure that you are reaching that goal. The Cool Eye is like the virus-protection program on your computer. It runs *along with* your other programs and keeps them running smoothly. You don't stop what you are doing to use your Cool Eye. You use it while you are getting on with your life.

Another form of practice involves the way you spend time. Our cerebral cortex is divided into the left brain and the right brain. Your left brain is a kind of data-storage device that is orderly, probability- and history-based, and invents the very idea of a past. Your right brain is a kind of data-storage device that is artistic and random, possibility- and future-based, and invents the very idea of a future. Equal use of both of these puts us in the present. All humans spend time in the past, present, or future in our minds, but we are only considered grounded, mindful, or otherwise, cool, when we are *present-minded*.

Have you ever driven to the store the same way you always do and arrived completely unaware of any of the turns you made or landmarks you passed along the way? Where was your mind during the drive? I'd be willing to bet that your mind was either in the past or the future, rather than in the present.

When you live in the past (regretting it or remembering it fondly), or live in the future (dreaming of it or worrying about it), you are effectively on autopilot in your life. You aren't cool. You can't make decisions in the past or future. You can't take actions in the past or future. You can't use your five senses in the past or future. You can only do any of these things in the present. When you are in the present, you are not on autopilot; you are at the steering wheel of your life. You are only in control of the present, and cool people are in control.

Rather than focusing on things out of your control, do something that allows you to *take* control instead—think about where you are *right now.* Hone your skills at taking snapshots of your current situation. How do you look? Why are you going where you're going? Are you prepared for what's happening later in the day? This will allow you to be in control of yourself and attentive to the people around you (especially that possible Mr. Right).

When we call people "cool," what we mean is that they seem to be at the steering wheel of their lives, present-minded, willing to change on a moment's notice if the social situation calls for it, and capable of going for what they want in their lives. They look as though they are politically savvy and gifted at social propriety, as if they were trained at some charm school or expensive prep school. In reality, they might not be any of these things, but they've mastered the use of their Cool Eye.

Throughout this book, you will learn how to use your Cool Eye to make yourself cool, desirable, and the director of your award-winning love story. This skill is vital to the first step you take in the Attraction Phase of getting Mr. Right: displaying beauty.

What You Can Learn from Paris of Troy

As we've observed in the last chapter, myths have been around for thousands of years. These are stories passed down from generation to generation and from culture to culture. They have withstood the test of time and humanity's social evolution for one simple reason: They contain essential truths about what is common to the nature of men and women. These truths are as relevant to us now—especially if we seek out their inner messages—as they were millennia earlier.

I'll share several myths (including some modern ones) with you in this book, because they speak eloquently about what is going on in our three brains. The first I'd like to relate is a story that illustrates the makeup of a man's reptilian brain and identifies the three secret parts that drive his animal instinct.

You might be familiar with the Greek myth of Helen of Troy, the "face that launched a thousand ships." The legend says that Helen was the most beautiful woman in the world and queen to King Agamemnon of Greece. When the Trojan Paris sweeps her off her feet, it leads to an epic and tragic war that claims the life of Paris.

Not many people know the tale of the story before the story, though. It is here where the true secrets lie. In this legend, there were three chief goddesses—Hera, the goddess of the earth (the queen of everything); Athena, the goddess of wisdom and of the hunt (success); and Aphrodite, the goddess of love and sex.

Hera, Athena, and Aphrodite were extremely competitive with one another and each thought her domain was superior to the others'. To settle the argument over who was the best goddess, they decided to hold a test to see which powers and skills in women were the absolute most desirable to men. They found their ideal test subject, a man known to be the most fascinating, handsome, successful, wealthy, and powerful young man in the land—Paris of Troy.

Each goddess went to work on the mind of Paris and offered him the lure of her powers. Hera offered him power over all the earth, and kingly station over all its lands—to make him the most alpha-male of all men on earth—if he agreed that she was the most magnificent goddess. Athena offered Paris the ability to win every battle with total certainty of victory. Aphrodite offered him the hand of Helen, the most beautiful woman known in the world, even though she was the wife of a rival king.

This was quite a challenge for Paris, because the three goddesses knew that three things drive the reptilian brain of a man more than anything else—alpha-male status (rank, power, and territory), winning at competition, and sex-charged beauty. Paris wanted all of these things, but he could choose only one. After long deliberation, he chose the thing that he wanted most. He chose the beauty of Helen. Aphrodite made it possible for him to steal her from Agamemnon, and, well, you know what happened from there.

Again, myths survive the eons because they capture essential truths about our reptilian brains. The truth in this myth is that all men want beauty, status, and competitive success, but they prize feminine

beauty (and the promise of sex that comes with it) above all. Therefore, it makes sense that the first step for all women who want to attract a man is to show their beauty to him. To accomplish this, you
must do your best with your physical looks and use your Cool Eye
to determine whether those looks are just what he craves. If he also
has a Cool Eye, he'll be able to take note of his desire for you. He'll
think, *Wow, she has just the look that gets my motor revved.* Remember that "Beauty is in the (Cool) Eye of the beholder," and a
Cool Girl with a Cool Eye deserves a Cool Guy.

The penalty for not having the skill to display beauty (and, more
important, to know whether he is cool enough to recognize that it is
to his taste) is harsh. It is the loss of years of your time, your energy,
and your money. Let's prevent that from ever happening again.

What You Can Learn from Penelope and Ted

Do you remember the story of Penelope and Ted that I told you at
the beginning of this book? Penelope was the vivacious French national who dated Ted, a surgery resident, for two years before the relationship fizzled out, and Ted let Penelope go back to France without
a fight. They were good together in many ways, but they never had
a real sexual spark. Here's the rest of that story:

As I told you earlier, Ted was much more attracted to Penelope's
friend, the gorgeous Rose. Since Rose was unavailable, and since
Ted liked Penelope, they started dating. They got along great and
they enjoyed doing many of the same things. However, Ted never
felt a strong sexual pull toward Penelope, and this ultimately under-
mined their relationship. Penelope never cultivated the Cool Eye to
notice that whenever she, Ted, and Rose were all together, Ted's eyes
lingered far more on Rose than on herself, regardless of the commitments they had made to each other.

Penelope had an attractive face, but she was also more than
twenty pounds over her ideal weight and tended to be somewhat lax
in her grooming and fashion sense. As a result, while Ted saw her as

a wonderful friend and companion, his animal sexual instinct never revved its motor around her. Friendship alone can never make up for a failed sexual attraction. On an unconscious level, Ted likely realized that without a sexual attraction for her, he could never truly move to the higher level of committing to Penelope for life. When Penelope's visa ran out, he allowed her to move back to France without him.

Penelope did many things right in this relationship, but because she failed to display her highest beauty potential to Ted and read in his gaze that he did not completely approve of her looks, she failed to execute the very first step of the first phase of courtship. As a result, there would be no permanent future for them.

I'm sure many of you feel frustrated and maybe even incensed by the ramifications of this story. You can rail against this all you want, but the reality is that men put a huge premium on beauty. The ages-old myth of Helen of Troy underscores this. It is simply how men are constructed; it's in our DNA. There's nothing we can do about it—we can't help that we have a walnut-sized reptilian brain inside of us—and you can't do anything about it, either. Sexual attraction is not logical. It is not some lofty, ethical part of gentlemanly character (which would be in our cerebral cortex), but rather is only an instinct in our brain stems.

I can't tell you how many women I know who want to be loved for who they are on the inside and never have dates. You can choose to be deluded and lonely, or you can embrace this reality. Remember, to succeed in finding Mr. Right, you need to accomplish all nine steps of this program *in order*. If you want an amazing catch of a man, as handsome, successful, and interesting as Paris of Troy, the first step is fulfilling his innate desire to have his reptilian brain fed by your beauty.

What Is Beauty, Anyway?

I am not suggesting that you need to look like a supermodel or a movie star to ignite a sexual spark in a man. Different men define beauty differently. "Beauty is in the (Cool) Eye of the beholder." Some men like short women. Others prefer tall. Some men go crazy over blondes while others lust for redheads. Different men find attraction in big eyes, long legs, curly hair, full lips, large breasts, *small* breasts, and an infinite combination of these and other traits. As far as men are concerned, there is no one standard for beauty, and few of us really believe we're ever going to come home to Angelina Jolie every night. It's not that we are willing to settle for less than perfection. It's that mature men are truly happy with less than perfection (as long as they believe you are making the most of your beauty). No matter what type you are, a large number of men will find you beautiful if you make an effort to reach your potential for beauty. It is *trying* that counts.

Some men do prefer women who are far above their ideal body weight, but counting on those few diminishes your odds of finding Mr. Right. The story of Ted and Penelope was not to highlight the fact that Penelope was overweight, but rather that the exact kind of beauty Ted's reptilian brain preferred simply did not match the kind of beauty she offered.

Many of her female friends actually found her quite striking in looks. Women confuse one another this way. Another critical thing for you to understand is that men define beauty in women differently from the way women define beauty in women. Women provide one another with the worst kind of disinformation on this topic. While many female friends of yours might tell you all kinds of details about beauty secrets, diets, and clothing—how to look like a waif, your perfect type of manicure, the right combination of protein to carbs in an organic meal, or the right cut in a blouse to suit your body type— men don't care about those details. They really don't.

The vast majority of men don't care if your manicure is French, American, or Lithuanian as long as your nails are clean and generally suit your hands. They don't care if you eat carrots, hamburgers, or wheatgrass as long as you look like you're in reasonably good shape. They don't care about how your clothes are tailored or how fashionable they are as long as you appear neat and well put to-gether. Men might know about and have opinions about all of these things, but when it comes to attraction, intellect has nothing to do with it. It's all about instinct.

The evolutionary psychologists teach us that the root of sexual attraction is reproductive heartiness. This means that men uncon-sciously find themselves attracted to women who offer the best chance of perpetuating their genes. I'm not suggesting that men understand this at an intellectual level. In fact, most men are not thinking about fatherhood at all when they see a beautiful woman. Remember, though, that the reptilian brain is all about instincts such as survival and reproduction. That means that the following things spark their sexual instincts:

- That your body creates a sexually appealing ratio of your chest to your waist and hips. Scientists have discovered that the waist-to-hip ratio (WHR) is a significant factor in judging female attractiveness. Men, regardless of their culture, invari-ably rate women with a 0.7 WHR (waist circumference that is 70 percent of the hip circumference) as more attractive. Such diverse beauty icons as Marilyn Monroe, Sophia Loren, Natalie Portman, and the Venus de Milo all have ratios around 0.7. The ratio signals fertility—as they age, women's waists thicken as their fertility declines.

- Envisioning you naked, most men would prefer that you exer-cise in a way that reduces cellulite, shows your skin to be clean and smooth, and if possible, demonstrates some muscle tone. The Body Mass Index (BMI) is another important universal determinant to the perception of beauty. The BMI refers to the proportion of the body mass to the body structure. The slim ideal does not consider an emaciated body as attractive (regardless of what your female friends might say), just as the full-rounded ideal does not celebrate the overweight or the obese. You say you hate to go to the gym or just can't find the time to work out? Get over it.

- Recent studies show that men find symmetrical faces (the same proportions on the right side as on the left) to be the most beautiful. Look at a photo of Charlize Theron or Halle Berry, and you will see nearly perfect symmetry between the right and left sides of their faces when you hold a mirror up to the midline. Facial symmetry is a universal determinant of health, so beauty is a signal to a man of the quality of your genes, which will contribute to the health of his offspring. Few people are blessed with such symmetry, but a hairstyle can create the illusion of symmetry. Makeup can help as well, and a good stylist will show you how to use both to greatest effect.

- Another feature is the degree of skin complexion on the spectrum of dark to light. People in Western cultures in the twentieth and twenty-first centuries consider tanned skin highly attractive. A theory for why this is so is that sometime during the twentieth century it became possible for those with greater incomes to travel around the world. Many of these people would travel to the French Riviera and, upon returning, have a nice tan. Thus, the tan became a symbol of status. Status in men suggests wealth, and wealth in men suggests all the resources a successful offspring could need. Tanning in women also gives skin a glow, which we find more appealing than a pasty (rather than pale) or rough complexion. In women, darker skin suggests healthy sun exposure, and sun exposure (in moderation and not from use of tanning booths) suggests better health and survival of offspring due to the need of sunlight to help in vitamin metabolism.

- Using your beauty in certain postures and physicality signals the man's reptilian brain that it is safe, and even desirable, to approach you.

- Exposing your neck, hands, and/or the undersides of your arms signals openness to sexual attraction. So does an upward gaze at him (as opposed to looking down at the ground).

- Doing something with your hair indicates that you are comfortable enough to "groom" yourself in his presence, something that animals do only when they are trusting of and intimate with those around them, or when they themselves are more powerful than any other in the community.

- Gaze at a man of interest for a time just barely more than what you might do to a stranger or acquaintance. This indicates comfort, an assumption that intimacy has already been established, or that you are open to it, and offers something out of the ordinary for him to pay attention to.

- A relaxed jaw and a slightly open mouth indicate comfort with his approach and security in your own sexuality.

Taking the First Step: Using Your Beauty

The first step in attracting a man involves making yourself regularly visible in a condition of heightened beauty. Again, I'm not talking about setting unrealistic goals for yourself; I'm talking about striving to achieve your greatest potential, keeping the above male sexual-instinctual guidelines in mind. If you do your best with what you've got, and learn the ways of screening out Mr. Wrongs that I teach you in the chapters to come, you will naturally filter out all the men who will not be matched to what you have to offer.

Wear attire that accentuates your body, or wear clothing that allows you to reveal something while leaving the imagination to work at filling in the rest of the picture. This is a very powerful technique; men's imaginations do remarkable things to their sexuality. Many men will go for a librarian type over a swimsuit model. It's all in the general presentation that accentuates your best qualities.

Don't be seen hunched down in poor posture. Display your hair, your face, your chest, and your behind proudly. Men find slouching seriously unattractive in women.

We've covered your eyes, hair, body, and the garments that adorn it. Two other deep, core tactics will take your sexual attractiveness to new levels.

The "Bad Boy" and the "Femme Fatale"

Many men find the woman who displays the physical behavior and body movement of a "femme fatale" beautiful, even if she does not have classical beauty by genetic good luck. Many women find "bad boys" mysterious and therefore sexually attractive for that same reason, often ignoring hints that these are men of poor character.

Men don't pay attention to things that don't change, move, or shift. However, they will pay attention to a change in their environment. These changes trigger an alarm that relates to his reptilian brain's desire to maintain territory. When he finds that a beauty rather than a threat is passing through his turf, the contrast will make you even more desirable. This is an important beauty tactic for you to remember, and an exceptionally powerful one, since there are two kinds of arousal in us all—danger arousal and sexual arousal. Any kind of arousal is an instinctual call to action.

The reptilian brain in men, even with all its masculine features that make it different in behavior from your own, has the same reptilian-brained goals for your welfare: survival and reproduction. Arousal of either kind in men and women triggers us to take action before our cerebral cortex even knows what is going on.

When you move or dress in a way that sets you apart from the crowd in terms of beauty, it triggers sexual arousal, which of course assists his *reproduction*. Yet if you were to suddenly appear in his close personal space, or alternatively have a mysterious danger about you—the femme fatale allure depicted in films like *Fatal Attraction* and in literature like *Vanity Fair*—you trigger danger arousal in him. This of course also assists his *survival* by preparing him to fight danger or run from it.

The unwitting man at first may notice that he is only generally aroused, until he figures out which type it is. Since you do not intend to kill him, you have his sudden attention, and, therefore, his "arousal."

Sexual attraction and perceived danger go hand in hand, because they both are the core survival and reproductive triggers of arousal. Show a sharp edge to your personality at times. After getting his attention with your beauty, let your sudden movement (as if about to leave his vicinity) be reminiscent of a cruel mother about to abandon her baby boy (the worst primitive fear and danger a male could imagine). You can surprise or shock a man to danger arousal then let him relax into sexual arousal when he realizes that you are no threat at all. You will not leave, but rather stay at his side. Arousal is just arousal to many an unsuspecting man. Pair your beauty with what is only *perceived* danger about you, and you'll find yourself doubly attracting Mr. Right.

With the scenario flipped to one in which the man has an air of danger about him, you'll find yourself sexually attracted to him in just as instinctual a way. This is the very source of all you know about bad boys and their particular seductiveness to many an unwitting woman. Yet as we will see in later chapters, bad boys are just that: boys who are bad, who have a sexual allure in a well-developed reptilian brain but lack the sophisticated and gentlemanly maturity of the higher brain. Cool girls are onto this facet of men's seductive ways, and they steer clear of the bad boys in favor of mature men who have only an inner edge of bad-boy nature under their genuine and genteel exterior.

Smile, and the World of Mr. Right Smiles with You

There is one super-secret power of beauty that all women have, regardless of their body type, height, hair, or skin condition. This power is the smile. Smiling dramatically increases your physical beauty to us. It naturally produces more symmetry in your face than relaxation of the muscles would otherwise do. Research indicates that in the first four years of their lives together, couples with lasting romances smile at each other *five times* more than those who will fail, so an early smile telegraphs behaviors that work in long-term, committed relationships.

Of course, if you're going to use your smile, you need to mean it when you use it. Studies of smiling behavior show two kinds of smile. The Duchenne smile is a genuine smile that indicates full honest joy, attraction, and interest, with all the muscles of the face and eyes participating, including the forehead. By contrast, the Pan-American smile, worn by stressed flight attendants just being courteous, shows only an artificial smile in the lower face and lips, without involvement of the rest of the face, eyes, and forehead. The latter sends the wrong message and generates no sexual interest in men.

Smiling works on a man's other two brains at the same time as it appeals to his reptilian brain. A smile is an indication of internal self-esteem, which I will show later to be a direct measure of happiness (an absolute requirement of Mr. Right's mammalian brain). No friendship lasts without some measure of durable happiness, and so your smile is the first unconscious hint to a man that moving to the bonding of Phase II is worthwhile. Meanwhile, a smile worn frequently, regardless of troubles in the environment, reveals a property of the higher brain known as strength in the Personal Boundary. Since both yours and Mr. Right's higher brains control your ability at Personal Boundaries and, ultimately, commitment, then by smiling frequently you are months ahead of the game, sending signals that you are strong enough to both tolerate and honor a commitment back to him.

Your Action Plan

You're ready to put Step One into action. Follow these guidelines and you will bring out all of your potential beauty:

- Stay in good shape. Eat well and make a commitment to exercise.

- Dress in a way that accentuates your waist-to-hip ratio, creates facial symmetry, and (most important) makes you feel comfortable and confident.

- Use makeup, and style your hair in a way that maximizes what you see in the mirror as symmetry. Hold a mirror up to your nose and see if each side of your face looks similar to the other. If it doesn't, consider adjusting your makeup or hair to create balance.

- Consider ways in which you can make yourself appear or behave as a bit of a danger to him, a bit of a femme fatale, yet in a way that still fits your particular personality.

- Be cool enough to spot a mature gentleman with an attractive edge from a real bad boy or truly dangerous man (more on this later), and choose the former.

- When you spot a potential candidate, walk into his gaze and turn briefly to meet his eyes. Maintain the gaze a little too long, relax your jaw, open your mouth ever so slightly, consider brief hair play, and tilt your head, exposing the neck. Smile briefly and genuinely, sending good energy to him in your eyes, then turn and walk on to some purposeful task, like getting a drink or greeting a friend. Notice whether he sees you and smiles back first. If so, you will have just created a moment, an intersection of your life story with his. It is now his job to pursue. If he doesn't, it may be that he does not have the mature masculine traits you will need in a Mr. Right, he may not find your looks to his perfect liking, or the timing may be wrong. Don't stress over this. Just go to another man in the vicinity who captures your imagination. Remember, there are 3.25 billion men in the world. Be a cool girl and move on.

Your Cool Eye makes all of these techniques stronger. It serves as your monitor, reminding you to stand upright, smile, make sure your outfit is straight and that your hair is where you want it to be. It will even let you know if you've been standing still too long and that it is time to move closer to, further away from, or completely out of the view of the man in question. If you keep your Cool Eye sharp and if you embrace the tools provided in Step One, you'll find quality men attracted to you with stunning regularity.

You'll know men are not attracted to you when they don't look at you, don't ask you out on dates, don't show body language that hints that they want physical contact with you, don't call you, page you, text you, e-mail you, or otherwise make suggestions that you continue the courtship process.

Following Your Story

As I mentioned earlier, there is an additional component to relationships that goes beyond the nine steps in this book. That component is the sense of story that sweeps you up with Mr. Right. Your life is a story. His life is a story. Your shared romance is going to be, I hope, the greatest story you have ever heard. This system of courtship is universal. It applies to all people ever born who have sought an exclusive love for a lifetime. Yet, your own story and that shared with Mr. Right are the very thing that give you uniqueness, that make you one in a million to him, and him one in a million to you.

The story of our lives and loves grows organically with our maturity level. This story guides you with signs and clues that trigger your intuition at every turn. Your Cool Eye gives you the ability to read your own story, to notice the clues and signs that come our way serendipitously. It is in these plot points, these shared moments with men, that we actually have the opportunity to shape our own destinies. Without your Cool Eye, you miss the clues and signs of your story's destiny calling you. You miss the shared moment and its opportunity for an entirely new direction of your story. You miss the countless potential Mr. Rights whom you let slip through your hands every day.

As we go along then, I'd like to share someone's story to show how the plot point in question affected it. In this case, we'll go back to Penelope. Penelope did not use her Cool Eye on this very first step of her story. She didn't identify that Ted lacked a serious level of attraction to her beauty from their very first shared moment.

The good news is that she learned from her experience. She activated her Cool Eye and learned to extricate herself from dating situations quickly if she felt a lack of attraction from Mr. Wrong. She also began to do her best with the striking beauty she already had, losing weight, changing her hair to suit her face better, and continuing to smile as brightly as she always had before the unfortunate situation with Ted. Soon she had a vast array of men who passed this first step with her. One was a man in her own country of France. Pierre was a businessman like her father, only more successful. He was tall and handsome and, more important, his story was far more right for her in every way than Ted's was—from his culture, to his manners, devotion, and mutual goals that perfectly fit her own. He was Mr. Right, and a year after marrying Pierre (three years after Ted), Penelope had a beautiful baby girl. That girl was the physical manifestation of two stories joined in perfect serendipity.

Obviously physical attraction is only the beginning of the process, but it must come first if you are to find Mr. Right. With a sense of story watched carefully by your Cool Eye, you're ready to move on to Step Two of Phase I. You may not look exactly like Helen of Troy, but empowered with the secret knowledge of the Greek goddesses, you will have a leg up on every woman who does not have what my system provides. In the end, you will *be* Helen of Troy to your own perfect Mr. Right. He will see you as your best possible self.

Just ask Penelope.

Chapter Three

Stand by Your Man

Phase I: The Attraction Phase
Step Two: Demonstrating Your Ability
to Raise His Alpha-Male Status

The most beautiful experience we can have is the mysterious—the fundamental emotion which stands at the cradle of true art and true science.
—ALBERT EINSTEIN

I CAN'T TELL YOU how many beautiful women come to me complaining that they actually can't get any dates. More often than not, it is because the vibe they give off is one that shows they are passive at best and unapproachable at worst. Of course, this is not to say that courtship is only about your moves. Mr. Right has an equal responsibility to keep things moving along between you. Now that you have displayed beauty, it is his turn to win you over through his own Step One of courtship. It is time to learn about the stage in the lives of men and women that sets the precedent for all future relationships with the opposite sex: the Oedipal period of around ages three to five.

In the Greek myth of Oedipus, a young man unwittingly kills his father and marries his mother. Sigmund Freud applied this tale to the first experience of competition by young males for the attention of a woman. The first woman in a man's life is his mother, and at this age, he faces competition with his father for her love and interest in a way that will have an impact on all of his future relations with

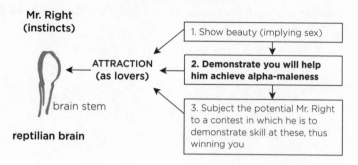

The Attraction Phase

**Mr. Right
(instincts)**

ATTRACTION
(as lovers)

brain stem

reptilian brain

1. Show beauty (implying sex)

**2. Demonstrate you will help
him achieve alpha-maleness**

3. Subject the potential Mr. Right
to a contest in which he is to
demonstrate skill at these, thus
winning you

Step 2 describes the female role in the Attraction Phase.

women. If successful at passing through this phase, he will find that he cannot compete with his father and instead decides to become like him, someday to find a woman of his own just like Mom. If he fails to grow through the Oedipal period, the boy will make an unhealthy durable connection to his mother that results in difficulty being truly intimate with mature women later in life. (More on this in the next chapter.)

Freud spent inordinate amounts of time detailing what happens to boys when they go through the Oedipal period to the relative neglect of the study of girls' development. The early life of a woman is obviously no less important than a man's, but the nature of it is somewhat different. To get a glimpse into that, we need to turn to another story—the story of Bluebeard.

What Bluebeard Tells Us About Women (and Men)

Bluebeard was an older, wealthy man who was greatly desired in his home country of France. He had been married countless times—at one point, he was thought to have had nearly a hundred wives—and each wife "disappeared" at a young age. He had a huge palatial residence with hundreds of rooms. He permitted his wives to go anywhere in the palace while he was sailing abroad for business—with the exception of one room. He threatened them with untold dire consequences if they didn't accede to this single rule.

When Bluebeard left the palace, he gave his wife a ring of keys to every room in the house. The woman would explore the luxuries of various dining halls and libraries, but invariably temptation got the best of her. Though she knew of the risks, Bluebeard's latest wife always opened the forbidden door.

And there, in the dim light, she would find the dead bodies of Bluebeard's *previous* wives.

As Bluebeard's last wife did this, she heard her husband's coach galloping home. She knew he would certainly kill her. Still, she managed to maintain her wits and dispatch a messenger for her sister.

When Bluebeard returned to greet his wife, he saw drops of blood on the key to the forbidden room and knew instantly that she betrayed him. He brandished his sword and swore to cut off her head. At that moment, though, the woman's sister arrived with two brothers in tow. They shot old Bluebeard to death and saved their sister. However, in killing Bluebeard, they also killed her marriage. (As did she, by going snooping in that forbidden room in the first place.)

In a surface interpretation of this tale, we can understand that the most primitive experience a girl has of her father is one of mystery about him. Every healthy girl has at least a brief time when she idolizes her father and professes that she would like to marry him one day. Yet in the Oedipal period, she is frustrated in her desire by the special nature of her mother's attachment and exclusive favor of her father.

On some basic level, a girl has an intuition that her father has some mysterious control over the heart, mind, and body of her mother. She might even sense that the center of that power lies somewhere in his loins. Yet she doesn't understand this. On a base level, the "secret door" of Bluebeard's mansion symbolizes her father's "fly." The girl who successfully gets through the Oedipal period gives up her exclusive adoration of her father in favor of someday solving the most central mystery of her life with another man more suited to her age and societal norms.

This sense of mystery has special resonance for us today. Romantic suspense novels—stories that combine love and mystery—have a seemingly permanent place on bestseller lists. Every popular women's magazine seems to promise "the secrets" of this or that (usually something related to men). Men think that women are at times strange or peculiar in their love of gossip sessions with one another, the special place in their lives with girlfriends where they can enjoy the sharing of secrets and mysteries. It is not silly at all, but the most primal need in the reptilian brain of a woman to crave secrets to know and mysteries to solve. It is at her sexual core to follow the mystery of what lies deep in a man's heart.

Obviously, then, women bring this need for mystery into their romantic lives. The man who is boyish and wears his heart on his sleeve, professing his undying love for you, soon becomes boring and uninteresting sexually. No matter how much women have wished for men to share more, be more sensitive, and truly connect with them heart and soul, they don't really want that at all. At least not completely. What you really want in Mr. Right is for him to hold on to a few secrets that he will never tell you. You want him to have an air of mystery surrounding him. You want access to all the rooms of the mansion of his psyche, but not that one, last forbidden room. He vaguely reminds you of your own father as long as he keeps you guessing about him. If he gives you the key to open his "secret room," his most unconfident experiences, his personal shames, and his insecurities, you enjoy a feeling of connected friendship but lose all sexual attraction for him. Opening that room of Bluebeard's house, you find the dead bodies: the shames of his past and the death of your mutual sexual attraction.

After you display a beauty that captures his attention, the very first thing a man must give you to be worthy of you is a sense of mystery that is likely to endure. Keep your Cool Eye open and aware of this. If you can figure him out in three minutes, he is disqualified from courtship with you. He is a little boy looking for a mother, a suffering soul looking for a therapist, or a psychological pauper clad in threadbare clothes looking for a financial or emotional handout. A secure, mature man is comfortable keeping some sense of privacy, individualism, and mystique.

Mr. Right knows the story of Bluebeard innately. He has a natural sense of mystery about him and is willing to keep you guessing just a little, even if you protest. If you find a man who can do this, you can both move on to Step Two of Phase I, which is your ability to demonstrate that you can raise his status among his peers.

Reminder: Mr. Right Can't Leap Tall Buildings in a Single Bound

Suzanne was a twenty-eight-year-old attractive, brainy computer executive. She had perfect skin, large brown eyes, shiny brown hair, a perfect car, perfect attire, and she owned a perfectly arranged house. Everything about her was perfect, in fact, except perhaps the way those pesky men in her life behaved.

Men were always missing something for her. They weren't tall enough, young enough, or sharp enough with their wit. Everything was competitive with her, especially competitions with men. She had her standards, and she announced them proudly on top of her television—where she kept a statue of Superman, her ideal man.

Suzanne didn't realize that others could easily see how painfully shy and quiet she was in social settings. She had very few friends and the ones she had were not particularly loyal. Most men did not find her appealing due to her lack of social initiative, her mousy-librarian way of dressing and style, and her Martha Stewart–like habits of cleanly perfection. She placed her parents on a pedestal, defending them harshly against any slight criticism from boyfriends, seemingly unaware that her mother was an alcoholic and her father was a socially inept dolt.

This did not bother Peter, a bright, attractive, ambitious, and kind attorney. He approached her with care and respect, seeing the natural beauty under her glasses and the intelligence in her eyes.

Suzanne had Peter at hello, with a display of beauty, followed by hours of quick-witted "difficulty" she hurled at him. Many women are good at playing hard to get, but for Suzanne, it was a 24–7 way of life. She believed she was always right, and she never let a man win an argument or even a minor debate of opinion.

Eventually, she left them in the dust, bleeding self-esteem all over the place. Tim, her former boyfriend, was a pro snowboarder who suffered a head injury, leaving him intellectually impaired. Within a month of his injury, Suzanne had forgotten Tim's longtime devotion to her and threw him out on his confused butt.

Suzanne had a habit of telling her boyfriends "Your stock just went up" when they did something to please her. Peter's stock rose precipitously in their early days—he did fix-it jobs around her house, he brought her presents, and so on. Then his law firm folded and his stock plummeted.

From Peter's perspective, much about Suzanne sexually attracted him, yet something was still wrong. He had some nagging intuition that there was something very unattractive about her, as physically beautiful as he found her. He began to lose sexual desire for her and slept with her less. Suzanne, in turn, used this as further proof that he wasn't man enough for her. Soon Peter didn't feel like sleeping with Suzanne at all, even though he felt intimidated enough by her to be available at her beck and call.

Soon after Peter lost his job, Suzanne broke up with him. Peter was miserable for a week but recovered quickly. He never noticed when he was with her, but it became clear when she was gone how very toxic for him she had really been. Her beauty was definitely not worth the cost.

Suzanne was great at Step One of Attraction, but she had no idea that a man needs to feel valued in a woman's eye or that to secure a man's sexual attraction in an ongoing way, a woman must find a way to raise his alpha-male status. Suzanne's standard was Superman, and she would never stoop to offer a *mere man* the relationship gift of Step Two. She would carry her habit along with her for years to come.

Understanding the Alpha-Male Thing

While the reptilian brain of women is concerned with connectedness and belonging (which as you will recall, ultimately preserves the safe destiny of her few hundred precious eggs), the reptilian brain of men is concerned not with connectedness so much as with having rank above other men. This alpha-male status gives him the highest opportunity to mate with many of the best genetic examples of the females in his peer group. In the wild, gorillas of highest social status dominate the territory and actually mate with 80 percent of the females in the social order, leaving the other 20 percent for the lesser gorillas. Rank benefits our male-genetic destiny because we have billions of seeds to sow.

Step Two of the Attraction Phase is where you personally hint or demonstrate your value to the man in terms of your help in elevating his rank (alpha-maleness), preserving (not invading) his territory, and shedding light on his masculine power. His goal at this stage of courtship is not exclusively focused on you; it is focused on you indirectly through what you offer him in assistance at power, territory, or rank.

Mr. Right finds you beautiful, but he remains aloof, detached, centered on his career and friends. He may have *lust* for you, but at this point, he still *loves* his dog more. Yes, you are beautiful, but there are many beautiful women in the world, and if men were nothing but reptilian, we would try to sleep with all of them. Step Two of Attraction is your opportunity to let him see you as special and unique among women through being the only one among them capable of raising him up in the eyes of his peers to the degree you do.

The most heartfelt example on the big screen of Step Two in recent years was in the film *Jerry Maguire*. The title character, played by Tom Cruise (the ultimate alpha-male in real life), was a sports super-agent who was fired suddenly, decimating his alpha-male status. In a career in which beautiful women were a dime a dozen, Jerry was surrounded by them, yet none of that beauty could save his suffering male ego after he was ousted from the firm.

In a classic early scene, Jerry marches through the huge agency's cubicle maze with the possessions from his cleaned-out desk. He announces that he is "fine" (not) and is starting his own agency. It is a pitiful picture of a lost man, one entirely powerless to alter his immediate fate. As he takes his last farewell steps through the office, he asks, almost in tears, "Who is coming with me?" When no one answers in the hushed room, he even goes so far as to grab two fish from the aquarium and says, "Okay. These fish. These fish are going with me. Who else? Who else is with me?"

Now from afar, Renée Zellweger's character has had her eye on the flighty, fast-talking, evasive Maguire for a long time. You might say he is quite a mystery to her. As a simple secretary prone to daydreaming of love, she does not understand the complex dynamics of a Super Bowl promotion or the contract negotiations of a star athlete. However, she sees something special about Jerry's mysterious power, some boyish idealism and weakness that she can't quite place.

Jerry heads toward the door slowly, stopping once more before saying good-bye to the company forever. He asks a last time, "Who is going with me?"

A lone hand rises. Renée Zellweger's character stands to the sympathetic grimaces of her coworkers. She speaks with firm intention but a trembling voice. "I . . . I will go with you."

Even Maguire is shocked at her boldness. After all, he doesn't even know her in a crowded room of women as beautiful as herself. He gazes at her appreciatively, and reaches out for her. At some level, he knows that one woman who stood by him may very well have saved his self-worth from falling into oblivion.

Of course, there was much more to the Jerry Maguire story just as there will be in your real-life romance. Certainly when women master only this step and none of the others, codependence, use and abuse, and all other kinds of trouble ensue. Yet leaving it out entirely is a setup for certain failure of the relationship or divorce. There is no way to complete any durable sexual attraction in a man except through this second step.

In a world where women truly can do anything a man can, many men feel that they have no purpose in the lives of women. Women can hire security systems to guard homes they themselves own as they go to work as the CEOs over male employees and are free, *Sex and the City*-style, to "have sex like men," sleeping with whomever whenever and wherever they choose. Women are quite empowered today and—very frequently these days—men feel they are not. What's worse is that we often feel we have no role, no story in your life, no place for us to provide you with what you cannot provide yourself.

What this scenario leaves men is this: an impossible choice between committing to a woman who doesn't need and admire us or a woman who only needs and admires us due to her relative immaturity. The former leaves us ripe to commit and then cheat because we never get that full sexual attraction to you. The latter leaves us with an overdramatic or at least guilt-ridden taboo: the sexual relationship with a woman who is more like a little girl on the inside than an equal and true lover.

Tom Cruise's Jerry Maguire feels like a million bucks because of Renée Zellweger's respect and admiration of him, her willingness to stand by his side even when the whole world is crashing down around him. She will be his teammate and his partner eventually. For now, though, he is wildly sexually attracted to her power to raise his alpha-male status, to remind him of the man he is inside.

That is what men need from you after they experience your beauty and give a compelling mystery back to you. That is what we must have, if you want us sexually attracted to you for life. We need you to shed your light on us, to remind us of who we are as men, even if you don't understand our ways, secrets, or mysteries.

Your Action Plan

If a man has been mysterious enough to capture your interest:

• Imagine that he owns a territory, a physical space, and spend time in it. Use your body in a way in which you both respect and belong to his territory. Touch him and not other men when in public, showing preference for him physically. Even you yourself, your body, your ideas and opinions, and your safety could come to be considered territory to his reptilian brain.

• As you get deeper into sexual attraction, signal him in nonverbal ways that you are his woman (therefore part of the territory he wants to keep exclusive). For example, show specific preference for him over other males, such as cutting off conversation with other males when he arrives, or telling your friends in front of him that you'll be spending the rest of the day with him and will have to see them later.

• Respect his territory. If he has a personal bathroom, den, or garage, don't go in there. Let him know in this way and others that you respect his privacy, space, experiences, and property.

• Cheerlead him in a way that shows preference over other males. Root for him to beat other men at work, sports, challenges of the intellect, and other competitions.

• Assist him in the background of his ambitions. If he is applying for a new job, get him coffee or offer a fresh take on his résumé design, even if you are a CEO over many men other than him. Your self-esteem need not be threatened by this. Remember that you're in a love relationship to *love,* not invest in stock. This step is one of the paths to him truly feeling loved by you. Don't offer him opinions from on high about his qualifications for the job. (Challenging him directly is the *next* step of courtship.) Simply *be there* for him.

- Be complimentary to him in word and complementary in action. Be his exclusive teammate in his quest for more power in society.

These may not seem to be in your basic nature at first. They may even seem demeaning on some level. I mean, *be a cheerleader*? Still, this is something that will benefit you as much as it does him. At this step of courtship, what your Cool Eye is telling you is that if you want him to continue to be sexually attracted to you and you alone, you need to do what Renée Zellweger did. When you make a man feel like a million bucks, he begins to see you not as a notch on his bedpost, but as a teammate and supporter he cannot do without. You will move beyond raw lust, and be one step closer to friendship and the love that exists only within that emotional bond.

The assistance he gets from you can only come from a woman. His buddies and coworkers can't provide the feminine light you shed on his ambitious struggles for rank, territory, or power. To his animal instincts, those men are potential competitors, not cheerleaders. A man's reptilian brain wants you to acknowledge his power and show him off to others as the alpha-male of the group. Whether he truly is the leader of any group or not, your simple vote for him will sexually attract him to you, and nudge you both further toward friendship.

Once again, his alpha-male status is precisely:

- his external rank among other men;
- his degree of territory, whether physical possessions or psychological space;
- his degree of internal power or ability to realize his ambitions and maintain them.

To attract him sexually in Step Two, simply demonstrate your power to elevate his status in each of these categories.

Demonstration 1: Be On His Arm and Raise His Rank Among Men

If you want to spur sexual attraction, you will want to let him be seen by his friends with you on his arm, looking your physical best. This automatically shows him to be of high rank, or alpha-male status. This is one way in which Penelope of the prior chapter failed. She didn't even get a chance to go on to Step Two because Ted did not often want to have her present when he was out with his friends. Now you know why. She was not beautiful to him in a way that triggered his reptilian brain. Her level of beauty did not give him an instinctual sense that his status among other males was raised because he was with her.

This process of assisting your potential Mr. Right to become more alpha-male is similar to the marketing term "social proof," coined by Robert Cialdini in his book *Influence: The Psychology of Persuasion*. Social proof is the notion that when people see a product sell in huge quantities, they see higher value in it. However, in the case of sexual attraction, you are the lone "consumer" of Mr. Right.

There is no more powerful external evidence of a man's social worth to his peers than a beautiful woman who is all his. I know it may not make sense to you. It's a guy thing. But if we are what you want, then this is what we need. It's not about how he looks to women other than you; it's how he looks to other guys.

Of course there are other ways to raise his rank among peers. For example, if you are a very together woman who has many friends and networks of people to rely upon for advice, help, and further notoriety in a social group, this also raises his rank. (Penelope of the last chapter was especially good at these particular resources.)

Your professional status *might* also raise his status in the eyes of his male peers, but only if this professional status somehow aids *his* career and resources—if you demonstrate that you are teaming with him to raise his rank among men by using your resources to assist his own in a way that other men's significant others don't. Every time his buddies comment on how lucky he is to have your true, fair, emotional support and money management on his side, you succeed wildly at raising his attraction for you.

Demonstration 2: Respect and Increase His Territory

One of the greatest secret fears of a man is that he will be over-whelmed by a mothering figure. He worries that his physical, psychological, and social territory will be taken over. This is why we cringe when you hang up pink curtains and pictures of teddy bears or buy any product made by Martha Stewart before we are ten years into a marriage with you.

In his book *Men Are from Mars, Women Are from Venus,* John Gray talks about how men like to go to their "caves" to solve problems. The "cave" represents the high reptilian value we place on territory to call our own, a space that a woman may not enter (let alone other men) unless the woman is fully in line with his exact rule of that territory. The man's ambitions in life are to grow and expand such a territory. Have you ever had a man get upset at you for calling him at work too often? Well, you violated his reptilian territory. Have you ever had a man consider his bathroom his private space that nobody is allowed in, not even to clean up? That's his territory.

Demonstration 2 is about showing him that you will not invade, overwhelm, or change his territory. Show that you respect his territory. Acknowledge and admire his personal spaces. Show that you recognize his territory outside the relationship—his career, social network among other men (yes, you better let him have ample guys' nights out), and his need to have a hobby, avocation, or spiritual interest in a cause greater than himself—and that you're even willing to help him *expand* that territory. If you can hint at some access you have to money, career advancement, or something else that would build his territory, it could go a long way here.

If you have preselected a man with solid boundaries (which we will learn how to do in your *challenges* to him in the next chapter), then you need not fear giving him a long leash in spending time with his friends, his hobbies, or late, ambitious days at the office. If he has a solid Personal Boundary, he will honor his promises and not cheat. Further, if you grant him wide and *expanding* physical and psychological territory and he knows it, it ironically draws him *closer* to you in his desire for you. This is the origin of the push-pull that women sometimes feel from men who demand more space. When in frustration you give up and tell him he's free to do whatever he wants whenever he wants, he wonders what is wrong and moves closer to you.

Striking a healthy balance between support of expanding his territory, and preserving your mutual intimacy is the sweet spot to shoot for. Remember not to let a husband too far, nor a bachelor too near. A husband too far may soon become a bachelor, and a bachelor too near may become your second (and second-rate) husband.

Demonstration 3: Cheerlead Him to Raise His Power

In this demonstration, you give him not just interest but admiration of his power, and show him that through eventual friendship and commitment to you, he will likely increase his power even more.

If you keep your wits about you and don't let your wildly growing sexual attraction get the better of you, you may notice something about men. At times, we can appear jealous. I'm not speaking about pathological jealousy. If a man's jealousy is so wildly out of control that it is constant in social situations, then he may have already failed future tests of character in his higher brain. In that case, you've already saved yourself years of pain and an eventual divorce. The jealousy I'm speaking about here is jealousy in the reptilian context of sexual attraction. This reptilian-brained jealousy is not a marker of immature or faulty character, but rather comes about when you yourself fail to do Step Two of Attraction. It is an outcome of him sensing that you are not willing to attract him in this step.

Most men can be spurred and coaxed at least a little by your purposeful use of this reptilian trigger, but we cover that in Step Three of Attraction. Once you do this, you ought to demonstrate preference for him. This makes him feel powerful.

Your preference for him is not just a complement; it is a clear biological signal to him that you recognize his power and will protect it and grow it. If you are in addition an active woman willing to pay for some things, approach others without fear, and confidently state your mind, you are simultaneously showing him that you literally have a kind of energy to blend with his, called confidence, which is stored in your mammalian brain. You will have given him the first hint that bonding with you in friendship will be to his advantage in the next phase.

This demonstration then, more than specifically raising his rank externally among other men as in the first demonstration, amounts to "cheerleading" him, having faith in him and his ambitions, simply believing in him in a way that makes him feel more powerful internally.

While Renée Zellweger's good looks are undeniable, her selfless action in support of Jerry Maguire raised his internal sense of masculine power when all external hints of his power and worth were crumbling around him. She stood by her man. Period. You may be a secretary like her, not of high financial means, not connected to royalty or hundreds of friends and notables like Penelope, or not of supermodel looks. Yet, in the simple act of *believing* in your man when no one else will, you raise his power among men, perhaps not so much in a flashy, external way that depends on the attention of other males, but in the deepest interior way. You make him feel like a million bucks, and make him feel like more of a man because of your simple faith in him.

Much of Demonstration 3 is primitive and ignores the fact that women hold power and are leaders, lawyers, politicians, and CEOs. This step is not intended to be a competition—that is left to the final step of sexual attraction. Remember, though, that in the Attraction Phase of dating, we are still dealing with the animalistic, primitive brain. In the wild, animals usually take these gender-specific roles. Humans are, of course, far more than animals, and we will address this when we get to the other two brains of Mr. Right later.

Meanwhile, your interest and effort at helping us see ourselves of higher external rank, greater physical and psychological territory, and stronger internal power—as alpha-males—practically drives us wild as animals for you in sexual attraction.

Following Your Story

What we can learn from Suzanne, whom we met earlier in this chapter, is that when a woman does Step One of the Attraction Phase, and skips over Step Two, she will cause a man to want to be with her for a short while, but sooner or later he'll catch on that everything is a losing game. Most men have more sense than Peter and will write off the Suzannes they meet as mean, or having low self-esteem. Yet nice women make Suzanne's mistake as well when they simply forget to give a man some kudos or make an effort to show a man that she can and will benefit his life.

What Suzanne might learn in the future is that this second step of courtship is an opportunity to use the Cool Eye again. A woman can look for signs and clues that it is time to show preference for a man, raising him up like Jerry Maguire. If he creates a sense of mystery for her or has secrets that intrigue her, the Cool Eye might kick in there to remind her that it's time to give back to the man. When she sees her man struggle with something outside his control, that is her opportunity to have a moment with him, a chance for two rich life stories to join as one—a chance to say, "I will go with you."

When a woman sees the drama of her romance story bring competition from other males with her potential Mr. Right, this is not her chance to bow out or back away. It is her chance to cheer him on, to show preference over those other males, to take the role in a story that only a woman can fill: to show him that he is yours and you are with him. If you believe in us, we are attracted to you. It is part of what makes being a man in love with a woman a vibrant, sexual joy.

When you see your story give you opportunities to assist him in this way, your Cool Eye is working, as the opportunity will arise with every mature man. A smart woman who masters Step Two improves the lives of both people—and works Mr. Right's sexual arousal for you into a frenzy.

The Attraction Phase

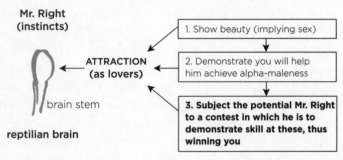

Step 3 describes the female role in the Attraction Phase.

Chapter Four

Playing Hard to Get

Phase I: The Attraction Phase
Step Three: Winning the Contest for You

When people keep telling you that you can't do a thing,
you kind of like to try it. —Margaret Chase Smith

After you have indicated your interest in Mr. Right by making him feel like a million bucks, you may notice that if he is a mature man, he doesn't disrespect you or take you for granted as some people might suggest is the norm. Immature men—bad boys and Mr. Wrongs—take and take and take to be sure, just as children do. You'll spot them quickly and get rid of them. Mature men appreciate being treated with respect and admiration. When we are treated this way, you arouse our reptilian brain and we naturally want to give back. We will want to display not mystery, but our own response to Step Two of sexual attraction: a bold action displaying our alpha-male status you have gone out on a limb to believe in in a way that helps you. You have been our devoted cheerleader. You had faith in our masculine abilities. Now we want to enjoy being the knight that saves the damsel in distress that is in you.

In Paris of Troy's time, he would have done dangerous deeds for the favor of a woman. Now, of course, that approach would seem both ill advised and a little cheesy. Instead, Mr. Right will respond to your cheerleading his alpha-status, with a use of that very status to assist you. If you want him sexually attracted to you for life, let him. We need to help you in ways you can't help yourself (even if you're capable of doing everything yourself). It makes us feel fully alive, and if we are fully alive, we are more available to you.

There are smaller, more everyday-life ways of doing this than actually slaying real live dragons for you. The way we might walk on the outside of a curb for you. The way we might hold a door or open a car door for you. The way we might simply put our ambitious to-do lists on hold for the day in order to quietly listen to your emotions, gripes, and fears—to be the symbolic shoulder for you to lean on. To be the one who defends your mistreatment by a boss or coworker, or the one who is even more annoyed than you by the rude clerk at the checkout or the car that just swerved in front of you on the way home. Even if you are a professionally powerful woman, you need to let us do this. If you want us to desire you sexually, you need to understand that our reptilian brains need it.

I once met one of the most powerful women in New York. For all of her power-lunch bluster, her millions, and her aggressive forwardness, I caught a seconds-long tender glimpse of sadness at the lack of true, lasting male sexual desire for her. She said, "There just don't seem to be any men in New York that are up to my standards, as powerful as me. So how can I win at this?" Her feminism forbade her to let a man help her in any way, which deprives all men in her life of one of the very things we need in order to be sexually attracted. That moment of doubt, of sadness, actually revealed what she couldn't see herself—that she does in fact need something that only a man can provide: a man coming to the rescue of a damsel who, while powerful, is still nevertheless very much in distress.

Athena's Gift: Slaying the Dragon Every Time

Of the three gifts offered to Paris by the Greek goddesses, we still haven't discussed one: Athena's gift of winning every battle. Men love sports. We love argument. We love to be right. The animal part of us loves to watch a good fight, to fight for our careers, our family, and our woman. We love to win. Winning contests makes us love all aspects of our lives with even greater electricity. That deep, instinctual reflex system in our reptilian brain loves a challenge, competition with other men, the ambition to overcome that challenge, and finally, winning a prize other men could not. This makes us feel like real men just as much as your standing by us, believing in us, or cheerleading us does. If you put us to a contest that we can actually win, our durable sexual attraction to you will be finally, securely, and completely yours.

By the time we get to Step Three, we have seen beauty in you, and felt like you can assist us in raising our rank, territory, and power. Now we need to rise to a challenge we can win. We need to slay the dragon for you. Winning with our bodies at sports is just an outward reflection of winning through wise strategy in our minds, which is ultimately a reflection of the winning potential of our genes.

Step Three is not just as simple as playing hard to get. Remember that women will always dangle the carrot of sex to get commitment, and men will always dangle the carrot of commitment to get sex. In this step of sexual attraction, you are going to use both of these angles to your favor. In developing your ability at beauty and the body language that goes with it, you are now going to be a difficult temptress who is hard to get (who dangles the carrot of sex), but at the same time *screen* him for the truth about just how worthy and capable he is likely to be in a commitment. High character equals the ability to commit, so you'll actually be able to assess the character of his upper two brains in the very same moves that you use to arouse his sexual urges.

Winning a contest for your sexual attraction is the most core affirmation that our genes are good enough to be passed on. If we win your contest, then you are attracted to us and unconsciously to the winning survival potential of our genes.

The third step of sexual attraction in my system also gives you one last chance to lock on the full arousal and sexual attraction of a potential Mr. Right. In addition, it offers a bonus—the opportunity to test a man's character (which resides in his mammalian and higher brain) as a way of reading the future of any potential friendship and partnership with him. It is time to put all three of his brains to an initial test. You need to see just how into you he is. You do this by putting him in a competition for your affections.

Go West, Young Man—and Leave the Woman Behind

Do you remember Amanda from the beginning of the book? She was the beautiful, petite epidemiologist from just outside Manhattan who wound up with Adam, the star salesman.

Everyone who knew Amanda described her as nice. Many women can associate with her. After all, our society often encourages women not to make any trouble. Amanda sure fit that bill, but she also had an even greater problem than her passive acceptance of the behavior of men. She was prone to being swept up in love, too over-accommodating, too easily won.

This is not to say that Amanda disrespected herself. She had good Personal Boundaries that make for a loyal future partner to a man. Still, when she met a man of great quality, she would consider it a done deal; when she was sold on quality, she was ready to be friends and to commit.

Amanda and Adam truly hit it off. They became fast friends, getting into a sexual relationship just as quickly. Amanda was a lot of beauty in a small package. She had a bright, wide smile, thick brown hair, large green eyes, and a fantastic body. She easily won Adam over in Step One.

The creative salesmanship that Adam possessed made him very mysterious to her. Amanda was very logical and left-brained, accustomed to numbers and figures. Adam's ways with humor and persuasion were all foreign social skills to her and his mysterious ways caused her to gaze at his antics in admiration when they were out on a date.

Amanda also was a truly caring person even while being respectful of herself. Her decision to enter into a sexual relationship with

Adam soon after meeting him was not based on some desperate need to cling to him, prove something to him, or keep him interested. She enjoyed sex and wanted to please herself as much as Adam. As such a giving person, she was prone to dishing out compliments and talking maturely of what good things she had to offer a man in terms of her professional status, her wide network of high-character friends, and her financial responsibility. In other words, she was great with Step Two. What capped it off for Adam was when he noticed other men looking at her when she was on his arm. Amanda was a knockout, and Adam could feel pride in her and in his own elevated status among men.

Adam at that point clearly demonstrated that he could hold his own in rank at his company. He was getting awards everywhere he turned. He treated all people with respect for their opinions, yet was the go-to guy for advice when his friends needed it. Adam treated his body, his home, and his property with respect. He had a powerful way about him, in his voice, his way of walking, and dominant body posture. It became clear to Amanda's reptilian brain that Adam was an alpha-male.

Amanda felt confident, jumping full into Phase II (Bonding in Friendship), the emotional-attraction stage of the overall courtship process we are learning. They were tight friends with lots of positive emotion to stir in each other. Yet she never looked back to the missing third and last step of the Attraction Phase. She never noticed it was missing because she was not very good at using her Cool Eye.

Amanda then quickly moved along with Adam all the way to Phase III of courtship: Commitment. She agreed to become his girlfriend. After all, they were already having sex and sex should come with a commitment, right? They were even becoming best friends, bonding over art, literature, and a shared love of urban living—it was perfect.

Except that way back toward the beginning, Amanda never put Adam to a challenge, a contest to win her over. They were together only a month when she took him to meet her parents in New York, and they had wild sex all over her parents' home when the older couple went off to do some shopping. She took him to a Broadway show and even paid for his ticket, easily afforded on her generous salary. This was not a threat to Adam's masculine needs for alpha-male status, given that he, too, was financially successful.

Amanda was so certain that Adam was right for her—a fast lover and friend in one—that she never challenged him. Because of this, he never became a true partner. When Adam's company offered to transfer him to their western U.S. office, he quickly jumped at the chance and did not offer to bring Amanda with him in a more serious commitment.

Adam disrespected Amanda on some instinctual level that told him she was somehow not enough for him. Not for life. Not after such a whirlwind romance that had had no time to develop naturally into a rich romantic story.

Amanda had not done any self-demeaning thing to cause Adam to disrespect her. She was happy and proud of herself, and had good boundaries and ethics. She simply failed to master Step Three.

Getting His Head into the Game

Step Three is your chance, at the right place and in the right time, to predict the future story of your relationship and its commitment potential by testing Mr. Right's character. You'll do this by giving him a hard time. If you don't master this last step of the Attraction Phase, then he won't be attracted to you in an ongoing way—and you won't remain attracted to him, either. Below are some tests of all three of his brains. Why give him challenges for all three now? Because if you only test his reptilian brain, you are only testing masculine sexuality. This contest requires more.

Millions of men in the world are in relationships that have wonderful emotional bonds and high moral standards where commitment is solid. Yet a large number of them have flagging sexual interest some or most of the time. Why? Many couples I've worked with who have endured infidelity on the part of the wife often describe a sudden and wild increase in sexual attraction in the husband after the fact. Why? The answer to both of these questions is that the reptilian brain of men absolutely positively needs a contest to win in order to feel like a "real" man.

Men who have a beautiful woman who adores and supports his status tend to get bored and tempted to stray even though the woman has everything he could want. I believe that a major contributor to infidelity is the simple absence of a woman's use of Step Three—not just once early in dating, but at regular intervals to rejuvenate the married couple's sexual attraction.

The Attraction Phase repeats for life. Note the stimulus steps and his response, which allow the sequence to continue, and even repeat, through meeting, dating, and beyond, into friendship and commitment.

Consider that when a woman does this step (which Amanda failed to do), it needs to be carefully performed and in a way that is appropriate for the actual time the couple has been together. Early in dating, when you haven't yet formed a friendship with a potential Mr. Right, you want to use this step as a screening tool to prevent

Mr. Wrongs from working their way into your life. Later in the relationship, when you are friends with a committed partnership, the man will have already passed your tests of him countless times. He has already proven his worthiness to be with you as a friend and partner. In a committed relationship, you are going to revisit Step Three only as a means of rejuvenating your sex life, not as a way of screening your devoted partner out of your life. That is long over—but sex had better not be.

That bane of society and trigger of our divorce crisis—infidelity—may very well have as a core cause the simple mistake of failing to revisit Step Three. When a woman is entirely oblivious to the need to challenge a man, she may eventually see the lack of sexuality bleed into bad emotions, which poison the friendship they have built. Further still, lacking friendship on top of lacking sexuality causes the relationship to start to resemble more of a hostile roommate situation, a business contract, or legal partnership that has no real humanity to it. The man originally committed to a love relationship—not a business contract—and somewhere inside may find enough excuses and moral gray zone to cross over into cheating. The man, lacking sexual attraction in his own wife due to her failure to be skilled at Step Three (the contest to win you), sees the friendship die, then the psychological commitment dies, too (regardless of the piece of paper you signed that merely states you are legally married). If he is mature and has good boundaries, he will divorce her. If he lacks mature boundaries, he very well may cheat on her and then find that when she cheats back, he is suddenly, wildly attracted to her again. Why? Because this is the very first time she has triggered that last and final step of the sexual attraction stage: She finally put him to a contest against other men. Unfortunately for both people, he probably won't win this contest. The damage to their trust in friendship and committed partnership is too great.

On the flipside, the women who lack Cool Eye ability may lapse into an innate sense that the sexuality and friendship are dying, and she's waiting for the man to make the next effort toward working on it. Yet it is actually her turn. It is time for her to challenge him without betraying him. This step is one of the two most solid things you can do to utterly cheat-proof your relationship or marriage (the other is selecting a man with strong, mature Personal Boundaries; I'll tell you much more about that later).

Your Action Plan

Let's begin with the reptilian brain. This means giving him tests for rank, territory, and power. You need to find out if you will be able to stay sexually attracted to this man for life. Rank tests assure you of that. Rank clearly states to what degree we are leaders or alpha-males. Test his leadership over other males. If he fails, you may want to find a better candidate for Mr. Right.

Approach another male near your man and simply ask a question of some sort. Any question, really. Gauge your potential Mr. Right's reaction. Does he allow this and do nothing, merely waiting for your return? Good so far. He is secure enough in his personal boundaries to remain calm, rather than getting jealous. At this point, jealousy would suggest a higher-brained character flaw, a clue to his inability to commit. He should no longer exhibit the reptilian-brained jealousy we talked about in the last chapter because you've already succeeded in Step Two.

Showing a man you are curious about how interested other men might be in you might seem counterintuitive. It is. It may not be your basic nature as someone who seeks harmony among people, but it is a crucial feminine skill in the art of flirtation. If you want to attract Mr. Right, you have to talk directly to *his* reptilian brain, not *yours*.

Now does he make his presence known to the other male in a non-desperate, non-needy way? Good. You also don't want a guy who is too afraid to show dominance over another male. Your man needs to have enough self-control and political savvy to rise in rank among other men.

Finally, what is the response of the second male? If he shies away, backs off, shows deference to your man, or attempts to befriend him, that is good. Your guy may be Mr. Right, and he will feel a reptilian thrill when he senses that he's won the test you just gave him—even though on the surface you have antagonized him. If, on the other hand, he gets in a fight over such a trifling thing or doesn't even monitor the intentions of the competing male, he may just be a Mr. One-Nighter or an outright Mr. Wrong.

Now let's try a territory test. One territory test is to observe whether he can protect you, himself, his property, his self-esteem, and his time. You might perform subtests of each of these. See if he respects his own time by arriving and leaving when agreed. Find out if he respects his own identity territory by throwing a playful teasing insult his way, which he will hopefully shoo off. See if he protects you by standing between you and any threatening elements in a crowd or in the street, such as strangers, traffic, or bad weather. If he clearly can't do these things most of the time, he has failed your territory test.

Try moving into his territory or personal space, and see if he allows it or maintains it. Most men who see your beauty will want you in their physical territory but do not want to be overwhelmed by having you in their psychological territory too much or for too long. If he keeps you there for a time, but then respectfully makes a break away from you to be alone, he is not being rude. In fact, he may very well be masculine enough to be Mr. Right.

Get close to him for a while, so much that you are clearly in his privacy zone. Then pull back suddenly to your own private space. Does he move after you without self-control? Does he start approaching your privacy zone trying to enter it? If this is blatant and constant, he is likely a bit too little boyish on the inside for your level of maturity. He needs your belief and approval of him too much, and has therefore failed your territory test.

See if he keeps a healthy, dominant space around his own body, even in a crowd, and if he handles incursions of it neither with passive defeat nor poor, politically incorrect politics with others (for example, if standing in a crowded bar, he decides to lead you to a table). If he can't do these things more often than not, he has failed your territory test.

Once again, you can use another man for a territory test. Move slowly to place another man between you and your potential Mr. Right. If your man deftly repositions himself aside you without seeming to be huffy, hostile, threatened, impatient, confused, desperate, or fearful, you have tested many of his character traits, and also seen appropriate, diplomatic territoriality. If he can't handle it, he has failed your territory test.

The final test of his reptilian brain function is the power test. Power tests tell you once again that you will be able to stay sexually attracted to the man for life; that he can not only protect you from outside threats, whether physical or psychological, but can protect *himself* and also preserve and even build the physical, emotional, and financial resources you will be collecting as a team in a shared life.

- If he is impatient, he is not powerful and fails the power test.
- If he is terrible at budgeting time, energy, or money, he is not powerful and fails the power test.
- If he is easily drained of energy, intellectually or emotionally, he is not powerful, and fails the power test.
- If he gets angry easily, he is not powerful and fails the power test.
- If he gets anxious easily or acts like a victim, he is not powerful, and fails the power test.

Notice that these tests do not rely on the man being ultra-wealthy or anything more than average in financial status. They are tests of his degree of inner masculine psychology. A man's means is not just a reflection of his inner psychology—it is also a reflection of the external circumstances he was born into or found himself in. He must be responsible enough to be self-supporting, yet power is not simply about the current amount of money in his bank account—it is about his skill at building and preserving energy, time, and money. A poor man with high character can build wealth more easily than a rich man with poor character can keep it.

Mammalian Brain Tests

In physics, energy takes many forms, such as electricity, heat, light, and nuclear power. In humans, though, energy is called self-esteem. Self-esteem is the energy that Mr. Right's three brains run on. It is the petroleum of the mind, the gasoline and oil of love. I define self-esteem as WELL-BEING + CONFIDENCE.

Well-being is a sense of satisfaction in having all of one's needs met: having enough. It is like soothing oil in the engine of the mind. Confidence is a sense of being able to take action, to defend, to tolerate risk, loss, or change. It is like the energized gasoline of the mind, the energy of *action*. You can test these by throwing out a provocative statement and seeing if he has the patience to respond slowly, diplomatically, and without loss of control in anger or in fear. Getting angry reveals a low level of well-being. A person gets angry when his or her needs are not met. On the other hand, getting anxious reveals a low level of confidence. Backing down from you in a victimlike way reveals a lack of confidence. An adolescent boy-man will lose it on you when you throw a lighthearted criticism his way, either attacking you back (directly or passive-aggressively), or shying away from you in fear and apprehension.

To test his anger:

- Disagree with him and do it with a smile. If he gets upset, he may be Mr. Wrong.

- Purposely do something small that he does not like (such as leaving your bathroom supplies in his bathroom). If he gets upset rather than diplomatically returning your items to you, he may be Mr. Wrong.

- Make plans for a date during an event that is important to him (such as the Super Bowl). If he gets upset, rather than asking for a future favor in return, then he may be Mr. Wrong.

- Ask him what makes him sad. If it is small things in life, be on guard. Depression is just another form of anger, and both hurt a potential friendship.

To test his anxiety:

- Put him on edge about an issue. Let him wonder about you. Don't call him back for a little longer than he was expecting. See if he gets anxious or worried. If he gets overly anxious, he may be Mr. Wrong.

- Call him as a joke and make up a comic tragedy, such as your poodle being crushed by a falling piano. Alternatively, ask to borrow his car for an hour, then return appearing upset and tell him you wrecked it. In the seconds it takes him to react, you may notice a tendency toward hysteria, anxiety, or worry. Take note, then laugh and say you were kidding (a second test, since a sense of humor is crucial to the friendship part of any relationship). If he laughs along with you, he may be Mr. Right.

- Jest about having to "break up" with him over something silly, like his pants being too short for his legs, even if you haven't even been on a first date. If he acts nervous or fidgety and doesn't know how to respond, take note. He may be Mr. Wrong, rather than a mature guy with a sense of humor.

- If he takes a victim approach to life, this is an especially nasty form of poor anxiety management called masochism. It is evidenced in his use of words like "should," as in "People *should* be more courteous," and phrases like "I don't know why this always happens to me." You can ask him if he thinks this or that "should" be a certain way, and if he is laid-back rather than judgmental or victimlike, he may be Mr. Right.

To test his ability to be a teammate:

- Invite him to play a game with you. Popular self-revelation games such as the Cube are useful. (You can find info on the Cube game with a Google search, right after searching his name for any criminal record.) Other games are Slaps, where you test to see if he can slap your hands when yours are placed on top of his. Tell him it's a test of intelligence after he fails to slap them. Look up physical games and comedy-improv games on the Internet. See if his mind works well with yours, and if it feels good to work as a team.

- Games are fun, but sometimes certain duties in life are not. Get more serious and ask him to join you in a joint project around your house, or volunteer to do one around his house. If things end in anger or anxiety (from either of you), you may not be very good friends in the future.

- Ask him to help you with an intellectual project, such as re-searching something that interests you on the Web, or invite him out to a date movie and tell him that it's for an article or college report you are writing. See if he can tolerate the subject matter and offer interesting insights.

Once again, all of these are meant to be tests—not ways of life. Getting too overzealous with these tests can accidentally give him the impression that you are a high-maintenance woman, a prima donna, or too difficult to be worth the effort. These types of tests are in the spirit of Ellen Fein and Sherrie Schneider's book *The Rules,* but I would like you to be difficult with men more as the exception than the rule. Otherwise, you are only doing one single step of nine in the overall courtship ritual.

Higher Brain Tests

The higher brain is about the ability to commit. It is sparked by sexual attraction and fueled by emotional attraction, yet it is the container for those kinds of attraction. It is the center of rights, privacy, respect, morality, agreements and compromise, beliefs, spirituality, identity, art, logic, humor, strategy, honesty, and all higher virtues. It is the center of keeping your word and the place where intellectual attraction is housed. It is what you are looking for at the end of the rainbow, the only skills that guarantee that a man can commit, now and forever, as a true life partner. Why not save yourself time right here and now, by pretesting his ability at intellectual attraction and, therefore, commitment? In the higher brain tests, you detect the man's ability to commit long-term but also his ability to be a great partner and companion for life, in which you keep a constant intellectual attraction.

The first higher brain tests are the Personal Boundary tests. Manufactured by the higher brain, the Personal Boundary establishes your preferences in life. It is comprised of your rights, your sense of privacy, and your ability to say no to some things and yes to others. It is what causes people to respect us or disrespect us. What good is getting involved with a man who doesn't know his own identity? I see thousands of men who let the women in their lives make most of the decisions. What movie will they see together? Whatever she wants. Where will they go for dinner? Whatever she wants. When a man defers to you constantly, this might seem appealing for a while. Ultimately, though, you want a man with preferences. You want him to be able to think for himself and make a commitment to those thoughts. Likewise, why go on to the Bonding in Friendship Phase with him if he doesn't have the boundary respect to treat you right? Certainly, you don't want to go even further, to the Commitment Phase, if he has a poor Personal Boundary or little respect for yours. That would mean he is not capable of commitment at all.

To test the strength of his Personal Boundary and how much he respects yours, consider the following:

- If he wastes time and is always late, he is not respectful and fails the boundary test. He will have a rough time being a truly committed partner later.

- If he is too easily controlled, he is not self-respectful, and he fails the boundary test.

- If he has trouble telling you no, he fails the boundary test.

- If he has trouble accepting no from you gracefully, he fails the boundary test.

- If he lacks preferences, he fails the boundary test. Ask him what his opinion or preference is on many things. If you get the impression that he thinks anything is okay, he may be Mr. Wrong because that is too vague a boundary for a man to have.

- If he is a poor budgeter of time, energy, or money, he fails the boundary test.

- If he wastes energy suffering over the things he doesn't control, he is not powerful, and he fails the boundary test. Notice if he says the word "should" a lot. The word "should" indicates that someone is trying to control what he doesn't.

- If he is controlling in a far greater degree than simple, ordinary masculine territoriality, he fails the boundary test.

In addition, there are several dos and don'ts associated with the boundary test, and these will show you that he has a good boundary simply by respecting *yours:*

- Don't be too available, but do be available somehow. (Mr. Right will take this in stride.) Your way of being somewhat available might be to be reachable by e-mail but not by phone, or by phone but not in person. In doing these things, you are exercising a boundary.

- Make direct eye contact, but turn away and walk away without warning. Willingness to walk away shows him that you have a strong Personal Boundary. If he doesn't react in a needy way, he has a solid boundary.

- When he asks for something, say no often through this step, with only a sprinkling of yes. If he takes humor or amusement in your difficult, overly strict limits, he gets it as far as sexual attraction. Just be sure to reduce the intensity of this eventually or he will think you're a prima donna or a high-maintenance woman.

- When the moment of a kiss comes, turn away the first two attempts, even if you are screaming inside to go for it. Then, give in on the third. If he coolly waits for this, he respects your boundary and must have a good one himself.

- Definitely, *no sex* of any kind early on unless that's all you will ever want from him. Otherwise, none until you have a commitment. If he fails these tests and you still have sex with him, he is going to move on to other women after the sex for sure.

The next higher brain test is a test of beliefs and goals. A belief is an idea tied to a packet of emotional energy. It is therefore a bridge between the emotional mammalian brain and the intellectual higher brain. Since emotional energy can come in either positive or negative form, it is important to notice whether a man's beliefs are more heavily negative or positive. Simultaneously, it is important to know whether you and the potential Mr. Right share common life goals. Why? Because negative beliefs can bring down the friendship you share (by one or both of you simply feeling bad most of the time) and the commitment you make (by negative energy torpedoing the goals you set together).

To test this:

- Ask the man what he believes about various topics that are important to you. Then pay attention to your own energy. Do you feel drained by his beliefs? Do they feel negative? If so, he may fail the beliefs test and will not be good at committing to you some day.

- Ask a man what his goals would be if he had unlimited time, energy, and money. If his answers match up with yours in a way that benefits you both, he may be Mr. Right.

Next come the decision tests. All decisions a person ever makes are either constructive or destructive—either to yourself, others, or both. Decisive people seem more alive because they have a strong sense of purpose. Mr. Right will be the most alive man you will ever know.

- If he is impatient and prefers immediate gratification, he fails the decision test.

- If he is wishy-washy about what he would enjoy doing with you, he may be Mr. Wrong. If he is decisive, he may be Mr. Right. Real men are decisive.

- If he gets truly jealous over more than just instinctual things like sex and competition with other males (for example, he gets jealous of your promotion, your new car, your new friends, and so on), he may be Mr. Wrong.

- If he feels that in order to be right, you must be wrong, he won't be able to commit someday. He fails the decision test.

- If he feels diminished by your success and you can feel it, he fails the decision test.

- Give him a conundrum, a mental riddle that has no acceptable choice. Ask him something like, "Would you rather die by fire or flood?" If he responds that neither is good, then he fails the decision test. If he responds with something of compromise, or even humor, such as, "Both—I'd be set on fire, but jump into the flood," then he may very well be Mr. Right.

This Is Only a Test

These three types of tests will spur him on to you like crazy if he is truly a mature man. These tests will also repel immature, adolescent boy-men, which is just as important. What is the man's experience of your testing him in Step Three? He'll see your behavior as unpredictable. This is a very good thing. If you get predictable, we get bored, not because you aren't desirable or are bad at the core, but because you deny us the deep psychological role we desperately need in our reptilian brains—the need to have ambition toward winning.

Remember that if you do *only* this step of courtship, you are setting yourself up to appear to be a mean, rude woman, and one of the biggest turn-offs men can imagine. Yet if you have already attended to maximizing your beauty and doing some cheerleading of a man you find both mysterious and an alpha-male, you must then find a way to raise the stakes for him by giving him a hard time in winning you over.

When it comes right down to it, we ultimately want your surrender to us sexually, but absolutely, positively not without a contest, a competition, or a heroic story for us to live. Give us that. Test us. Give us the opportunity to win, and therefore *value* you, and the joys of the sexual connection we will eventually share.

Following Your Story

Adam's departure may have actually saved Amanda years of wasted time on a relationship that would have lost sexual spark eventually. Then again, had Amanda known about Step Three, the relationship might have gone the distance. That is the importance of your shared story together. Like all men, Adam wanted to be a hero to his woman, but he desperately needed to win a contest for her affections. Amanda made Adam her hero without even putting his abilities to the test. Unwittingly she deprived him of one of the most desired experiences of being a man.

In Amanda's story, she had plot choices. Those choices would ripple into the distant future, giving her a whole new path to her destiny. Amanda's choice was sleeping with Adam very soon after meeting him. Many women enjoy sex for the sake of sex. Maybe they learn something new about themselves this way. Maybe some get a brief self-esteem boost. Maybe some of them are just addictive types and sex becomes the drug du jour. If you followed *Sex and the City* closely, even when Sarah Jessica Parker's Carrie character tries out "having sex like a man" (one-night stands, followed by moving on without emotion), she still ends up with an empty feeling. I have known, seen, or treated many women who have had one-night stands and have yet to meet one who didn't eventually feel somewhat empty inside about this. What seemed like a thrill at the time felt like eating spoiled food by the morning. Still others will tell me they don't have a second thought about one-night stands and feel quite confident about their identity and self-esteem. Most often, these women are still living in their own reptilian brains and have a way to go in their development of a full, rich mammalian brain and higher brain.

Remember, men will always dangle the carrot of commitment to get sex, and women will always dangle the carrot of sex to get commitment. Amanda gave away the sex too soon and would have to wait and grow awhile to reach a new level of sexual attraction ability. Still, she eventually met an attorney who found her beautiful, whom she secretly idolized for months before dating, and she gave him four months of resistance before deciding that it was time to sleep with him. This one was a keeper, and her four-month test of his endurance gave them ample time to become friends with an emotional bond and then make a commitment enriched by intellectual connectedness.

All this was possible for her because she finally cultivated the skill of the Cool Eye enough to gaze down on what she'd lacked in Step Three.

The Bonding Phase (Emotional Attraction)

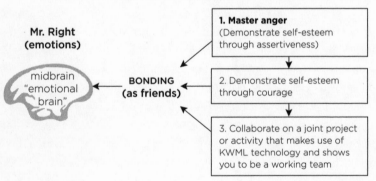

Mr. Right (emotions)

midbrain "emotional brain"

BONDING (as friends)

1. Master anger (Demonstrate self-esteem through assertiveness)

2. Demonstrate self-esteem through courage

3. Collaborate on a joint project or activity that makes use of KWML technology and shows you to be a working team

Chapter Five

A Friend in Need

Phase II: The Bonding in Friendship Phase
Step One: Demonstrating Mastery of Anger

Hell hath no fury like a woman scorned.
—William Congreve

THE REPTILIAN BRAIN is the human unconscious, the reflexes and instincts we automatically do without thinking, the things we have no conscious choice over like the drives for survival and reproduction. When our Cool Eye is turned off, the reptilian brain can take over our behavior and leave us behaving like animals. When the Cool Eye is turned on, however, we can actually tame the reptilian brain and put it to work for good purposes in our lives.

On the other hand, we *do* have choice over the mammalian brain. We have more natural ability to use our Cool Eye when we are in this brain, because it is all about emotions and emotions tend to call us to attention, telling us to look at ourselves and understand why we feel the way we do.

We now enter the second phase of courtship: emotional attraction. This phase is all about friendship—determining if your potential Mr. Right has the emotional ability to be the kind of best friend you need for a lasting relationship. This phase of courtship is the only place where you and Mr. Right can reach the state that we call being in love. How? Through understanding a simple, elegant point about friendship: Friendship is mutually shared, consistently positive emotion.

The mammalian brain is the seat of emotion. To go back to our car engine analogy, the mammalian brain is the gas tank, the place where emotional energy is stored to fuel relationships. Anything about your life that involves emotion brings in the workings of your mammalian brain, and the relationship fuel within it called self-esteem.

Crucial relationship skills that involve emotion include the following:

Friendship, which is simply being side-by-side with someone in a state of consistently shared, positive emotion.

Self-esteem, which is positive emotional energy. It is what causes people to be *emotionally* attracted to us, rather than just *sexually* attracted.

Love, which is the donation of self-esteem from one person to another. The central act in friendship is loving. Of course, to feel that the other person is worthy of our love, that person needs to attract us sexually first.

Communication, which is the combination of an idea with a certain amount of emotional energy sent out into the world for someone else to hear.

Valuing, which is the amount of positive or negative emotional energy you place on an idea, possession, or person. A guy can be sexually attracted to you but still not value you. Valuing you can't happen until this phase, and actually *respecting* you can't happen until the next phase.

Beliefs, which are the amount of emotional energy you invest in ideas, possessions, and people. They are what you hold dear.

Through beliefs, you interpret everything you see or hear, and attach meaning to them. If you and Mr. Right don't share a majority of beliefs, you won't be able to cross smoothly into the commitment phase.

⁓

We tend to be friends with people we love and value, and who love and value us back. When we are around friends, we feel good, have a sense that our self-esteem is raised, and seek out communication and contact with those friends even more. Have you ever spent time on a man with whom you do not feel loved, valued, or happy? With whom your self-esteem tends to be knocked down a notch? With whom you feel less happy, more down on yourself, or upset after most attempts at communicating? If your answer to any of these questions is yes, then chances are you are not meant to be very good friends with this person or that at least one of you lacks high self-esteem and therefore the ability to raise the self-esteem of the other person.

A friend is not necessarily someone you sleep with. A man who has a one-night stand with you does not *love* you or *value* you. He can't, because sexual attraction is about instinct, not emotion. There has not been enough time to develop positive shared emotion. He is in *lust*, and lust, while necessary in a relationship, cannot be love.

A friend is also not someone to whom you necessarily owe anything, have a contract with, or make promises to keep. You don't have to have a commitment to your friends. Friendship is *always* voluntary. Your friends like you simply because they feel good around you. When legal agreements, contracts, and promises fail to give us total security, the bond of friendship always gives us peace.

Love means giving positive emotion or self-esteem to another person. By definition, friendship is the only phase of human courtship or relations where love (as opposed to lust or sheer duty and honor) can possibly exist, because love is the giving and receiving of emotional energy.

If you are in a relationship that has commitment—an agreement, promise, or even a legal tie that binds—but no friendship (or therefore love), you are in quite a predicament. This would be like being mere roommates, stale, cordial business partners, or worse. In this situation, you might tend to honor agreements, try to communicate or spend time together, but only out of a sense of duty or obligation, the chance to profit monetarily, or the threat of legal repercussions. None of these is particularly binding or durable psychologically.

Your mammalian brain is powerful, dramatic, and carries the very glue that binds a relationship tighter than any law of the land, religious dictum, political policy, or physical threat. This is why this phase fits so perfectly between the potentially impersonal lust that is sexual attraction and the potentially passionless promise that is commitment.

Emotional Energy

Consider energy. It gets things done, protects, heals, warms, illuminates, and transforms one thing into another. Yet it is colorless, weightless, invisible, uncontainable, and mysterious. Nothing in the world changes without energy. In fact, without energy, such as that of the sun, nothing new happens at all, and all living things die. Our relationships run on energy—the energy of self-esteem within the action of loving.

Emotional energy can be positive or negative. Positive emotional energy is called *self-esteem,* and fills us with happiness (a sense of well-being and confidence). Since friendship is consistently shared, mutual *positive* emotion, you can't be a good friend without ample amounts of well-being and a sense of confidence inside you. Likewise, a man cannot be a good friend to you if he lacks these two types of self-esteem in himself; he can't be Mr. Right.

Negativity, on the other hand, causes friendships to fail. Negative emotional energy is called *stress.* It infuriates, depresses, and puts the recipient on edge, creating barriers to friendship that are often too substantial to overcome. Stress in your environment actually comes in only two varieties: hurt and loss.

Have you ever been hurt? Have you ever been insulted, made to feel "less than"? Have you ever been made to feel like a loser, or a fool, or been "used"? Have you ever been made late by a man and lost time, a connection, or an opportunity? Have you ever had your life tarnished, belittled, or held back from being what it was meant to become? Everything you have ever labeled stressful has been bad energy coming in to hurt you (like an insult), or coming to take something from you (like an employer with layoffs in mind).

If the negative energy of hurt gets into you, that very same amount is now the amount of *anger* you feel. If the negative energy of loss gets into you, that's the exact same amount of *anxiety* you feel. This negative energy kills friendships.

Anger and anxiety are the only two pure negative internal emotions. Learning to master and understand these emotions allows you to avoid sending negative emotional energy into Mr. Right while at the same time screening out the Mr. Wrongs who are sending this kind of negative emotional energy into *you*. Once you have mastered these, you can learn to team up with the potential Mr. Right to harness good energy to your mutual benefit. Proficiency in these three steps *in this exact order* offers a lifetime friendship, and, therefore, a lifetime of good communication and love.

Friends Don't Let Friends Get Negative with Anger

The first step in Phase II is mastering anger. Anger is usually the first obstacle a new couple encounters after they've passed through the sexual attraction phase. Anger in and of itself is not a bad thing. Any good story has a plotline that sees the main characters encounter some early challenges that set the stage for a rich adventure. This plotline often involves having something that is amiss or missing—a job that is beneath us, a failed dream, a sense of insecurity. When we are lacking something in life, it causes anger. Anger is simply a signal telling us that something is wrong, specifically that some of our needs are not being met.

However, if anger is managed badly, it sends very negative energy to the person who is the object of your anger. Since, as we discussed earlier, friendship is consistently shared, mutual positive emotion, the negative energy of anger—if not used productively—is a great danger to a budding friendship. To ensure a growing friendship with Mr. Right, you must master your own anger and be a quick student in spotting mismanaged anger in men who will eventually prove themselves to be Mr. Wrongs.

Too Pissed for the Little Blue Box

Caroline was an outright daddy's girl, the darling dear to her father, a recovering alcoholic and manager of one of the largest department stores in the western United States. She was also a partying, heavy-drinking worker bee in an advertising agency. Caroline loved money more than anything—old money, new money, and especially somebody else's money.

Caroline was stunning. She looked like a younger Jennifer Connelly, and she *definitely* knew how to display her beauty. She'd go drinking in the most crowded sports bars of Phoenix, turn heads, cause fights for her attention, and drink some more. The alcohol had her so loose she'd draw twenty guys a night to her with a pucker of her full, red lips.

Chad, a well-to-do veterinarian, found himself on the receiving end of one of her faux kisses. Fresh from surgery on a dog with an enlarged spleen, he was tired, but he pepped up when he saw that very first glimpse of her beauty. Caroline smiled at him widely, and he imagined taking her solid, athletic, five-foot-eight body in his arms to kiss for the rest of the night. When she complimented him on his height, his build, and his Tiffany money clip as he paid for her drinks, he noticed how all the other men stared at her, and how all the other women seemed to know her. They'd pass by, tap her in recognition, and seem to linger in her glow. When Caroline turned her attention to another of her many male suitors but allowed Chad to reclaim her, she'd swiftly moved him through all three stages of sexual attraction. She'd won him with her beauty, raised his alpha-male status, and given him a competition to win. Chad was totally hooked.

Unfortunately, while their sex life was lusty, the rest of their relationship was tempestuous and nothing more. Caroline had a childish, pouty, manipulating way of dealing with anger. She'd either sulk passive-aggressively when Chad didn't let her have her way or shout Chad down in public. Whenever Caroline felt that her needs weren't being met, she let loose, and Chad was the unfortunate recipient. Amazingly, they were together for more than a year before Chad realized what was happening. Like many men, he'd been blinded by sexual attraction.

Just before Chad woke up to reality, it was Valentine's Day, and he had somehow convinced himself that it was time to pop the question. Caroline had essentially browbeaten him into this, even specifying in her angry, demeaning way which restaurant he should use to propose and the exact Tiffany ring she expected from him.

Chad and Caroline never had a friendship. They were lovers only (and the sex *was* spectacular). They had navigated quickly through the Attraction Phase of courtship but never got any further. Now Chad was on the precipice of moving on to commitment—when suddenly he saw Caroline for who she really was. At dinner that Valentine's Day, Caroline had several quick drinks, and something Chad said triggered her anger again. She delivered a withering remark, and Chad heard her as though she was speaking for the first time. Perhaps the little blue box in his pocket picked up some signals he'd previously missed. Whatever it was, he excused himself to go to the men's room. When he returned, he told Caroline that he was leaving—both the restaurant and her life.

Saving Failing Friendships with the Anger Map

Neither Caroline nor Chad knew how to deal with anger. Because of this, their friendship, and, therefore, their relationship, was doomed. If they'd had my Anger Map, however, they might have stood a chance.

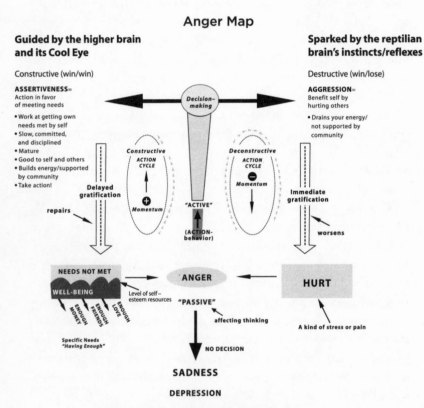

Anger Map

Guided by the higher brain and its Cool Eye

Sparked by the reptilian brain's instincts/reflexes

Constructive (win/win)

Destructive (win/lose)

ASSERTIVENESS=
Action in favor of meeting needs

• Work at getting own needs met by self
• Slow, committed, and disciplined
• Mature
• Good to self and others
• Builds energy/supported by community
• Take action!

AGGRESSION=
Benefit self by hurting others

• Drains your energy/ not supported by community

Decision–making

Constructive ACTION CYCLE

Deconstructive ACTION CYCLE

Momentum

Momentum

Delayed gratification

Immediate gratification

repairs

⊕ *Momentum*

"ACTIVE"

(ACTION-behavior)

worsens

NEEDS NOT MET

WELL-BEING

Level of self– esteem resources

ANGER

HURT

ENOUGH MONEY ENOUGH FRIENDS ENOUGH LOVE

"PASSIVE"

affecting thinking

A kind of stress or pain

Specific Needs *"Having Enough"*

NO DECISION

SADNESS

DEPRESSION

In the mammalian brain or emotional brain

The Anger Map explains any and every difficulty you have ever had with anger, depression, aggression, abuse, hurt, or lack of your needs being met in life. All of these things have a direct connection to one another through this map.

Causes of Anger

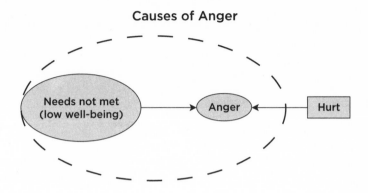

There are only two causes of anger in the world. Everything you have ever experienced with a man that caused you anger was either:

- an emotional stress coming from outside you, called hurt; or
- a need not met inside yourself; a lack of well-being.

A hurt coming from outside of you can be as small as a slight insult from someone or as large as a physical attack. Hurt causes anger if you let it get into you. When a man is late to meet you, makes a negative comment about your appearance, implies that he is better, smarter, or a harder worker than you, or anything else insulting, he puts negative energy into your friendship. As a result, you value him less, and your friendship diminishes. Go back to the definition of love I gave you earlier (positive energy). You actually love this person a little less because of his negative energy.

The other way that we can become angry is when our own needs are not met. This means we are low on well-being, that type of self-esteem that lets us feel nurtured and in a state of having enough. Unlike hurt, this is entirely our own fault and responsibility. When you were a little girl or Mr. Right was a little boy, a nurturing, motherly figure used to provide for your needs as if by magic. Some of us believe that our lives should always be that way. We sit around and wait to be fed, wait to have our minds read by our romantic partners. We become high-maintenance like Caroline. This kills our chances of having deep, mature friendships.

Anger can be quite toxic when dealt with the wrong way. What's the right way? Anger is nothing more than negative energy that needs to be turned to positive energy. Anger is just a helpful signal telling you that you need to act. They key is *how* you act. You can use anger in one of three ways:

Depression.   Being immature, passive, and self-destructive. Depression is the prime link from negativity in the ideas of the higher brain to the emotion of the mammalian brain (when your Cool Eye is turned off).

Aggression.   Being immature and actively destructive of others. Aggression is hurting others to help ourselves, and the prime link from the reptilian brain to the mammalian brain (when your Cool Eye is turned off).

Assertiveness.   Being actively constructive with decisions. This is the only mature path to deeper friendship with others and simply amounts to going out and getting your own needs met without using or hurting others. It also has a link from good ideas in the higher brain (when your Cool Eye is turned on).

Depression and aggression always cause you to generate even more negative energy out of anger. This means that they eventually spell doom for any friendship. Assertiveness, on the other hand, always raises the value of both the friendship and you in Mr. Right's eyes.

The Three Uses of Anger

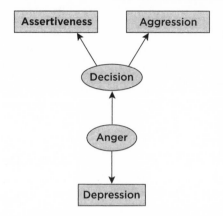

There are only three uses of anger in the world—depression, aggression, and assertiveness. Only assertiveness gets you toward your passion and fulfillment as a woman. (Better discard depression and aggression from your life!)

Depression Sinks Friendships

Have you been in a relationship or friendship with a man who was frequently depressive, pessimistic, or negative? Have you yourself been depressive, pessimistic, or frequently negative? If so, you were watching your friendship die every moment you absorbed that energy from each other.

The very first thing I ask a depressed person in my office is, "What is causing the depression? What needs are not being met?" I do this since hurt is something that happens in the present and rarely something currently happening when we are depressed. If you are depressed about a job, there must be needs you have that the job doesn't meet, such as having a nice boss, high pay, or low hours. Similarly, feeling depressed about a guy means that somehow the relationship fails to fulfill your needs.

You alone are responsible for fulfilling your needs. Do you need companionship? Be a better companion to yourself. Do you need more sex? Masturbate if necessary. Do you need to be heard and understood? Take up public speaking and keep a journal where you can be more understanding of yourself.

Depression in both men and women has been the cause of many a divorce, and most of us don't even realize this. More than half of all depression goes untreated, yet being in a relationship has proven benefits at keeping not only depression at bay, but prolonging your physical health. How could we so blithely miss the fact that in our failure to catch our own minor depressions and nip them in the bud we are housing a silent killer of our own marriages, and ultimately of our own mental and physical health?

Here is how it usually goes:

- The marriage is beautiful and the newlywed period blissful.

- The normal stresses of life grow—the kids, the dual incomes, the debt.

- The husband or wife gets a little twinge of depression when that stress keeps seeping in, over months or years, and finds his or her partner supportive and reliable as a shoulder to lean on.

- They don't do anything about the stress. It grows.

- Eventually, the other spouse turns weary of being that shoulder and also becomes a bit depressed or resentful.

- With the friendship fading in a once-beautiful marriage, the wife feels less valued and less prone to want to have sex. The husband feels less valued and less prone to do things that demonstrate how committed he is to her.

- The husband feels no commitment or love anymore, and loses his desire for sex with her. After all, it has been a long time since she showed how turned on she is.

- The wife feels no sexual attraction or love anymore, and thinks about giving up on her commitment. It has been a long time since he showed how committed he is.

- Cheating might happen, irreparably damaging the strained relationship.

- Divorce.

What kills a relationship in this scenario is not directly the amount of stress this couple is under or even the eventual depressions caused by it. What kills it is a lack of knowledge of the exact definition of friendship, the passiveness in letting it die, or the lack of understanding of what needs to be done to fix it.

If you are clinically depressed, you need a local professional to help you consider medication. However, if you have only little fits and spurts of it, you need to learn more about aggression and assertiveness and then get into *action*.

I always tell patients that it is better to be angry than sad. Anger itself is not a good or bad thing. It's just a signal that something's wrong: namely, that your needs are not being met. You are low on well-being, that nurturing kind of self-esteem. Letting anger just sit in you to stew and turn to depression is not the way to go.

Early psychiatrists described depression as anger turned inward. Depression is like a passive pot of anger that you just store up inside.

When you do this to yourself and your potential friend in Mr. Right, you are being a poor friend. When you hold grudges and store up anger and resentment, when you beat up on yourself instead of declaring what you need, you are being a bad friend. You are poisoning the friendship you have started or could have had with negative energy.

Depression is a passive stance in life where you see that you have needs and you do nothing to meet them, often under the influence of negative ideas stored in your higher brain. If you had bad experiences in your past that you've never dealt with through a psychoanalyst, they may have led to negative beliefs such as "I'm a loser and I might as well not even try anymore." This kind of thinking might encourage you to be passive. You wait and wish for someone to

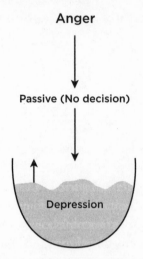

A Depression Tank: Stored-up Anger
(All depression is simply anger.)

come along to make you feel better. Maybe it will happen. Maybe Mr. Right will read your mind and give you everything you desire. Don't count on it, though. This kind of clairvoyance is uncommon. You need to take a more active stance.

Friendship is voluntary and nobody owes it to you. To get it, you need to remember the definition: consistently shared, mutual positive emotion. If you let yourself stay depressed, you have no positive emotion to share, and so you cannot emotionally attract Mr. Right.

Aggression: Keep Your Friends Close and Your Enemies Closer

The first step in getting out of depression and being a better friend is to get outwardly angry instead of passive. Once you do this, though, it is not okay to go blowing your top all the time like a little girl (nor should you accept his doing the same thing to you). It is

Options for Anger: Aggression

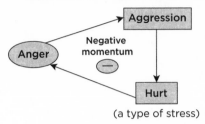

(a type of stress)

The "cycle of violence" brings
negative momentum to your life.

indeed better to be angry than sad, but aggression is just as destructive to a friendship as depression.

You get into a cycle of violence when you argue destructively. Doing so tends to manufacture new anger through hurt, rather than transforming the anger into positive energy. You might feel better having released some of your anger, but your partner receives such a strong dose of negative energy that he loses nearly as much as you win. Ultimately, you lose as well, because the friendship suffers a devastating blow.

Here is how it usually goes:

- The marriage is beautiful and the newlywed period blissful.

- The normal stresses of life grow—the kids, the dual incomes, the debt.

- The husband or wife gets a little twinge of depression when that stress keeps seeping in, over months or years, and finds his or her partner unsupportive and unreliable as a shoulder to lean on, because the spouse has stresses of his or her own.

- The husband or wife snaps, insulting the feelings of the spouse or assaulting them physically. The spouse is then hurt, and slowly becomes angry, but out of fear of more of the same, shuts up and buries the anger in ever-growing depression.

- Eventually, the abused spouse turns weary of burying the anger in depression and also becomes aggressive, fighting back through sabotage, physical violence, or through passive-aggression.

- With the friendship destroyed in a once-beautiful marriage, the wife feels completely devalued and totally avoids sex except to prevent more hurt. The husband feels further devalued and ever more possessive.

- The wife feels no sexual attraction or love anymore and thinks about giving up on her commitment. It has been a long time since he showed how committed he is.

- Cheating might happen, maybe even a criminal act, irreparably damaging the strained relationship.

- Divorce.

Not cool. This process would never get beyond the beautiful marriage part if someone had a Cool Eye turned on. If a man makes you a deal in your relationship, it is always either a win/lose deal or a win/win deal. Has he ever suggested that you clean his place without offering anything back? Has he suggested going only to restaurants or movies he likes without considering going to an equal number of the ones that you like? Has he ever expected you to listen to his gripes but is too busy making a living to listen to yours? These are all win/lose deals. Such deals can be amplified to terrible extremes when anger gets involved. The Cool Eye stops bad deals in their tracks.

Aggression is always a win/lose way of using anger. Every decision we ever make is either constructive or destructive, or else it really wasn't a decision at all. Being destructive is the same as being win/lose, which is the same as being immature. The Cool Eye is the only skill that lets us recognize a win/win situation from a win/lose one, and when we are immature, the Cool Eye is turned

Aggression: A "Win/Lose" Deal

off. Immaturity kills good friendships through anger. It happens through being aggressive, which takes bad ideas from the higher brain and uses them without purposeful thought (with the Cool Eye turned off).

Caroline did a terrible job of dealing with her anger with Chad. She lashed out at him regularly. Eventually, she did so one time too many, and Chad walked out of her life with that little blue box firmly in his pocket. She failed to understand that, as an adult woman, her needs were hers to attend to—and she could have done so through that amazing power of friendship and self-care that every woman has inside: assertiveness.

Assertiveness: "Good" Anger

Assertiveness is the ability to go out and get your own needs met for yourself without having to hurt others, use others, or manipulate others. It is a mature, patient, slow, and disciplined approach and can only be accessed if you have your Cool Eye turned on. When you do that, you can actually access good ideas from the higher brain that encourage you rather than bring you down. Assertive people are cool.

Options for Anger: Assertiveness

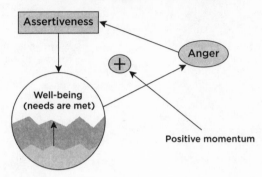

Example: List of Needs
1. Nice boss
2. High pay
3. Low hours

Are you feeling hurt, depressed, or needy about your man? Assertiveness is the cure—and amazingly, your potential Mr. Right will think of you as a better friend. Your depression will lift, you will fight less, and you will find that there is a real friendship growing between you via consistently shared, mutual positive emotion.

When we are children, we need mothering. We need to be nurtured. We need someone else to get our needs met for us. Unfortunately, some of us become stuck there, and we bring this into our adult relationships. It's a heck of a surprise for a person in this situation when he finds out that his partner wants nothing to do with parenting him. In the end, we are all forced to learn how to mother ourselves. That is exactly what assertiveness is.

Assertiveness is the only way that adults can take care of their needs in a mature fashion. Do you need more money? Go train for a better job or start a business. Do you need more companionship? Do something that allows you to make new friends. Do you need a different kind of guy in your life than the one you're with? Speak up about your needs and see if maybe he really does have it inside to be what you need. If not, you can mutually agree to break up and save yourself years of time, money, energy, and pain on therapy and a divorce.

Remember, the Anger Map works for both you and your potential Mr. Right. It is no more acceptable for him to treat you with depression or aggression than it is for you to treat him that way. If you feel that your man is too aggressive, rude, or dismissive, show him the Anger Map. If he doesn't understand it or does but won't change, this is a very clear sign that he's Mr. Wrong. This guy will never be your friend, and you can't have a real and durable love without being true friends.

The Two Deadly Sins of Anger

The Mike Nichols film *Closer,* starring Julia Roberts, Jude Law, Natalie Portman, and Clive Owen, detailed the worst of the worst of human anger in relationships. It was the story of two struggling couples who had started out as friends. Throughout, the film provides a deep understanding of the core destructiveness of immaturity with anger in relationships.

The movie does a masterful job of showing the connection between sexuality and anger. What begins as a juicy exploration of sexual attraction—all the idealism, the tingle in the loins, the innocence, and seemingly honest, heartfelt admiration of the other—turns to bitter contempt, jealousy, and emotional violence.

Natalie Portman's character, Alice, is a refugee of the New York sex industry who goes to London to start a new life, where she meets a struggling writer, Dan, played by Jude Law. There is instant sexual attraction when they breeze through all three steps we have learned.

Dan writes a book about Alice and it's a hit. On his book tour, though, he seeks to have an affair with a photographer named Anna, played by Julia Roberts. When she rebuffs him, Dan plays an aggressive, dirty trick on her by connecting her through e-mail to the porn-addicted dermatologist, Larry, played by Clive Owen. Larry and Anna, however, actually hit it off.

From there, what could have been the beginnings of real love between the men and women in these two couples turns away from friendship and deep into the nastiest kind of aggression. The film is so real, because it shows the jealousy, revenge, and immature manipulation that relationships based on sexual attraction alone can foment. Scene by scene, you can see the workings of the Anger Map gone wrong. When Dan is foiled from exacting his revenge on Anna for actually striking up a fledgling friendship (love) with Larry, he has no other place to channel his aggression and becomes depressed. This then poisons any chance of real love and friendship with Alice who, neglected, encounters Larry and is seduced by him. When Anna feels Larry's retreat from commitment, their friendship and love diminishes, and she finds herself finally giving in to an affair with Dan. Larry himself now becomes depressed, and then seethes jealousy at Anna. He finds a route to exercise his anger further through tormenting her with cruel words and mentally castrates Dan in a confrontation that joins all the characters in a growing cycle of emotional violence on one another.

This film illustrates a fascinating facet of anger for us in showing where two deadly sins—revenge and jealousy—are located on the Anger Map.

If you think about what is considered destructive in spitting negative emotional energy into your friendship, it always involves struggling to control something that cannot be controlled. Aggression is a win/lose action. If you have ever followed a sports team, you know that not even the worst underdog team can be forced to lose. That's why betting on sports is a gamble. We don't *control* making someone lose. We don't control making someone suffer for rejecting us any more than we control making the Cowboys lose a football game (although I relish it when they do).

We don't control the past or absolutely control the future. What this means is that since the past is gone, any emotion you have about wishing it were different is only going to damage your friendship. Trying to control things is destructive or immature win/lose behavior.

The form of aggression we call *revenge* can lead nowhere but to more hurt for *you*. Just check the Anger Map and you'll see. Even most families who attend executions of murderers of their loved ones cite that revenge does nothing to soothe the hurt they feel over the crime. Every time you take out revenge on something your guy did, you are poisoning the potential friendship with him. Every time he brings up something he didn't like about how you handled his friends wrong, left your stuff in his private bathroom, or didn't somehow meet his needs in the past, he is poisoning the friendship you share.

The other deadly sin that *Closer* demonstrates for us is jealousy. Jealousy is anger directed toward the future, and we don't absolutely control the future, either. Jealousy is a type of aggression we hurl at others when we think that the world is a place of scarcity, that there isn't enough love to go around. If we see our ex move on with someone else, it feels like he has won and therefore we must have lost. We think that in the future, he might have more happiness than we will, and our jealousy silently wishes that this would not be the case. Jealousy is an aggressive wish to control the future, where we can fantasize that if someone fails to get his needs met, maybe we will get ours. The characters of *Closer* were so bent on winning that friendship in their relationships was an utter impossibility.

Following Your Story

What this means for you is that when you turn on your Cool Eye, you might at times catch yourself being jealous or pick up on it in your guy. Every time you do it, you are contributing to the end of your friendship, and, therefore, the end of the very glue that connects sexual attraction to commitment.

There is one crucial thing for women to remember about this, and I can't stress it enough: Men who appear jealous might appear that way for a very healthy reason or an unhealthy one. When men seem jealous but are really just being territorial—because of their reptilian brain's need to establish and keep territory—that is a good thing for you. It means they are sexually attracted to you. Respond by coming back into their territory. The way to tell if what looks like jealousy is more of the bad kind, the one that speaks to emotional immaturity in them and therefore poor fitness to be your friend, is if they are disrespectful or controlling and can't let it go.

When a man is just stating his limits, establishing his territory, and is fine with leaving you if you cross those limits, he is sexually and emotionally mature. But if he fights as if for his life when you reject him or his advances, when he is constantly controlling or irritable, and vents that irritability on you, when he is prone to stressing you all the time, he is emotionally immature and has the bad kind of jealousy as a character flaw. This will make for a bad friendship and, therefore, a bad potential marriage. There is a subtle difference in what you see on the outside, but this is a crucial thing to understand about men and maturity. Many an otherwise healthy relationship has failed because the woman thought the man was being jealous when he was really only doing the mature masculine thing: defending his territory or even your safety.

In *Closer*, the only redeeming actions by the characters are near the end. Larry, having brutally defeated Dan for the affections of Anna, becomes more assertive. He states honestly what he really wants with her but is beyond trying to control her anymore through his vengeful tactics. When he drops his jealousy for good, she is back in his arms, though spent from all of the destruction. Alice, having suffered under Dan's tyranny and treachery, finally gives up punishing him silently through passive-aggressiveness. She gives up wishing he could be the caring gentleman he was in the past, gives up her wish for revenge over his affair, and is simply appalled at what she sees in him. Their relationship is done in her mind, and she is free to go out into the world independently to get her own needs met.

Like the couples in *Closer*, Caroline and Chad were another casualty of ignorance about how friendship is the cornerstone of anything worthwhile. Neither Caroline nor Chad was particularly effective at using their Cool Eyes. Caroline couldn't see that the way she pulled back from Chad in depression or lashed out at him in aggression prevented them from becoming anything more than sex partners. Had she been able to step back a bit, she would have noticed that she was hurting Chad with this behavior and that all of that pain would ultimately take its toll. At the same time, Chad did nothing to change the way Caroline treated him. If he'd been more cognizant of how Caroline made him feel and what caused Caroline's anger in the first place, he could have been more assertive about helping her find a more effective way to meet her needs. Eventually, Chad simply walked out when he realized he couldn't take it anymore. Could they have made it together? By failing to master Step One of Phase II, neither gave it a real chance.

Caroline's story was not to be with Chad. Her story would eventually take her through alcohol rehab, years of therapy, and then to a very different kind of man. This man didn't have the money Caroline always coveted, but he had the high character to follow her growth all the way to maturity. With this new man, Caroline learned to take assertive responsibility for her needs—and to bond with him in a deep and abiding friendship.

Spectrum of Unhappiness

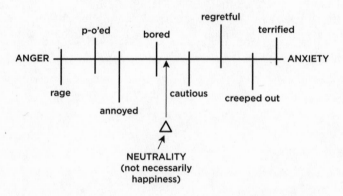

Whatever word you use, every uncomfortable emotion
you ever feel exists somewhere on this spectrum.

Chapter Six

~

If the Cowardly Lion Can
Get It, So Can You

Phase II: The Bonding in Friendship Phase
Step Two: Demonstrating Mastery of Anxiety

You must do the thing you think you know you cannot do. —ELEANOR ROOSEVELT

YOU'VE LEARNED HOW to master anger. If friendship is simply consistently shared, mutual positive emotion, then you have exactly half of the key to total mastery of friendship with a man. You know how to turn anger and depression into assertiveness, and then turn assertiveness into a positive emotional energy crucial to friendship, called well-being, a nurturing energy that comes with having your needs met. Well-being is one of two types of self-esteem.

I have never known a patient with a chronic state of unhappiness to have a high, durable level of self-esteem. Unhappy people don't go around proud of who they are, cheering up others. I have also never known a patient who has durably high self-esteem to get depressed or be unhappy for very long. Think about the people you know and remember the keys are the words "chronic" and "durable." It would seem that there is a direct relation between happiness and self-esteem. In fact, I argue that happiness *is* self-esteem. They are the same positive energy.

I've come up with an equation for self-esteem:

$$\text{SELF-ESTEEM} = \text{WELL-BEING} + \text{CONFIDENCE}$$

It really is as simple as that. You already know about well-being. Now we'll talk about confidence, and you'll have the two keys to lasting friendships.

Emotions exist on a spectrum. As a woman, you are always either more of one thing or more of its opposite. From serious on one end to silly on the other, from shy on one end to sassy on the other, you are always a bit more like one thing than its opposite.

If you could imagine a spectrum of unhappiness (of negative emotions), then anger would be on one end and anxiety on the other. Have you ever been out-of-your-mind angry, but then something frightened you and the anger evaporated? Have you ever been in a frightening, abusive workplace or relationship with a man, but you finally got so angry about it you didn't feel afraid anymore? When you are unhappy, you're either more angry, or more anxious. Try this on any negative emotion you have ever felt.

If you mix blue and yellow, you get green. These waves of light that carry color labels show us how green is both a certain amount of blue and a certain amount of yellow depending on the particular type of green it is. Emotion is the same. This easy way of classifying all negative emotions as part anger and part anxiety is extremely useful to us in understanding your friendship with Mr. Right. Once you understand the opposite ends of this spectrum, you can handle everything in between. Get total control of anger and anxiety in your life, and you will be able to transform any unhappiness, any negative emotional energy. All you need are the Anger and Anxiety Maps.

The Only Thing We Have to Fear (About Mr. Right) Is Fear Itself

We just learned in the last chapter that anger stored passively as depression kills your potential friendship bond or connection with Mr. Right, as does the destructive use of anger as aggression. These negative energies destroy a friendship, and therefore love. When you act in an immature way with anxiety—through being impatient or impulsive, or playing the victim—you deliver the same death sentence to friendship. These create more negative emotion. Master anxiety in addition to anger, and you can solve any and every negative emotion that hampers your friendship.

Evolutionary psychologists Leda Cosmides and John Tooby have a fascinating way of describing the evolution of the mind as it relates to anxiety. People developed into social groups originally as a defense against danger, such as tigers hunting us. We had to form alliances, which today you might call friendships. Since our brain anatomy hasn't changed much in the last few thousand years, what worked back then gets applied to new situations today.

Cosmides and Tooby describe how forming alliances is not an easy task, with the main difficulty being that members of the group can defect from it. (Remember that a friendship does not require loyalty and allegiance for all time, but just consistently shared, mutual positive emotion.) An alliance is an "I'll help you if you help me" arrangement. This is called *reciprocal altruism,* another way of saying that friendships need to be a win/win arrangement.

Yet as friendships go on, a problem threatens this arrangement. This is known as the free-rider problem: Someone in the social group can subtly take advantage of the favors offered and not give anything back. This is win/lose behavior. This causes most friendships to falter. What all of this means is that when we are in romantic relationships, the friendship part can only work well when both the man and woman are mature enough to be equals in a reciprocal-altruism exchange of positive emotional energy (which is science babble for "being in love").

You need a friend with a mature higher brain to be your love, and he needs you to be his as well. Many a self-help guru has lectured about how we either live in fear or live in love. Now you know exactly why fear and love cannot coexist. One is negative energy and one is positive. Anger is half of all negative energy and anxiety is the other half.

It is necessary to use an Anxiety Map to figure out this other half

Anxiety Map

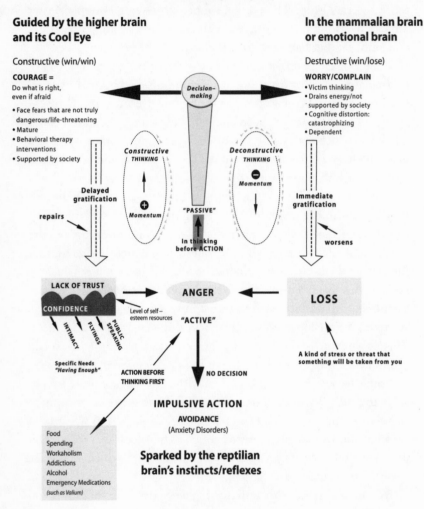

Guided by the higher brain and its Cool Eye

Constructive (win/win)

COURAGE =
Do what is right,
even if afraid

• Face fears that are not truly dangerous/life-threatening
• Mature
• Behavioral therapy interventions
• Supported by society

Delayed gratification

repairs

Constructive *THINKING*

+ *Momentum*

Decision-making

"PASSIVE"

In thinking before ACTION

Deconstructive *THINKING*

– *Momentum*

In the mammalian brain or emotional brain

Destructive (win/lose)

WORRY/COMPLAIN
• Victim thinking
• Drains energy/not supported by society
• Cognitive distortion: catastrophizing
• Dependent

Immediate gratification

worsens

LACK OF TRUST

CONFIDENCE

INTIMACY   FLYINGS   PUBLIC SPEAKING

Level of self-esteem resources

Specific Needs "Having Enough"

ANGER

"ACTIVE"

ACTION BEFORE THINKING FIRST

NO DECISION

LOSS

A kind of stress or threat that something will be taken from you

Food
Spending
Workaholism
Addictions
Alcohol
Emergency Medications
(such as Valium)

IMPULSIVE ACTION

AVOIDANCE
(Anxiety Disorders)

Sparked by the reptilian brain's instincts/reflexes

of friendship, because if we don't, it is very possible that you have your anger and depression very well managed, but are destroying a potential tight friendship with Mr. Right by letting anxiety get the best of you and dumping it into him.

No Place for the Weak Willed

Linda was a nurse in the town of Milwaukee, and she did quite well for herself. She was of Puerto Rican descent, beautifully brown-eyed, with thick, luxurious hair, and slender. Her self-respect was so strong that she vowed that she would never marry because she didn't need to.

One night, Linda went with her friends from the hospital to a local country music bar. There she met Jon, a local firefighter with the big burly arms of Popeye and just enough hair on his open-shirted chest to show he was a "manly man," even before Linda knew that he saved lives for a living.

Jon was, of course, taken with Linda's beauty. Step One of the Attraction Phase complete. She was too timid to walk up to him first, but she beckoned him with her eyes. One flutter, two, three, and he approached her as he'd approach a wall of flame—fearlessly.

Once they started talking, Jon found that Linda was closely connected to the arts community through her hospital's charity department. She loved going to art shows, as did he, because Jon was a closet oil painter. He was impressed with her numbers of friends, the fact that they were in the art world, and her status as a professional in medicine.

Intrigued by this Renaissance man's desire to change careers someday soon, Linda listened intently as Jon described his plans to move to New York with all the money he'd saved over the years. There he would start his new life as a painter and only volunteer for the fire service to keep up his skills.

While Linda was quickly falling in love (but not slow, patient, mature love), she suddenly felt a pang of dread. What if this wonderful man changed her world? She'd only known him a few hours, but what would it be like if she went off to New York with him? Then, what would it be like if he left her there alone someday because he died in a fire or wound up cheating on her?

Filled with sudden anxiety, Linda darted from the table and went to the bathroom without explanation. Jon was left waiting ten minutes, twenty, an hour more. Soon he got up to pace the bar looking for her. He felt a sense of protectiveness for her already, and he felt attraction.

As handsome as he was with his chiseled face and body and his dimpled chin, Jon could have any woman in Milwaukee he'd ever want. Yet more than any of them, he found himself wanting this missing, soft, feminine young nurse. Little did he know that she'd fled the bar, concerned that falling for a man like him could lead to even more anxieties than she'd already imagined.

Linda had unwittingly taken Jon through all three steps of the Attraction Phase: displaying beauty, alpha-male assistance, and putting the man to a contest to capture her. Unfortunately, Linda did none of it with the Cool Eye.

Two weeks later, when he ran into Linda at the grocery store, the normally levelheaded firefighter lost all wits about him. He approached her carefully, tapped her on the shoulder, and asked what he'd said to offend her.

"Nothing," Linda said. "I just had to go." Her sense of independence and composure was back. After a brief conversation, they decided to go out together.

Linda and Jon dated and got along famously. A friendship was born. Linda was even-tempered and could be assertive when she needed to be, almost never letting her anger get out of control. She was not a fit-thrower, given that all of her medical training had been about keeping one's cool. Step One of the Bonding in Friendship Phase was complete. They went on to find they shared many interests and values.

In a short time, Linda lost all sense of worry and took back her vow never to marry. With each shift of his muscular frame, Jon seemed to show her with his body that she was safe. With his soft voice, he'd tell her his stories of rescuing babies, pulling people—and their cats, too—from flaming buildings. She was safe with him. With each glance from his deep brown eyes, she came to know that she—a nurse who had never been out of state—would soon be living in New York.

Once in the Big Apple, however, all hell broke loose.

Linda had never attempted such a massive overhaul of her life before, let alone for a man. Her friends were only occasional voices on a cell phone, and her job was harder in Brooklyn than having three nursing jobs in Milwaukee. She was drained, and stressed, and soon began a terrible new habit.

Linda started to complain, one of the options for anxiety in our lives. She complained about her lack of friends and fretted openly about her lack of job security in a big-city hospital with a glut of nurses available at a day's notice should they fire her for some reason she couldn't fathom. Then she learned a habit of worrying, knowing that every night she came home to Jon, his huge firefighter's arms would cradle her until the worry ended in sleep. It only took three months of this anxiety habit for Linda to kill the budding friendship with Jon. Consistent anxiety cannot sustain a friendship, because it does not create positive emotion.

Jon moved out of their three-thousand-dollar-a-month little box of an apartment and into the YMCA. There he found impoverished peace. *At least,* he thought, *the people here don't complain all day and night.*

If You Give In to Loss, Then All Is Lost

What was going on with Linda? She was a bright, attractive, intelligent woman with a great career. She was well mannered, diplomatic, and didn't lose her cool. She knew what she wanted and went for it. She was sexy and beautiful. Yet her relationship with Jon ended up miserably. This happened because she didn't understand the importance of Step Two of the Bonding in Friendship Phase of courtship.

In this step of friendship, just as in Step One, a woman finds that the negative emotion in her comes from one of two causes. In the case of anxiety, the source is either experiencing a loss or a having a lack of confidence in the first place.

When Linda moved, she suffered the loss of many friends. She lacked confidence about how a woman gets about in a new city. She

Causes of Anxiety

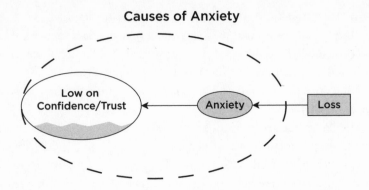

also lacked confidence about living with a man for the first time. So much was new and frightening to her. This led to a great deal of negative emotional energy.

As we've already discussed, one form of stress (negative emotional energy coming from outside you) is hurt. The other form is loss. A loss can be as little as a big bill arriving in the mail (a loss of money), or as huge as losing a whole person from your life. Being fired is a big loss, as is getting a major physical illness like diabetes (a loss of health). A divorce or breakup may be both a hurt (insulting, angering) and a loss (of companionship, money, security).

Linda suffered the loss of living far from her many friends, but by failing to master anxiety in her life, she had an eventual even bigger loss: the loss of her potential Mr. Right in Jon.

Once you are anxious as a woman, you can do only three things with the emotion:

Get *impulsive,* addictive, or avoidant. This is the passive way to let anxiety have its way with you (via the reptilian brain). This behavior is the link from the reptilian brain to the mammalian brain and happens when your Cool Eye is turned off regarding anxiety.

Get *masochistic,* needy, or take on a "poor me" attitude. This is an immature, destructive way to deal with anxiety, spurred on by negative ideas that are stuck in your higher brain. These bad beliefs can get the better of you when your Cool Eye is turned off.

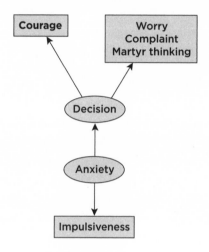

Courage

Worry
Complaint
Martyr thinking

Victim thinking, including helpessness, hopelessness, worry, complaint, regret, and a "poor me" attitude

Decision

Anxiety

Impulsiveness

Use courage. This is simply doing the right thing, no matter how bad you feel. It is encouraged by finding good ideas, or positive beliefs in your higher brain, with your Cool Eye turned on. It is the *only* path out of anxiety, addiction, and living like a victim.

Addicted to Anything but Love

When we have a passive stance in life, our Cool Eye is often turned off. When that happens, emotions run amok. This is like letting the reptilian brain's spark plug ignite the gasoline of the mammalian brain in an explosion rather than using the gasoline to fuel an engine.

The first type of thing that can then happen with anxiety is impulsiveness, a reflex driven by our fight-or-flight response to life-threatening situations. As you know, the reptilian brain is the center of instincts and reflexes. When you have anxiety present and just let the reptilian brain have its way with you, you tend to act without thinking first—which is exactly what impulsiveness is.

Anxiety is different from anger in how it is used. While anger that sits passively in us just gets us even more physically stationary, anxiety that we are passive about tends to jump us into impulsive, undirected action.

Options for Anxiety: Impulsiveness

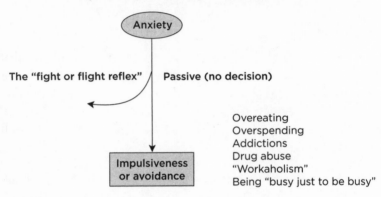

Impulsiveness is taking action without thinking. You actually need this ability when dealing with a threat to your life. If a speeding car is coming toward you, it is not time to sit and wonder what to do. It is time to dive into unplanned reflex action without thinking. When we are passive about life and fail to employ our Cool Eye skill, we tend to let our anxiety control us. This sends us into panic attacks, addictions of all kinds, avoidance of doing the things we really need to do, and a host of other problems. All of these are impulsive.

When we get very anxious and yet passive, we tend toward addictions—eating every donut we see in the workplace break room, smoking, drinking, and overspending and getting into debt, among others. Some people even become addicted to work as an impulsive response. Ironically, this kind of action tends to lead to greater anxiety in your life—and Mr. Right's. As long as this negative energy stays around, it does severe harm to a friendship. This is equally true, of course, if you see this kind of behavior in the man you are in a relationship with. It is a clear sign that your long-term future is in jeopardy.

Here is how it usually goes:

- The marriage is beautiful and the newlywed period blissful.

- The normal stresses of life grow—the kids, the dual incomes, the debt.

- The husband or wife gets a little twinge of anxiety when that stress keeps seeping in over months or years, finding his or her partner supportive and reliable as a shoulder to lean on.

- The husband or wife doesn't do anything about the stress. It grows.

- Eventually, the other spouse turns weary of being that shoulder, and he or she also becomes a bit anxious, perhaps even feeling victimized by his or her spouse's inadequacy.

- Now both are anxious, and one of them finds comfort in some addictive activity like pornography, alcohol, drugs, or something as seemingly tame as workaholism.

- The addiction robs more and more time, energy, or money from the relationship, a loss that amplifies the other spouse's anxiety until he or she also develops an addictive behavior.

- With the loss of attention (and time, energy, and intimacy), the negative energy of anxiety grows. Friendship fading in a once-beautiful marriage, the wife feels less secure and less prone to want to have sex. The husband feels less secure and less prone to do things to show how committed he is to her.

- The husband feels no commitment or love anymore, but also

feels fearful that she may be having sex with someone else. It has been a long time since she showed how turned on she is.

- The wife feels no sexual attraction or love anymore, but also feels fearful that he may be developing a commitment to someone else. It has been a long time since he showed how committed he is.

- Cheating might happen, irreparably damaging the strained relationship.

- Divorce.

Some years ago, there was a tragic but touching film about love called *Leaving Las Vegas,* starring Nicholas Cage and Elisabeth Shue. I have seen dramas such as this acted out in the real lives of women and men countless times in my practice. *Leaving Las Vegas* shows us a romantic triangle of sorts between prostitute Sera (Shue), failed Hollywood screenwriter Ben (Cage), and Ben's terminal addiction to alcohol. He's lost his wife and family in a sea of alcoholic self-destruction and arrives in Las Vegas planning to drink himself to death. Instead, Ben meets Sera, and they develop a strong attraction. However, Ben warns Sera that no matter what, she can never ask him to quit drinking. Lacking a Cool Eye, she agrees, ignoring any higher-brained intuition because she is so enthralled in their growing love. These are two people whose lives intersect just as they've reached their lowest depths of despair, a brief joining of the stories of two desperately needy people who together find sexual attraction but only a brief friendship. They accept each other as they are, with no attempts by one to change the other.

While some may see *Leaving Las Vegas* as a dark but beautiful love story, it points out something to us about the nature of anxiety, addiction, and the four types of love.

Four Kinds of Love, but Only One Can Lead to Mr. Right

There are, then, actually four kinds of love in the world, identified by everyone from the ancient philosophers to the troubadours of Renaissance times to directors of modern romantic comedies. They are the following:

Eros.   A one-way desire for sexualized love, which lovers might call unconditional. There is, of course, one significant condition: that you give in to the desire of the one who pines for you.

Agape.   A one-way giving of love, as a parent gives to a child. The only true unconditional love. There is no such thing as unconditional love in a soul mate relationship. Unconditional love is not a feature of mature relationships. It is a feature of parenting, a one-way giving to your child. This is the kind of love you agree to when you become a parent—a one-way deal where you give good emotion and the child receives your good emotion.

Philos.   Brotherly love, a two-way giving of love by equals, without a sexual component.

Amour.   Mature romantic love, a two-way giving of love by equals, with a sexual component that sparks the bond beyond just an ordinary friendship.

Have you ever longed for an inaccessible man? Eros is the kind of love you were feeling. Eros is the one-way, fiery, possessive desire of a sexually needy person for a sexually powerful person. It is essentially desire by the immature for the mature, like a child in need of parenting. Unfortunately, many, many couples feel this love for each other at the beginning of a relationship, do no step-by-step courtship whatsoever, and mistake this love for mature romantic love. Eros is actually not love at all, but desire, or sexual attraction igniting the reptilian brain. Eros is what drives all addictions. It is not shared, but is rather a one-way deal (a win/lose deal) where one person pines for the love of another and in some cases the object of desire might begrudgingly give it. Since it is not truly shared love, it fails our definition of friendship: consistently *shared*, mutual positive emotion. This is the main kind of love the characters of *Leaving Las Vegas* felt for each other. It is the kind of love shared by Romeo and Juliet, guided mainly by the reptilian brain without any higher brain skill.

Agape is the love of a parent for a child, or the love of God for humanity. It is the companion to Eros as a type of love. Like Eros, Agape is not shared. It is given one-way and is therefore not a form of friendship either. Our parents are not our friends. They have a different role and provide us with a different type of love.

Agape is a response to the Eros of another person but does not have a sexualized component. Eros and Agape are the source of unrequited love, and a mirror of the early Oedipal period from boyhood and girlhood, when little boys have to learn that Mommy belongs to Daddy and little girls learn that Daddy can only belong to Mommy in that secret, mysterious way. The bottom line on Agape is that it cannot be truly given if a person does not already have quite a full tank of self-esteem from which to give. In other words, people are not ready to be parents until they have more than enough self-esteem stored up inside to afford this kind of one-way giving called Agape. Agape is a kind of lofty, proper, ethical, safe, orderly love given with boundaries and limits, as a parent sets down rules and God sets down laws. In this sense, you might see Agape as a combination of both mammalian-brained love and higher-brained love.

Philos is different from Eros or Agape in that it is *shared* between two people of equal value and status. It is a pure emotional brain experience, a real love in the mammalian brain, rather than the sexualized version of it in the reptilian brain that we have called Eros. Even though I use the phrase "brotherly love," this is the kind of love you have for your girlfriends, classmates of either gender, or your close colleagues. It is the most common emotional meaning of the word "friend." It truly is consistently *shared,* mutual positive emotion.

Yet there is a special love we all want like no other, a kind of love that is not just fantasy, that is full of spark and magic, a promise of sexual joy and adventure, and yet not just lust. Amour is just that; not just sexual, not just familiar and full of happiness, but the kind of mature romantic love that can only be felt with Mr. Right. Amour is a two-way love between equals, full of both real friendship and sexuality. It is both a lightning bolt and familiar and comfortable— the state of being both true sexual lovers and emotional friends. Amour involves all three brains. Amour—mature romantic love—is that rare experience of having everything in one couple: the sexuality, the friendship, and the commitment.

Someone with a tendency toward addictions tends to love more in the form of Eros, because Eros is desire. Being romantically involved with someone like this is unfortunate because the desire he feels will gradually be directed away from you and toward the thing he is addicted to. One of the most subtle hints to an addictive personality in Mr. Wrong and in you is *avoidance.* When he doesn't like to talk about the tough stuff as mature people bring themselves to do, when you don't dare to try new activities together, or when you both run away from the question, "Where is this going between us?" you may already have your answer. You are both having problems with anxiety that are being used in the impulsive, addictive, and especially avoidant down-arrow of the Anxiety Map. This is what codependent people like the ones in *Leaving Las Vegas* do: They help each other avoid the reality that the addictions and reptilian-brained impulsiveness of Eros need to be kept in check if we are ever to find the mature romantic love that is Amour.

I want you to start acting like a relationship detective. Do you see how all these little pathways I am teaching you actually allow you to solve a grand mystery about relationships? Who would have guessed that workaholism actually perpetuates anxiety in a relationship, and therefore kills the friendship part of it? Who would have guessed that besides killing the sexual attraction of Phase I, overeating also kills the friendship bond in Phase II of courtship? By this point, *you* should be able to guess this.

Masochism: Otherwise Known as the Victim Attitude

Have you ever played the victim card? Have you ever been with a man who did? Have you ever complained, whined, moaned, had a pity-party, felt dependent, needy, hopeless, or helpless (even though you are a fully functional, walking, talking adult)?

Trust me; you're not alone. The second way we all use anxiety in our lives is a destructive, immature style of thinking called masochism, or playing the victim. This route for our anxiety actually has a link to negative ideas stored in the higher brain a long time ago. Beliefs like "I'm a loser," "Why bother?" and any other negative thought about yourself can steer your anxiety this way whenever you have your Cool Eye turned off.

Think of the Cool Eye as being totally off in the reptilian brain, partially on in the mammalian brain, and totally on in the higher brain. Masochism, passive-aggressiveness, and playing the victim card are at least a more conscious way of spending our anxious energy than impulsive addictions and avoiding things are. In fact, if there is any good side to masochism it is that it means that at least the person is thinking before she acts on her anxieties. The problem is that while masochism is active—a kind of decision—it is still a destructive decision.

All human beings have been masochistic at one time or another, because as children these traits of character are built into us for a very specific reason: They bond us to our mothers or other custodial adults. Why? Because as children, when we behave in ways like dependency, neediness, whining, fretting, worrying, helplessness, or with a poor-me attitude, our caregivers respond in positive ways. In small children, these behaviors might even seem cute and tug on our

Options for Anxiety: Worry

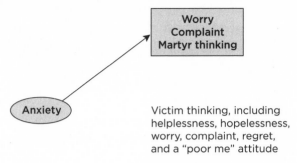

heartstrings. There is actually a pituitary hormone called oxytocin released in mothers in response to dependent behavior in their young. Oxytocin has been called the bonding hormone because it facilitates a bond between mothers and children.

People tend to respond much less positively to adults acting this same way. It sends them running from you, sometimes in repulsion. When you are frequently needy, worried, helpless, fretting, regretful, and overapologetic toward Mr. Right, or he is to you, it is a huge turnoff. A woman using her Cool Eye understands this and understands when she kicks over into this mode. She catches herself and puts a stop to the behavior with a reality check. *How old are you?* is what she asks herself and others.

Sometimes people's psychological ages fail to match their chronological ages. Many things cause this—traumatic experiences, immature parents who couldn't guide us to act any more mature than they were, a lack of resources or free time to be self-reflective—but only skill at the Cool Eye causes people to grow up. Without the Cool Eye, people get developmental arrest (they stop growing) or regression (falling backward in maturity level).

A woman lacking in Cool Eye skills doesn't grow or change. She keeps using masochistic methods right into adulthood. At this point, she is looked down upon as childish, immature, annoying, needy, prone to codependence, and avoided instead of bonded with in true adult friendship. Is this what you want Mr. Right to see in you? A little girl to take care of? A daughter to raise? I don't think so. The same goes for him, of course. If a man gets needy, dependent, constantly whines, moans, worries, gets hopeless or helpless even though he is a grown man, you may still be physically attracted to him, but your friendship with him will suffer interminably until one or the other of you changes your ways.

Here's what happens when you get into a cycle of masochism or worry:

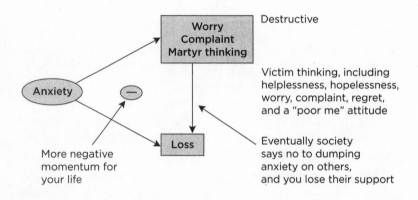

Say that your candidate for Mr. Right stops talking to you as much as usual and goes out with his friends more often. Since you are in the dark, of course you start trying to figure out why he's doing this. You imagine that maybe he is looking at other women, and it feels like a loss of love to you. Now you are anxious.

If you think before acting, you'll worry about it, complain to your friends, imagine him doing all kinds of horrible things, and start to feel helpless like a little girl. Suddenly, you have even more anxiety and more feelings of loss. You begin to push Mr. Right away by having Eros for him, by forcing him to be "Mr. Right Away." Little girls are dominated by Eros. They want what they want and they want it now. Your desire comes from a place of inequality because you have put yourself in an emotional state that is much less confident than his is. This forms a kind of loop. Say that you take yourself through this repetitive, obsessive worry process ten times:

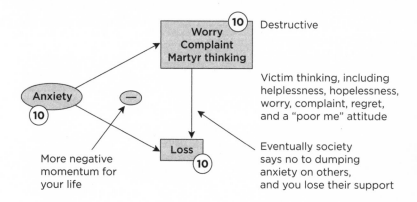

What happens in your brain? You feel as though you've experienced the loss ten times. Therefore, you have ten times the anxiety. All from the observation that your man talks less and goes out more.

Meanwhile, it's entirely possible that your potential Mr. Right has no idea that you're feeling any of this. When you finally dump on him how horribly worried you are about what he is doing behind your back—with all of the pent-up negative energy of your looped anxiety—you're going to send him running in the other direction. As a result, you cause yourself a genuine loss, just as Linda did when she moved to New York City.

Here is how it usually goes:

- The marriage is beautiful and the newlywed period blissful.

- The normal stresses of life grow—the kids, the dual incomes, the debt.

- The husband or wife gets a little twinge of anxiety when that stress keeps seeping in, finding their partner supportive and reliable as a shoulder to lean on.

- They don't do anything about the stress. It grows.

- Eventually, the other spouse turns weary of being that shoulder, and he or she also becomes a bit anxious, or even feels victimized by his or her spouse's dependency.

- With the friendship fading in a once-beautiful marriage, the wife feels less secure and less prone to want to have sex. The husband feels less secure and less prone to do things that demonstrate how committed he is to her.

- The husband feels no commitment or love anymore, but also feels fearful that she may be having sex with someone else. It has been a long time since she showed how turned on she is.

- The wife feels no sexual attraction or love anymore, but also feels fearful that he may be developing a commitment to someone else. It has been a long time since he showed how committed he is.

- Cheating might happen, irreparably damaging the strained relationship.

- Divorce.

If you respond to anxiety with impulsiveness or masochism, you cover your friendship in negative energy, suffocating it. So how do you deal with anxiety in a way that generates positive emotional energy? It takes courage.

Courage: The Cure for All Problems of Anxiety Within a Friendship

Courage is defined as "doing the right thing no matter how it feels." No matter how scary, hurtful, or difficult it is to do something that you fear, you still have the ability to do it. Courage is simply a decision. If you are living and breathing, you are capable of making a decision. In fact, the only time you don't want to use courage is when your life is truly in danger. Under those circumstances, *definitely* act impulsively. Let your reptilian brain do what it was designed to do—to keep you alive. For everything else you fear, you will win confidence every time you use courage. The definition of courage is to go out and do the right thing.

Options for Anxiety: Courage

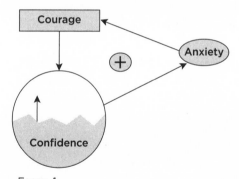

Do you see the plus sign in the diagram? Courage builds a momentum of positive emotional energy in your friendship, the energy of self-esteem called confidence.

Are you afraid to approach a man you love to address his alcoholism? Courage is the cure. If you don't use it, you are contributing to the destruction of your friendship through what is called enabling behavior—enabling an alcoholic to continue to pour new anxiety into your former friendship together.

Are you afraid to break up because you will be alone for a time? Courage is the cure. It's very uncomfortable, but if it is the right thing to do, you will become more confident and give yourself the chance at a better life.

The courage to be honest about what you want and expect, the courage to walk away from a date that feels disrespectful, or the courage to just say no to what you don't want, gives your potential Mr. Right a huge go sign for moving the relationship from mere sexual attraction into the emotional attraction of friendship. Courage and its reward of confidence are enormous signs to men of your emotional maturity and fitness to be a friend rather than just a one-night stand. A majority of real men (the type you consider potential Mr. Rights) are more gifted at courage and confidence than assertiveness (asking for what they want) or nurturing and well-being. Your ability to display courage and grow confidence makes a man think of you as a "guy's chick," the type he can truly bond with and feel totally understood and at peace with. Courage and its reward of confidence are the home-base emotions men tend to be most comfortable with. They make us feel as though we have known you all our lives emotionally. We want to befriend you.

You can use this to build up your life in a practical way. Right now. Try it out. Take anything you fear about men in general or your specific man. Feel the anxiety. Notice how you almost feel like pacing around (impulsively), or walking away from the fear. Notice how you then start thinking and thinking about the fear, and you see it grow into a big monster under the bed. You amplify it by worrying about it.

For example, perhaps you fear telling him that you want to move to a different town to find a better job. You worry about how he will react. You complain to your friends about how he isn't the type of guy to support you through such a hard transition—even though you've never raised the subject to him. The more you think about it, the more you become resentful that he might not support you. If you now look at how you feel about your friendship with him, you notice that he doesn't feel as much like a good friend. You start to feel more distant from him and less loving. Yet you are the one making all of this up in your masochistic thoughts. He doesn't even know you're thinking about this.

Finally, with all of your energy draining out of you and creating more tension and anxiety in you both, you try out courage. You approach him, sit him down, and tell him how you feel.

Ahhhh. . . . Even if he is not going to support your changing jobs or towns, you miraculously feel much better. You got it out on the table. You know you could do it again in the future. You survived. It didn't kill you to open your mouth and tell it like it is.

Interestingly, you find he is drawn to your bravery. He feels like you deeply understand men. For the first time in a while, he sees you as an equal, a force to be reckoned with. Even if at first he didn't like the idea of making such a radical change, he is willing to consider it. You hold fast to your desire and remain courageous as your confidence grows. You may even go so far as to say politely that if he can't move or support your dream, you understand, but you will have to go anyway. What a leap of courage that would take for you! You need to learn to risk the death of the relationship in favor of your dreams.

He thinks about this and realizes he would not want to lose you over a job you want and dream you must have. He agrees to team up with you and find a job of his own in the new town. Your dream comes true, all because of your willingness to be courageous. Ultimately, it doesn't make a difference whether you move or not. Knowing that he would have moved with you takes your relationship to a new level.

Confidence is the only way for a woman to learn to father herself when there is no daddy around to face her fears for her. It is a crucial, priceless power that every woman needs. Once you have mastered your ability to handle anxiety—and identified that your potential Mr. Right is capable of doing the same—you can move on to

Step Three of Phase II: mastering the ability to work as a team emotionally.

Following Your Story

What did we learn from Linda's story with Jon? We learned that anxiety could snuff the life out of any relationship regardless of how powerful the attraction. Linda let her sense of loss get the best of her. She lacked the skills to face her stresses courageously, instead relying on the much weaker—and overwhelmingly more negative—response of complaining. She choked her love affair with Jon to death by doing so.

Linda's story was not to be with Jon for life. It was to return to Milwaukee and her friends. She felt safer there and this sense of safety gave her the chance to build upon her life. Over the course of the next few years, she would learn that courage was the one and only cure for anxiety. Not long after, she found a doctor on a different hospital floor from hers. This would be her Mr. Right. He found her looks and physical presence sexually attractive, and her sense of bravery extremely emotionally attractive.

There is a wonderful story that helps explain how to make anxiety your ally in friendship. It is the story of Psyche.

Psyche was a mortal so beautiful that the goddess Aphrodite became jealous, and decided to wed her to Death. Dispatched to assure the ceremony took place was Cupid, the son of Aphrodite. Yet when Cupid laid eyes on fair Psyche, he accidentally pricked himself with one of his own arrows of love, falling for the human maiden completely.

Thinking she was to marry Death, Psyche was stunned when she awoke in a perfect paradise married not to the cruel god of the underworld, but rather to a man who would not allow himself to be seen by her as his prime rule of marriage.

The jealous goddess Aphrodite, mother of Cupid, put Psyche to a series of challenges in order to maintain hold of her anonymous son and god. These challenges are the very initiation rites of a girl destined to become a mature feminine woman. The ultimate challenge was to face the ultimate fear: the fear of death. Psyche had to go down into the bowels of the earth, to the underworld of Death in Hades, and steal a vial of perfume from Persephone, the wife of the king of the underworld. Psyche then needed to return to the world of the living to give the perfume to Aphrodite. If she failed, she could not keep her husband.

Psyche receives two coins with which to pay Charon, the boatman responsible for ferrying the souls of men from the world of the living to the afterworld. She also receives two barley cakes for sustenance. Psyche is challenged by lost souls and beggars in the underworld who are hungry for her barley cakes, or who ask her for the coins for passage back to the living. If she gives these (which is basic in her feminine nature), she will have no way back from her mission, and no way to lure the three-headed dog, Cerberus, away from his guard post at the gates of Hell. What she learns here is that a woman must at times courageously forsake others in order to fulfill her purpose in life. She must move beyond the regrets of the past and worry over the future to choose instead just the hopeful uncertainty of the unknown.

We have discovered the meaning of courage in friendship: to do what is right, no matter how bad it feels in order to eliminate the anxiety that would tear your friendship down and ultimately bring down the entire relationship. For men, this most often will involve going out into the world to face the fears that threaten your mutual welfare. For example, he must face his fear of flying in order to preserve your long-distance relationship. For women, courage most often involves daring to risk your connectedness with some others in order to be with him. For example, you may face the fear of saying no to your mother's wish for you to remain in your hometown rather than run with him to the big city.

For Psyche, the ultimate fear was that of death itself. For women, failure to face the death of the illusion of security in this world, of

constancy, and the flow of life through various friendships, relationships, and faraway places that beckon you to grow, where you may
find Mr. Right, or as important, find yourself, leads to being perpetually lost. This leaves you halfway between the security of childhood
and the certainty of a joint story with the man of your dreams. Ironically, the very thing you may hold most dear—the youthful security
of connectedness to others—may be the very thing you must courageously give up in order to find the very same thing in a more mature,
adult security in a new life, a new city, a new path that surprises you
with how close it takes you to what you were really meant to do with
your life all along. The ability of your Cool Eye to read Serendipity's
clues and signs gives you faith in yourself. This ever-present friend
will tell you, "It's time to do courage. You'll be utterly alone when
you do it, but never alone again afterward. It will be all right."

The lesson for your story as a woman is that while courage may
seem a frightening, lonely thing—when every part of your feminine
being screams for connection and assistance from others through a
hard time—courage provides a joyful escape from the prison of the
past and the lost confusion of being in between, at a fork in the road
of life. The path your Cool Eye will whisper for you to take is the
one that requires the most courage. Do so, and you will find Amour.
The marriage vow says, "For better or worse, 'til death do us part."
This is not a tragic agreement on a day of fear. This is a vow of
courage in a relationship meant for life with Mr. Right.

Having cultivated the assertiveness to mother yourself, and now,
the courage to father yourself toward being a good friend, you are
ready to find what could only be called best-friendship with Mr.
Right as a self-sustaining team.

Chapter Seven

~~~

Opposites Attract

Phase II: The Bonding in Friendship Phase
Step Three: Demonstrating Teamwork and Complementary Personality

We don't accomplish anything in this world alone . . . and whatever happens is the result of the whole tapestry of one's life and all the weavings of individual threads from one to another that creates something.

—SANDRA DAY O'CONNOR

THERE ARE ALL KINDS of friendships. Of course, women and men shade the distinctions differently. For women there are bar buddies, acquaintances, *friendly* acquaintances, coworkers, guy friends, gay friends, and regular girlfriends, not to mention best friends. This is all going on in your mammalian brain, the place of emotion and friendship; yet this brain is influenced a little by the instincts of the reptilian brain much in the way that coffee is influenced by the sugar you put in it. While the reptilian brain of women is all about connectedness to others, the reptilian brain of men is about independence—the ability to stand alone. So most women have a whole variety of friends, and most men lump all friends into one category. To them, everyone else is either a stranger or an enemy.

Friends with whom men share mutual positive emotion are usually of similar rank to us because of how our reptilian brain influences our social choices. In other words, women can feel natural being friends with other women who may be of widely different

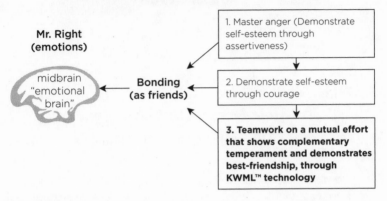

The Bonding Phase (Emotional Attraction)

socioeconomic status as long as they share something highly valued in common. For instance, a wealthy woman and a poor woman may bond over the fact that they are both mothers. For women, it is about belonging. Yet when men befriend men, we rarely associate with guys who are of much lower social status than ourselves, because that can ultimately bring down our own status in the eyes of other males, even if we share something of high value to us, like a love of sports. Likewise, we rarely associate with men who are of significantly higher social status, because these men make it difficult for us to feel valuable, unless they officially agree to mentor us the way a father might. Otherwise, they make us feel the shame of lesser status by comparison.

Given these differences, how in the world are men and women to find friendship with each other, and therefore love? It turns out that as the differences we have in our reptilian brains actually fit us together like puzzle pieces in sexual attraction, the same holds true for us in emotional attraction. Only this time, the notion of opposites attract has less to do with gender and more to do with simple personality style.

This last step of the Bonding in Friendship Phase is one of two bridges from emotional attraction to intellectual attraction. People of any personality style can be just friends, because all that requires is shared positive emotion. Yet to be best friends, something more is required. You have to have something the other person lacks and vice versa, something opposite not only about your types of emotional energy, but intellectual style as well. Think about anyone that you have considered a durable best friend. You'll likely find that while you are more gentle and nurturing emotionally, your friend is more outgoing and more confident than you are. While you are more logical and analytical intellectually (left-brained), your friend is less so—more carefree, humorous, and innovative (right-brained). This is true for friends Ben Affleck and Matt Damon, the couple Brad Pitt and Angelina Jolie, and a host of other creative teams and couples, regardless of whether romance is going on between them.

You might then notice that one of the differences between the people we call friends and those we call best friends involves the degree of chemistry and teamwork we engage in together. Someone you see once a month in a bar is less involved with you in a collaborative way—and certainly not in creating something with you—than a person with whom you jointly work on a project (whether that project is related to work, play, or some other avocation).

This is the goal of Step Three of the Bonding in Friendship Phase: to bond a man to you as more than just your basic friend who merely shares positive emotion with you consistently. After all, your pet cat can bond with you emotionally. This step takes you to the very edge of true commitment by showing that the people with opposite emotional and intellectual abilities make the best team members and the best friends.

The one true Mr. Right cannot just be a dinner friend or a shopping friend. He must absolutely qualify as your best friend in the world—the one who is a more valued, trusted, and collaborative friend than even your dearest girlfriends—your most-prized companion for life. This is one of the challenges we saw given to Psyche—that in Aphrodite's last test, she had to forsake her connectedness and charity to other women on the road through Hell. If Psyche didn't forsake all others to pursue her life's goals and her marriage, she would not survive. She would never see her husband, Cupid, again. Of course, in real life you may have many friends and even women as best friends. However, if it became clear to your husband that he was not ranked as the best friend among even your best girlfriends, you will have then already broken your relationship at Step Two of Phase I. (He will innately feel himself to be lower status in being with you and the sexual attraction would then die underneath your friendship with him.)

Think of our journey so far as one where we rise higher and higher through the three brains stacked in the head of Mr. Right. Then it makes sense that in this last step of friendship development, we begin to address not only the sharing of positive emotion, but a good matching of intellect as well, the domain of the higher brain's cerebral cortex. Why? Because contrary to what you have ever learned about birds of a feather flocking together, what I have learned from the tens of thousands of people I have treated, befriended, or communicated with is that opposites attract as well. To find a true Mr. Right, birds of a feather flock together in the shared beliefs and values of the higher brain, but in this brain opposites attract in the kind of teamwork we all call best-friendship.

Some Relationships Don't Balance Out on the Ledger

Do you remember Carl and Cathy from the introduction? They were mature people who worked for the same accounting firm. They were physically attractive, middle-class African Americans who liked many of the same outdoor activities in California and were quite skilled at the Attraction Phase with each other. Cathy displayed her beauty well, was fit, and raised Carl's status as an alpha-male by virtue of her father being the head of their firm. Other guys sought after Cathy, which led Carl naturally into a competition to win her over in romance.

Everything between Carl and Cathy was great for three months.

They had no big fights and no worries. They had fun together, and it was a time filled with sexual attraction and mature handling of the stresses that might have caused negative emotion and killed their friendship. Things were going so well that they decided to move in together.

That's when the problems started. They found they couldn't work together to find the right fit. They were too identical in psychological skill. Both were analytical accountants, so when they searched for a place, it had to be of such analytically perfect fit for the both of them, they couldn't agree to sign the lease. Both were nurturing people emotionally, so no one was more gifted at daring to make the first move on settling on a place. In fact, they both could have used more confidence.

After looking for six months, they finally agreed on a place, but in moving in together, neither could decide how to best decorate it. Soon there was a growing competition, because they were once again too identical. Every decision—whether it was about curtains, the color of the bathroom, or where to put the television—became a long-drawn-out and increasingly contentious negotiation.

Though they were mature, in good spirits, and cared about each other, Carl and Cathy broke up. They had started in a positive emotion-filled friendship, but they were too similar in personality. These similarities—and the conflicts created by seeing the world too similarly—slowly drained each other's confidence. Eventually, it was in such short supply that the friendship died.

Carl and Cathy failed to utilize their Cool Eyes to realize that, while much of their relationship was very good, they didn't have the foundation for a best-friendship. You can avoid having this happen to you if you check your personality to be certain it is the healthy opposite of that of your potential Mr. Right. People with opposite, complementary skills survive the most in a marriage. In fact, opposites are the only way to durable emotional good times, and the only pairing that can guarantee the good teamwork that leads to the next and last phase of courtship—the Commitment Phase.

The concept I am about to teach you is a profound way to rapidly analyze the personality of any man you are interested in and see if he is a great match for you or not. It is also a way to predict the likely future of your relationship as being one of long durability or certain breakup. It is easy to understand and identify the exact, deep emotional connection between soul mates.

KWML™: Kings, Warriors, Magicians, and Lovers

Is it possible to have a great sex life with a man and at the same time feel like something's missing? Have you ever felt like a man was physically loyal, but cheated on you emotionally? Did it ever feel like a man wasn't there for you emotionally, even though he physically did everything he could to be supportive? Did it ever seem like you couldn't be fun together unless other friends were around? Did it ever seem like doing things together, solving problems together, or trying to coordinate your lives tended to drain one or the other of you? The problem in all of these was a poor KWML™ match.

As we've been continually noting, friendship is consistently shared, mutual positive emotion. In securing frequent positive emotions with a potential Mr. Right, it is important to be assertive—to turn anger into well-being—and to be courageous, to turn anxiety into confidence. Essentially, when we do these two things we manufacture the only two ingredients of what we all call self-esteem, which is both a nurturing energy of having enough, and an outgoing, action-prone energy of handling what life throws us.

If well-being is a feeling of being nurtured and having our needs met the way a good mother would, then that means that assertiveness is the only mature, adult way to *mother* ourselves. Yet if confidence is a feeling of being able to withstand risk, change, and growth the way a good father would teach, then that means courage is the only mature, adult way to *father* ourselves. If a woman is more gifted from birth at being a nurturer, and a man is more gifted from birth at taking risks and tolerating changes in his life, it means that as a couple or as a team, they have a complete set of emotional skills.

They make a self-sustaining friendship team and don't have to cheat on each other emotionally, compete with each other destructively, or have an unhealthy number of fights or disagreements. When your emotional traits complement Mr. Right's, you have an indomitable combo.

Of course, emotional energy dominance is not a gender-specific thing. There are many emotionally nurturing men and superbly confident women. The point is that, when it comes to emotions, opposites attract. Opposite emotional skills create a perfect, self-sustaining friendship.

Have you ever felt extremely *un*confident about something that was coming up, such as a business presentation when you have not done much public speaking or a social event that you need to attend by yourself? When you have a fear such as this, what tends to happen? If you're like most people, you procrastinate, make excuses, and do everything you can to avoid the thing, even if you know deep down it will benefit your life. You let the time pass and the opportunity is gone. You don't get the promotion. You miss the social event and a chance to meet new friends (maybe even Mr. Right). As a result, your self-esteem plummets.

Now what if there was a man in the picture who is extremely confident? He encourages you and listens to your fears, but then says, "Enough. Now get out there, do your presentation, and make me proud." He doesn't do the thing for you. He treats you like an equal rather than a child, but also offers a shoulder to lean on. As you talk to him, you feel more energetic. That energy is called confidence. He has lent you his huge storehouse of confidence, and that little nudge has gotten you to go out to generate your own courage.

This is an example of emotional teamwork—the kind of teamwork emotional opposites generate for each other.

The need for emotional teamwork manifests in myriad ways. I recently worked with a woman who was *supremely* confident. She is an attorney who has won many awards and is an undefeated partner in a well-known law firm. Yet she is sad beyond belief because she is alone romantically. Men are afraid of her power and status, feeling they can never rise up to her level of alphaness.

This woman labors on so energetically in her career in part because she has a secret belief that there is some reward at the end of the rainbow for all her aggressive work. If she can just prove herself well enough in the world of men, she will somehow qualify for a husband who's right for her. He'll just drop out of the sky like in some silly car commercial. She believes that if she takes up male-dominated sports and takes "their" jobs away from them, then maybe men will love her. All the while, she is working herself to an early death. She has no loving man in the picture and not even any friends. All she knows is work, ambition, and accomplishment.

What she doesn't know is KWML™. She thinks all men ought to provide her confidence, not realizing that she has more than enough confidence for five people. She doesn't think to look for a nurturing man, a man who is full of well-being. He is not the hard-driving attorney type. He is a poet, dancer, writer, counselor, or schoolteacher. He is the type of Mr. Right that serves as the perfect emotional opposite and complement to this confident woman. What she needs to learn is that to find a Mr. Right who is capable of being her best friend and teammate, she needs to embrace the notion that opposites attract.

This is as true with intellectual *style* as it is with emotion. Everyone knows that we tend to care for others who share something in common with us (like attracts like—"birds of a feather flock together"). Yet your intellectual style is like nothing more than an idea tank to fill with ideas. As such, your *style* is different from the *content* you fill it with. You may have heard that there are left brain–dominant people in the world and right brain–dominant people. In intellectual style, the left-brainers are the ones who are logical, orderly, analytical, and always on time. They care about history and neatness, and never let you forget the past. On the other hand, right-brainers in style are intellectually creative and artistic, employing the spontaneous, flexible thinking of the musician, performer, actor, sales chief, creative director, or politician. They help you envision a future.

These two styles are also a best friend, soul mate pairing to look for in the potential Mr. Right. If you are a left-brained accountant who is overly analytical, and he is as well (like Cathy and Carl), then some day you are going to bore each other intellectually. You don't solve problems together well as a team, since you approach problems the same way and miss the crucial ability to creatively navigate your way around obstacles, which the right brain allows. If you are a right-brained musician who has trouble even balancing a checkbook and your potential Mr. Right is the same way, you're in for a future failure of the friendship part of your relationship. You'll both miss the need to have the targeted, detail-oriented planning skill that the left brain allows. Things will often be overstimulating, with drama wherever you turn. How will you remain friends who have consistently shared, mutually positive emotion if you're always either over-analyzing the tiny details of life or worrying about whether your house will be repossessed?

One of the things that women have told me about special men in their lives is that there's something more than just positive emotion in the friendship. They get each other. They seem to have an effortless connection of some kind and complementary problem-solving skills. When the woman is down, the male friend might offer a detailed plan (left brain) to lifts her spirits. When she can't solve a problem, he seems to have a creative solution (right brain) and is willing to hear her out as far as the emotions she feels.

Some friendships seem like a lot of work, peppered with some boredom here and there and excitement once in a while. Other friendships are more than just that. They are emotional and intellectual and somehow always seem interesting if not always exciting. People in these friendships tend to challenge each other and yet love each other more deeply all the time. They make each other feel like more of a man or more of a woman because of the way they know each other and do things together. (This kind of special friendship doesn't have to be romantic, of course. The romantic part of romantic friendship comes from the Attraction Phase, not the Friendship Phase. It is, however, critical for a lasting romantic relationship.)

In finding the kind of emotional and intellectual chemistry between friends I am talking about, women need look no further than the hugely successful TV show *Sex and the City*. The creators of that show did an amazing job of creating an ensemble of friends in which the four main female characters represent examples of all four variations of the feminine personality. Charlotte (played by Kristin Davis) is nurturing, conservative with emotion, and left-brain dominant. Carrie (Sarah Jessica Parker) is also nurturing and full of well-being, yet she's creative and right-brained as a romantic columnist. Miranda (Cynthia Nixon) is more confident and outgoing emotionally than either Charlotte or Carrie, yet intellectually left-brained and targeted like Charlotte. Samantha (Kim Cattrall) is overconfident, not very nurturing at all, and yet right-brained in her wild and unpredictable escapades.

People aren't such simple types in real life, though, right? Of course not. Since human beings can't be pegged in little boxes of personality style, but rather live on a spectrum in a quantum psychology, we have something priceless here if we *cross* two spectrums: the emotional one and the intellectual one. We take a line that has extreme emotional giftedness at nurturing (well-being) on one end and hard-driving action (confidence) on the other. Then cross it with a line that has extremely obsessive left-brained analytical intellect on one end and extreme unpredictable, wacky, dramatic, creative right-brained intellect on the other.

This leaves us with four quadrants or zones on a circle, each of a different style of emotion and intellect in one package. I have given names to these zones of a person's psychological temperament, or style of dealing with the world, communicating, behaving physically, and romantically relating. The names I enjoy using for human temperament are King (for men) or Queen (for women), Warrior, Magician, and Lover. Note that by using the term "Lover," this time

I don't mean it to indicate someone with whom you necessarily have a sexual attraction to or have sex with. I mean it this time to refer only to the emotional and intellectual nature of their *personality*.

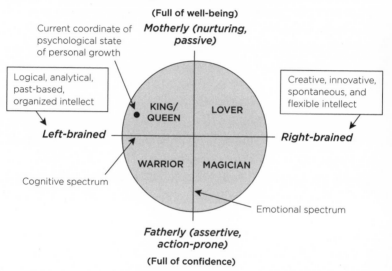

The Cognitive Emotional Spectrums Defining All Human Behavior

(Full of well-being)

Current coordinate of psychological state of personal growth

Motherly (nurturing, passive)

Logical, analytical, past-based, organized intellect

Creative, innovative, spontaneous, and flexible intellect

KING/ QUEEN   **LOVER**

Left-brained   **Right-brained**

WARRIOR   **MAGICIAN**

Cognitive spectrum

Emotional spectrum

Fatherly (assertive, action-prone)

(Full of confidence)

In my reading, I once came across a book on Jungian psychology, *King, Warrior, Magician, Lover* by author Robert Moore, and I rather liked the names as they paint a picture of four very different social roles for men. They also were common to a particular culture in history associated often in literature with romantic love: the medieval times of knights, castles, and fair maidens. Moore's book was set in one particular school of psychology (Jungianism) and was written for men interested in their spirituality. As I constructed my system for you, I brought in systems and processes from nearly all modern schools of psychology and wanted to synthesize them to help both men and women with dating and relationships. Applying these many principles to the four names that sounded so romantic, I discovered a direct connection to combinations of both my two types of self-esteem and the two types of intellectual style called right-brained and left-brained.

This was a completely new way to use the names of King, Warrior, Magician, and Lover, by combining Jungian psychology with every other branch of psychology seen in my diagrams. One could use these four names to describe four differing classes of human temperament, which I would like you to think of as a sort of starting point for growing a more complete, mature, sophisticated personality.

Temperament

In newborn babies, the term "temperament" refers to the basic, undeveloped nature of a child's personality. We say that some babies are "colicky," "happy," "curious," "shy," and so on. The same is true of full-grown men and women. We have developed personalities as adults, but these personalities are grown on top of the original temperament we were born with. As we grow more mature, we all become more difficult to label with a particular temperament of youth. Still, you can see remnants of it in people.

There are four unique variations in style of temperament for human beings, and we all slowly grow a complete and mature personality by practicing the skills of the other three temperaments as we go through life. The King (or Queen) temperament is nurturing and analytical. The Warrior is assertive and analytical. The Magician is assertive and creative. The Lover is nurturing and creative. In terms of emotional and intellectual attraction, the perfect pairings of these people's styles are their opposites, across the healthy center point of the circle where a completely mature and well-rounded person operates. Nobody you will have ever met can have perfect maturity or a perfect personality. We all are at least a little bit imbalanced in these four at best, or out there, off-kilter, or off our rocker at worst. Yet in best-friendships and committed relationships, we can help each other grow more than we ever could alone. Certainly, this is what you want in Mr. Right. Kings (or Queens) pair up perfectly in a relationship with Magicians, and Lovers pair perfectly with Warriors. They need each other.

In *Sex and the City*, you might clearly see that Charlotte is a Queen by temperament. She is more passive and nurturing than either Miranda or Samantha. She tends to be orderly and proper, remembers details well, and lives her life by rules (all left-brained), yet is not the first one to easily dive into a social setting and be the life of the party; rather, she's better one on one as an adviser to her friends (less confident and more full of well-being). She also has her anger more under control than her anxiety.

Miranda is more outgoing and confident than either Charlotte or Carrie, though not as much as the wild and dramatic Samantha is emotionally. She is organized, living her life by rules, like Charlotte (left-brained), yet is willing to dive into a conflict and be the first to speak up (confident). She, on the other hand, has her anxiety more under control than her anger. She is a Warrior.

Samantha is outgoing and confident, more so than either Charlotte or Carrie, but not more so than Miranda. Her right-brained ways make that confidence unpredictable and politically magical. She always knows where the party is and always has a creative way to solve her problems with men, sometimes in ways thought to be outlandish by the other women. She is a Magician.

Carrie is the star of the show, a nurturing, romantic, dreamy writer who is more caretaking and motherly than either Miranda or Samantha, and yet different from Charlotte in that she doesn't force herself to be quite so proper, organized, and dignified. She sees the symbolism and deep meaning in the world in a way that clearly shows her right-brained intellect. She serves as the example to the others of some of the deepest mistakes and rewards possible with men. She is a Lover.

If these four women didn't have personality hang-ups, there wouldn't have been six seasons of the show. We are lucky to see how

The KWML™ of *Sex and the City* Women

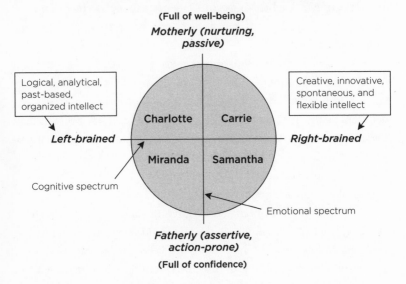

(Full of well-being)
Motherly (nurturing, passive)

Logical, analytical, past-based, organized intellect

Creative, innovative, spontaneous, and flexible intellect

Charlotte   Carrie

Left-brained   *Right-brained*

Miranda   Samantha

Cognitive spectrum

Emotional spectrum

Fatherly (assertive, action-prone)
(Full of confidence)

it is that they meander through various failed relationships and get closer and closer to relationship maturity by the very last episode—one where they all marry or are about to. With the technologies in this book, you can see why each of their relationships failed until the last TV season. They start to resemble one another by the end of that season because they have each grown from functioning in the outside areas of my circle above toward its center as they mature.

In my diagram above, the outer reaches of the circle signifies an emotional and intellectual imbalance of skill, which one would see in human immaturity. To the center, a person starts to find balance of the two parts of self-esteem—a complete and mature self-esteem—and there they find the maturity in a balance of both left-brained planning skill at details of life and right-brained skill at flexible thinking, spontaneity, thinking on one's feet, and creativity. In other words, toward the center, all mature people begin to look like all other mature people, each balanced in their emotional and intellectual abilities. We see

The KWML™ of *Sex and the City* Men

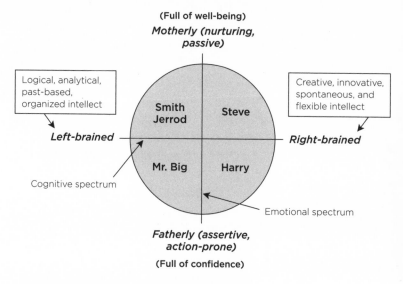

(Full of well-being)
Motherly (nurturing, passive)

Logical, analytical, past-based, organized intellect

Creative, innovative, spontaneous, and flexible intellect

Smith Jerrod

Steve

Left-brained

Right-brained

Mr. Big

Harry

Cognitive spectrum

Emotional spectrum

Fatherly (assertive, action-prone)
(Full of confidence)

the same four temperaments in the four boyfriends of the *Sex and the City* women.

The men in *Sex and the City* have much to learn as they grow more balanced in the other three temperaments that will make them ready for marriage. Mr. Big learns more sensitivity and Lover-like appreciation for the emotional side of life (of which Carrie is a natural master). Steve has to weather the challenges of life that a Mr. Big would find effortless and to become more of a tough guy himself. Smith Jerrod, the model-turned-actor, must develop the skill at publicity and outgoing physical presence that are the natural skills of Samantha the Magician. And Harry, the outgoing Magician male who lacks social propriety and attention to detail, must master these very things that are the natural skills of his eventual wife, Charlotte.

Carrie grows more Warrior traits in her Lover self and finds herself better suited for the soul mate, Mr. Big, who is himself a male Warrior in temperament. By doing this (while he grew toward

The Warrior and the Lover on the Cognitive Emotional Spectrums

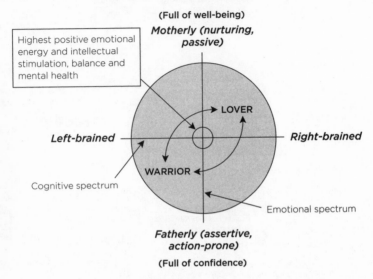

being more sensitive and having Lover-like skills), they got close enough in personality on the two sides of the circle's center to "get" each other, and bond for life. The same was true of Miranda, the Warrior female who marries the soft, cuddly, nurturing, distractible right-brained Lover Steve.

Samantha, the wily, outgoing Magician female pairs up with the organized, thoughtful, nurturing, and trusted adviser on life, Smith Jerrod, who is a King in temperament. In parallel, Charlotte the Queen marries the wild and crazy attorney, Harry, a Magician male.

Opposites attract. A Lover is best with a Warrior and a King or Queen is best with a Magician. Carrie (Lover) dated Aidan (a Lover), Alexander (King), and Berger (another Lover). Charlotte (a Queen) was wed to a doctor (who was a King), divorced him, and spent the rest of the show in unsatisfying relationships until she found a true Magician in Harry. Miranda (a Warrior) dated various

The King/Queen and the Magician on the Cognitive Emotional Spectrums

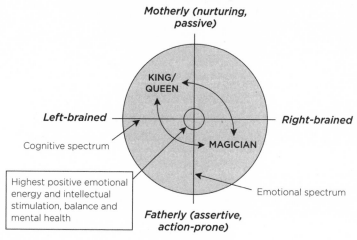

Motherly (nurturing, passive)

KING/QUEEN

Left-brained

Cognitive spectrum

Right-brained

MAGICIAN

Highest positive emotional energy and intellectual stimulation, balance and mental health

Emotional spectrum

Fatherly (assertive, action-prone)

jerks (Warriors) until she found Steve (a Lover). Samantha (Magician) tried her hand at Mr. Big (Warrior) only to be rebuffed, Richard Wright (Warrior) only to be cheated on, until she found Smith Jerrod (who was a King).

Part of the reason *Sex and the City* felt so real to women is that the personality dynamics are true to real life. Across the board, not according to their hobbies, religious beliefs, and political leanings, but simply by personality style, a Queen pairs well with a Magician, and a Warrior pairs well with a Lover. Why? Because they cause each other to grow toward psychological health, with more emotional and intellectual balance. They are natural coaches to each other, teammates in life who, without any special training at all, naturally encourage the maturity of the other just by being themselves. By being a *best friend*.

As you get skilled at identifying men quickly according to these classifications of personality, you will save yourself literally years of

Sex and the City Relationships

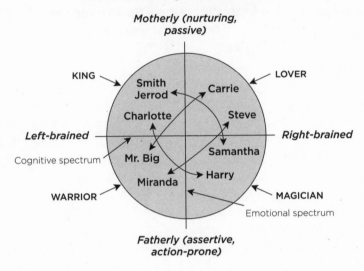

time spent pursuing, dating, and even marrying the wrong men. To have a best friend and soul mate, you want to find your perfect opposite in personality. That is not to say, though, that pairings of other temperaments—even identical ones—could not work out for you. It would just take a great deal more work since you would often need to go outside the relationship to other friendships in order to fuel up on the kind of emotional energy and style of thinking that doesn't come naturally to you. For example, a King and Queen will be both so overly serious, lacking right-brained ability at humor, that they will at times get into a rut or feel bored with each other. Two Warriors may tend to lack right-brained ability to be flexible and spontaneous, letting a minor misunderstanding escalate into a serious fight instead of dropping it. Two Lovers may kill each other with kindness and sensitivity, not able as a team to pull out the necessary Warrior's skills for solving life's most serious problems. And two Magicians might outperform each other to death, neither able to be grounded enough to nurture each other emotionally or calm down to the details of life intellectually.

Let's go deeper into why I choose the names King/Queen, Warrior, Magician, and Lover to apply them to my new model of personality for men and women both.

Imagine a medieval castle where there are all kinds of people and duties. A King or Queen watches over the land. He or she makes rules and has plans to grow the kingdom in a systematic way. He or she is nurturing (full of well-being) for the people of the kingdom and cares for their welfare. Kings and Queens are the top advisers people go to for justice, planning, and permission to try new ideas. In real-life relationships, men and women with this temperament contribute these gifts to their friendships.

A Warrior guards the land, protecting the people (with confidence) and taking targeted action when unpleasant things must be done. Warriors are the enforcers and therefore respect rules, though they don't necessarily come up with the rules themselves. They have very few friends, but they are very close to the ones the have. Warriors take orders from the King or Queen, team up with the Magician to solve the problems of society, and wage their wars to do honor for their Lovers. They fall in love with the Lovers, if for no other reason than because this is the only other human temperament capable of making them truly laugh.

The Lover is also like a poet, a court jester, or, when very immature, a fool, and as the nurturing, creative/artistic type, the Lover is the provider of the works of fine art (full of well-being) for the kingdom. The Lover creates the paintings, poetry, writing, and the soft music of the dining halls. He or she is the only one who can dare point out to the King or Queen that he or she is misguided or wrong. The Lover is funny yet mysterious to the rest of the people in the kingdom, especially the Warriors. Kings inspire people with knowledge and rules, Magicians inspire people with spectacles and fireworks, and Warriors inspire people by winning battles, but Lovers have the unique and sometimes soft, subtle gift of winning people over with emotional words, poems, and stories. This is so different and opposite from what Warriors do that it baffles them, and yet is very emotionally attractive to them.

Finally, the fourth type of temperament in men and women, the Magician, is all about a confident display of creative (right-brained) physical action. Sparks fly, and the opposite sex swoons over them. They are the great salespeople of the kingdom, the masters of ceremonies, the stars, the performers on stage, and the public workers of miracles. They are emotionally confident and intellectually spontaneous, creative, and flexible.

Keys to Emotional Attraction Using KWML™

If you see yourself as a Charlotte type, then you are a Queen, and your ideal best friend or soul mate in a potential Mr. Right is a Magician like Harry. The best way to test and emotionally attract a Magician on first meeting is to do something that puts the man to a test of his performance ability. Try the countdown technique. Get his attention with your hands, raising two fingers to his eyes, then yours, to get him to look and stand still. (Magicians are rarely seated because they are so active and prone to disappear.) Next, count from three down to one and then say, "Go!" Do this without any further guidance as to what he is to do. If he breaks into a performance of some sort or any kind of public display that is entertaining, then he is a Magician, and you will have given him exactly what he needs emotionally to be your friend—a chance to perform for you. You will have given him a sign of exactly the positive emotional energy—the definition of friendship—that he needs and lacks, which is well-being (nurturing).

If you envision yourself as a Miranda type, you are a Warrior, and your ideal best friend or soul mate in emotional attraction is a Lover, like Steve. The best way to attract a Lover emotionally is to get his attention by touching him lightly, perhaps on the shoulder. He will likely have been looking down at the ground, because Lovers tend to live in their own heads, but he will light up a bit at the touch. Speak in soft tones, letting the fire of your Warrior-woman ways burn in your alluring eyes, and say, "I can tell you have a lot of feelings and stories with feeling. Can you tell me one?" That's it. You will see him light up even more, warming to you due to your emotional sensitivity. This advice may seem vague and mysterious, but to a Lover, saying "I can tell you have a lot of feelings" makes him feel understood. He has passion for the world even though he doesn't jump around in it confidently and physically the way a Magician would. Lovers are the storytellers of the world and shine best when sharing feelings through stories. Give them this opportunity (but do it one on one, since they can seem shy or private), and they will feel that you are the best friend they ever had. You have created exactly the kind of positive emotional energy they need (confidence).

If you see yourself as a Samantha type, then you are a Magician, and in emotional attraction to a best friend or soul mate, you need a King, like Smith Jerrod. The best way to attract a King emotionally is to ask for advice, since Kings are the best advice-givers in the world. They run their kingdoms (and their lives) by rules, and are very educated, loving to read. When you ask Kings about their favorite books, or about which book would help what problem, they almost always know of one from deep inside their storehouse of knowledge. They are the perfect people to get your crazy physical Magician activity in balance with the needs in your life. When you ask a King for advice, it gives him everything he needs in friendship. It gives him a chance to nurture you with well-being, to give his left-brained, educational advice to you, and makes him feel needed and important. All these are good feelings that create positive emotional energy he needs (confidence).

Finally, if you see yourself as a Carrie type, you are a Lover, and in emotional attraction to a best friend or soul mate, you need a Warrior, like Mr. Big. The best way to attract a Warrior emotionally is to approach him carefully in respectful body posture, swoon, and say, "I feel your power." If you do this in a funny or even sarcastic way, he will warm up to you immediately even after being hostile to everyone else in the room. As the defenders of any kingdom, and feared, respected knights, the Warriors of the world want one thing most among other men—the high rank associated with power. They want respect for their physical prowess. In medieval times, the term "gentleman" never applied to a "gentle man," but one of genteel heritage and high character, both courtly in a way proper and respectful to ladies, but also fearsome when confronted with enemies or threats to the safety, dignity, or happiness of their ladies. When you approach a Warrior in the way I suggest, you both sexually attract him (by offering recognition of higher alpha-male status) and emotionally attract him (by giving him the positive emotional energy he needs to receive from you—well-being, which he lacks).

Opposites Attract Because They Make Us Grow

The ultimate lesson of KWML™ is that people of the opposite temperament from ours are our best friends in life because they make us grow into more complete, well-rounded people. They have an endless supply of exactly the kind of positive emotional energy we desire and an endless supply of exactly the kind of intellectual stimulation we need.

Friendship, of course, is about *shared* positive emotion. "Shared" means that friendship isn't just about you being on the receiving end. It is about mutual gifts of emotion and ideas (shared altruism). Even though you may have bar friends, shopping friends, and every other kind of friend, it is only your temperament opposite that has an endless supply of both what you need and a willingness to accept what you have to give.

The reason soul mates have a kind of eternal bond is that they not only share the gifts that each needs, but they also make each other grow. So many people go out into the world out of balance in their psychology, pretending to be what they are not. Most often, men who on first glance go to extra efforts to show how ambitious they are tend not to be ambitious at the root. Men who pretend to be docile and passive are aggressive and hard driving, and men who pretend to be intellectuals actually lack knowledge.

In one school of thought, called Self Psychology, we call this "putting on false self," which is pretending to be what you are not. When men or women do this, they are trying to overcompensate for the lack of something in their temperament by going overboard. Deep down, however, we have a need to grow toward the center of my circle, to cultivate the skills, ideas, and self-esteem of the other three temperaments that each of us lacks. This is a place of being that psychologists call the ideal self, or psychological integration.

We all have a real and genuine psychological place. Psychologists call this true self. If you were a Queen, like Charlotte, it might look like this:

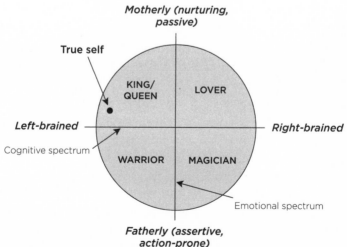

"True self" as both a specific "position" of behavior, and also being within a zone, or "spectrum" (quantum psychology)

Yet somewhere along the line, we might feel incomplete, not good enough, or get to hiding our true self, overcompensating, by pretending to be the opposite of what we really are. In the diagram below, it would be like Charlotte trying to be like Samantha:

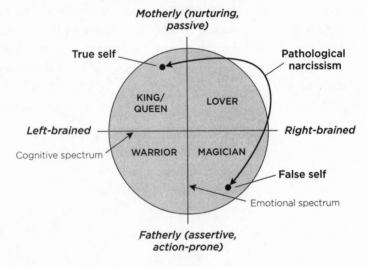

"False self" as "pretending to be the opposite of what you really are" (pathological narcissism)

Imagine when you were a little girl how you pretended to be a princess, a great actress, or a model. Everyone knew you weren't really those things; that you were just pretending, expressing a wish for what you could grow into some day. If a grown woman tried to convince her friends or a potential Mr. Right that she *is* a princess, a model, or an actress when she isn't, she'd be laughed at, scolded like a child, or avoided like the plague by men. Don't put on false self. Be who you really are.

The same goes for a potential Mr. Right. If you notice that a man puts on a facade as if he's something he's not, you have just spotted an immature guy who is definitely Mr. Wrong. You are going to learn in Phase III that an immature guy is not capable of a commit-ment. Someone coming across in a fake way like this does not make a good friend, as he will tend to need you or use you to keep being who he is not. This drains your positive emotional energy and your self-esteem rather than raising it—the opposite of friendship. Guys with tons of false self are like emotional vampires who drain your emotional blood.

A true best friend or soul mate is willing to grow because of you. He is willing to slowly, patiently move toward the center of my circle where psychological health, balance, and integration are. Certainly, you have heard of a person being called "a little off," "off-putting," "imbalanced," or "out of whack," versus being "cen-tered," "grounded," or "balanced." Our psychological target in life is to be centered in the place where our emotions and intellect have

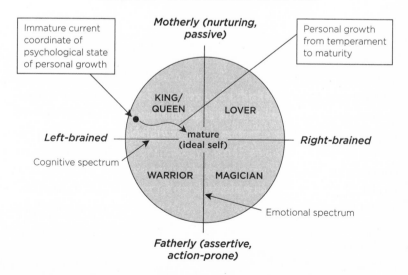

**Growth and maturity of personality =
the "slow road" from "true self"
toward the real adult skills of
"ideal self" are a balance of all four**

ideal skill and maturity. That target is the thing that psychologists call ideal self.

Ideal self is the best you. It is the full realization of your potential in psychological maturity, the sum total of all skills, feelings, mastery of emotion, and intellect you achieve over a lifetime. It is the slow, patient, disciplined practice at the other three temperaments you lack so that you grow into a whole woman. For a man, aiming for ideal self is the pinnacle of being a gentleman. It is being integrated or having integrity, which does not mean simply being honest (there are many naive and honest fools in the world). Ideal self is all this, and yet it cannot ever be fully reached to perfection, just approached with the effort of a lifetime.

In a best friend or soul mate, you are looking for the person of opposite traits to your own because their true self naturally causes you to move toward your ideal self. The reverse is true as well since a friendship is about mutual positive emotion. Yet what is better about a soul mate or best friend than about any old friend is that there is not only an emotional attraction, but also a core foundation for intellectual attraction, too. What you lack in education, your soul mate in Mr. Right has. What he lacks in experience and creativity, you have. You start a sentence and he completes it. When Jerry Maguire tells Renée Zellweger's character that she "completes him," this is a conversation between a Warrior and a Lover feeling that love that comes from a soul mate–friendship bond.

These are the gifts of the Bonding in Friendship Phase of courtship: that the love in friendship is always on tap, that anger and fear are always just a short period that gets solved maturely, that teamwork is a value and naturally built into your natures as a couple, and that empowered with a person of your opposite temperament, you are free as a couple from the challenges and stresses of the world. You truly do complete each other, and you are a self-reliant, self-sustaining team with more than enough resources to face the world together, ready for a true, lasting, and durable commitment.

Following Your Story

Carl and Cathy's story is a story you never need to repeat if you use your Cool Eye to identify your opposite in temperament. It took some time, but Carl and Cathy ultimately learned that their story wasn't for them to be together. They both were mature enough to see that what was fun and exciting for the short term could not possibly last for a lifetime if they couldn't navigate through as simple a project together as picking an apartment appropriate for them both. They couldn't act as a team because their personalities were too similar. They couldn't offer what the other lacked because they lacked the same things. As a result, they drained each other dry of the positive emotion. If you remember what we learned about reciprocal altruism, it will make sense to you how, in matters of love, birds of a feather cannot *emotionally* flock together in terms of energy type. We do well with significant others just like us only in terms of sharing the same belief systems we cover in later chapters. How can you be altruistic to someone in friendship if you don't have anything to give that he doesn't already have? How can someone feel grateful and want to give back if you don't have an emotional energy he needs or style of intellectual skill, humor, or creativity he doesn't already have?

Carl and Cathy's relationship failed due to a failure of Step Three of the Bonding in Friendship Phase of courtship: the ability to team up together in life in a self-sufficient way. Their stories would diverge from each other, leading both of them to marry stage actors eventually. With what you know now, this makes perfect sense. Stage actors are outgoing performers who are the opposite of reserved, analytical accountants who dwell in cubicles all day. Right-brained stage actors are also the intellectual opposites of the left-brained accountants. When Carl and Cathy found their temperamental opposites, their lives moved toward completeness.

Diving deep into this new way of looking at best-friendship, you might be tempted to cry, "Oh no! I'm doomed to be alone if I don't find my opposite personality type!" Not so. Some of you might worry, "Oh no! I'm a Queen type of girl married to a King type of guy. Now I'm stuck!" Not so. Remember that this is a kind of quantum psychology where a person can be described with a *general* term, and yet still holds on to all the unique *individuality* that is hers alone. You don't have to worry that your marriage will absolutely fail because you aren't the exact opposite temperament as your mate, but you will have to do more work gathering ideas and maintaining friendships outside the relationship in order to keep it strong. You'll have to infuse what you share with the fruits of your life outside the partnership.

On the downside, this model does explain why for some people, the relationship feels so strenuous, such hard labor at times to maintain. For others, the ones we gaze on with amazement at their soul mate connection, it shows exactly why things are so easy and smooth, why they always seem to be prospering as a couple with minimal struggle. If you are still single, I would like you to choose well before you even go on that second date. I would like you to be one of those people whom others consider lucky. Now you can make your own luck by choosing well from day one.

The four temperaments of KWML™ need not take any of the mystery and romance away from your relationships. To say so would be like saying that the plays of Shakespeare are ruined for us by knowing that they appear in five acts, or that our favorite films are ruined by knowing that there is going to be a beginning, middle, and a climax. In fact, the nine steps of courtship are merely markers of progress in your story, not the rich, dramatic, challenging, or joyful *content* of it. The mystery of how, why, and when the details of your tale of love plays out are yours and yours alone to decide and enjoy.

If you followed along the path of courtship this far, you will have locked in both a thrilling sexual attraction and a rich, secure, vibrant emotional attraction in friendship. You are now ready to see if your love has what it takes to go through the final phase of courtship: intellectual attraction in commitment.

Chapter Eight

⌒

A Line Drawn in the Sand

Phase III: The Commitment Phase
*Step One: Demonstrating Mastery
of the Personal Boundary*

*How fair is a garden amid the toils and passions of
existence.* —BENJAMIN DISRAELI

We've journeyed all the way through the reptilian brain and mammalian brain of Mr. Right and yourself. As we have done so, we've gone from a place where we have little say over what happens between men and women to having more decision-making power and unique individuality. We've gone from a place where all men are alike (as is true in the reptilian brain) to a place where we begin to see more differences in individuals. We've also gone from a place that is distinctly adolescent, as the reptilian brain is the least mature of the three brains, through a place approaching maturity (the mammalian brain is the center of the friendship and emotional skills of young adulthood).

When we get to the higher brain, though—the place of intellectual attraction and commitment—we come to the center of full adult maturity in behavior. It is here in the most mature brain that we see the greatest individuality and personal identity in Mr. Right and ourselves. Here we begin to see uniqueness, rooted in an individual's personal tastes and preferences, his or her education, vast array of experiences, use of emotion, and the ability to make sophisticated

The Commitment Phase (Intellectual Attraction)

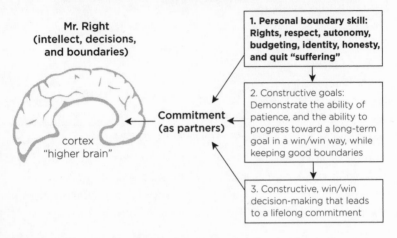

Mr. Right
(intellect, decisions,
and boundaries)

cortex
"higher brain"

Commitment
(as partners)

**1. Personal boundary skill:
Rights, respect, autonomy,
budgeting, identity, honesty,
and quit "suffering"**

2. Constructive goals:
Demonstrate the ability of
patience, and the ability to
progress toward a long-term
goal in a win/win way, while
keeping good boundaries

3. Constructive, win/win
decision-making that leads
to a lifelong commitment

agreements with others. While all men are essentially the same in their reptilian brains (and all women are in theirs), and all people have some opposite emotional energies in their mammalian brains, the complexity, sheer size, and variation of the higher brain makes us all unique from one another. The higher brain is the only area of the brain in which we reach true and full *partnership* with a mate. There is no permanent commitment for you and Mr. Right without these last three steps of human courtship.

Have you ever felt as if the man you're with did not respect you? Have you ever felt like he was wasting your time, your energy, your money, or your attention to him? Have you ever felt as if he was overly entitled to boss you around, or tended to say no to most of your suggestions? Have you ever felt as if a man you were with had a tendency to be overly agreeable to everything you suggest, while having none of his own preferences, to the point of making you feel as if you don't even really have a sense of what he's all about? Have you ever had something about your relationship that troubled you, yet was ill defined, vaguely annoying, overwhelming, lacking "something," or otherwise leaving you confused as to what to do to understand it better? If so, these and dozens of other mysteries about your relationship are explained in this chapter on Step One of the Commitment Phase: Personal Boundaries.

We enter the higher brain of Mr. Right now on a rich adventure full of complexity and discovery. We ask questions of it with a bold spirit of individuality rather than sameness. It is because of that very individuality that there are so many choices of mates in the world, regardless of your personality type. If human beings were nothing more than animals that have sex, cheat and get cheated on, fight each other for resources, and move through sexual encounter after sexual encounter, there would be no point in solving the mystery of Mr. Right at all. All women would be equally suited to mate with any man who comes along.

If human beings were nothing but advanced mammals who are actually able to cry and fret, start wars, crave addictions, get depressed, or otherwise lean on each other emotionally, then there would also be no point in caring about your unique story in life. Any Magician would be suitable for any Queen, and any Lover would be suitable for any Warrior. People would simply pair up as they do on those online dating services, take a test that says who "the One" is, and marry him without any deep thought or heartfelt story together.

We are more than this though, aren't we? We have personal stories and personal choice in those stories. We have serendipitous moments of encounter where two people's stories cross briefly, and it is our Cool Eye—resting in the higher brain—that allows us to recognize those moments and become the main characters in a personal love story with choices, challenges, and victories.

The higher brain carries a whole host of abilities for our love lives. It contains our intellect, our decisions, and the classes of things we value. It has our language, our art, our memory, education, life's experience, and identity itself. It is the headquarters of our Cool Eye and holds the crucial skill without which no relationship can last in commitment—the Personal Boundary. The higher brain is ultimately what separates us in sophistication from animals. It is the only part of us capable of making a man a gentleman, a woman a sophisticated lady, or any of us mature.

As we begin our ascent into this brain responsible for all social politics, rights, agreements, honesty, virtue, and civilization itself, we come to one other thing it contains: yet another bridge from the mammalian brain. This bridge is known as our belief system.

Beliefs, Value, and the Nature of Good Investments

The higher brain gives us rights, individuality, and identity, and it gives us beliefs. Yet those same things are what cause us to have a need for communication and compromise in the world. None of us believes exactly the same things as anyone else. This is a blessing, giving us all the variety of personality and stories in the world. It is also a curse—the source of most conflict, suffering, and misunderstanding. In the next chapter, we are going to go deep into the nature of beliefs and communication with Mr. Right as you make goals together. First, in this chapter though, we need to see how beliefs have an impact on your Personal Boundary—your special skill that actually controls the degree of intimacy in your commitment to each other.

If you have ever butted heads with a man and it seemed there was no way to resolve it—no matter what you did or said, you just didn't get each other—you can be sure there was a difference of belief systems. However, if you are to find true commitment with Mr. Right, you will need to find a way to select a man with a similar belief system or worldview as yours and then find a way to negotiate and compromise on whatever inevitable differences remain.

We have already crossed the first bridge to the higher brain: the KWML™ technology, which explains how humans need a balance of emotion (mammalian brain) and intellect (higher brain) in order to feel healthy and keep growing toward their potential. There is both a measure of and impediment to that health in one's belief system. As the second bridge we must cross, your belief system serves as the filter that interprets all incoming data and guides your actions according to what you *believe* is possible. All of your beliefs together form your worldview, your frame of reference, and your reality. This provides you with the *value* you place on ideas, experiences, and even people.

The difference between a belief and an idea is that an idea is just a piece of data, a lone bit of information that may be important to some people and not to others. In fact, an idea by itself is nothing more than words. There is no emotional value attached to the meaning of the words.

If I say "pencil" to you, does that ring with importance? Probably not, unless you are a teacher or writer. A pencil is just a thing.

How about if I say "cat"? If you are a cat person, you might feel a certain warmth inside thinking about the cats you love. If you are a dog person, however, you'll probably exhibit no emotion at all.

How about if I say "ex-boyfriend"? You likely *will* have emotions connected to that word. Maybe even bad emotions.

The point is that ideas are just data. A belief, on the other hand, is an idea to which there is emotional energy attached. You might then say that a positive belief is simply a dearly held idea, and a negative belief is either an angrily held idea or an anxiously held idea. Beliefs are composed of data and emotional energy in one package, glued together in the same way a communication is. In fact, you might say that all communication is simply the outward expression of one's beliefs held inside.

In this bridging between the mammalian brain and higher brain we are also going to focus on the nature of value, because it has to do with both friendship and with the ability to move on to the Commitment Phase of courtship.

Most people don't go into a commitment with someone they don't value. It's hard to believe in what you don't value. It's hard to communicate about what you don't value, and it's hard to set goals for what you don't value. Still, in this rapid-paced, eight-minute-dating, Internet-matchmaking world, some of us go into relationships without ever stopping to think about what we really value or why. When you lack a Cool Eye that lets you take a step back and analyze why you do what you do, sometimes you end up with what you (and he) are not sure you want. Friends may come and go, and guys you're sexually attracted to may be surrounding you all the time. However, when you get to the phase of relating that we call commitment, your very first step needs to be to take stock of what you *believe* a relationship needs to be to work for you and what you would exactly *value* in a perfect Mr. Right for you. That takes some higher-brained detail work.

A belief is like a table, with the main idea (dearly, or tightly held) being the tabletop. It could be the idea "My ex-boyfriend sucks," or, "I'll never amount to anything," or, "Cats are wonderful buddies,"

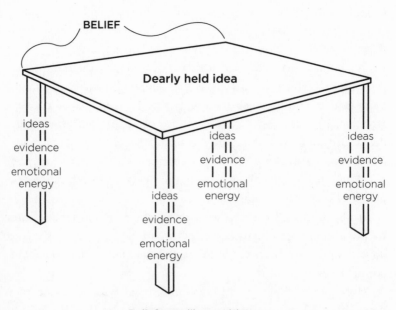

Beliefs are like a tabletop:
supported by chair legs called "evidence"

or, "Life is good." Whether there is a negative belief in you about yourself and the world or a positive one, a belief is still like an idea on a tabletop supported by facts, figures, experiences, and evidence. It is then superglued to the floor of your mind by emotional energy. The amount of emotional energy locking it down is the amount that you *value* the idea on the tabletop (value can be negative or positive of course).

The first key to understanding whether friendship is ready to move to commitment is identifying whether the potential Mr. Right has a greater relative amount of positive energy trapped in his beliefs than negative energy. This will then determine whether you open up your Personal Boundary to lasting intimacy with him.

You can tolerate a bad attitude in just a friend—even a chronic bad attitude—because there need not be a commitment in friendship. Yet if a man is constantly negative in his beliefs (therefore full of negative emotional energy), you will be hard-pressed to commit to him. He has already proven himself a Mr. Wrong, and the friendship itself will eventually die, too.

The key to beliefs is that they are incredibly hard to change, and yet they trap emotional energy inside them—just like supergluing a table to the floor traps the table to the floor. Have you ever worked with a man on getting his anger, anxiety, or addiction under control? Was it easy and simple? No. It was slow, difficult, and maybe a lost cause because often the negative energy we carry around is trapped to the floor of our minds. This stored, negative emotional energy is poison to a friendship and to the ability to fully enter into commitment. Negative beliefs like this are what we all call our baggage.

Negative beliefs start with a bad experience—a breakup, domestic abuse, being fired, being neglected by a mom or dad at a key moment, and so on. This puts an idea in your head like, "I'm not worth it." From here, a table leg of evidence or two props up the idea. "After all, I did get bad grades on my report card." The bad experience happened for *some* reason, and at the time, you had a significant amount of negative emotion attached to the event. This negative emotion (anger or anxiety) locks down the idea, "I'm not worth it" to the floor of your mind. Over time, you saw more data drifting by you, had more experiences where you were abandoned, neglected, or let go. The new ideas lend further support—more table legs—to your growing belief.

As far as negative experiences and the beliefs that feed on them,

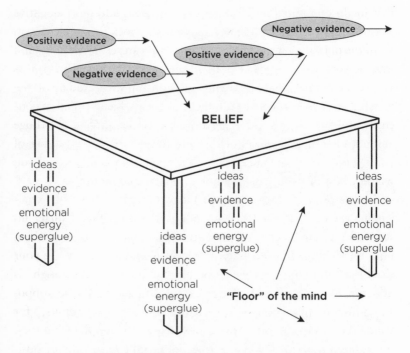

Thousands of beliefs are locked to the "floor" of an individual's mind and compose the sum total of what is termed one's reality, worldview, or frame of reference.

If the majority of these beliefs is composed of beliefs with positive energy, then the individual's overall worldview is a positive one. If the majority of these beliefs is composed of beliefs with negative energy, then the individual's overall worldview is a negative one.

As a belief grows in strength and dominance, it becomes more facile at collecting positive evidence, e.g. evidence that the belief is true, and rejecting negative evidence, e.g. evidence that the belief is untrue.

human beings are natural lumpers, not sorters. We lump the data and energy of negative experiences onto ever-growing lumps called beliefs. Your failure at a job equals "I'm bad." Your failed relationship equals "I'm bad." In fact, every failure to reach a goal begins to equal the idea "I'm bad." Since the belief acts as a filter of reality for every event of life that comes your way, you unconsciously focus on ideas that provide more support for this belief and ignore other ideas that might contradict it. These supporting ideas add more negative emotional energy, providing new superglue to lock that table down.

In the diagram on the previous page, you can see how a woman's overall worldview is composed of all the beliefs she has. The same is true of the man you date or are in a relationship with. Add up all the beliefs in a person and you add up all of his most emotional experiences and his interpretation of those experiences. This is a huge amount of trapped emotion, either positive or negative. If either of you is more negative than positive, the friendship will fail, and you will not be able to successfully go on to a true commitment.

You can start to chip away at your own negative beliefs by challenging them. Your Cool Eye actually lets you become a sorter instead of a lumper. A common negative belief among women is "I am not pretty enough." To counter this, you would purposely use your Cool Eye to look for new evidence that "I am not pretty enough" is not true, and then build a new belief that is positive and the opposite of the old negative belief. Something like "I am gorgeous," for which there is likely just as much evidence in the world if you look for it. Soon a new belief begins to grow, a positive one full of positive emotion. The old belief then begins to die like a cancer that's deprived of a blood supply.

When we are intimate with someone over an extended period, we naturally take on some of the evidence and emotion stored in their beliefs. When we do that, we agree to let intimacy bring other people's energy and ideas into our lives. We literally begin to share a reality. This is why over time, we tend to become like the friends we commune with most. If you share your reality with a man who has intensely negative beliefs, this can be poisonous to you. Of course, the man could work on those beliefs, but you don't control whether he does or how fast he does. If you put your life on hold during this time, you may very well wind up wasting your life. However, if someone is clearly willing to change and grow, and shows evidence of this by taking up new habits that stick, or by going to seminars, or by taking other productive actions, there is a chance he will become a more fit friend and potential committed partner.

Value and "Fair Deals" with Mr. Right

Have you ever felt like being with a man was a bad deal for you on some intuitive level? You couldn't put your finger on it, but your time and energy seemed all for nothing. In our introduction to friendship, we discussed what it means to place value on something or someone: It's simply the amount of emotional energy we invest in that person. I'm now about to reveal to you an invisible social economy. Just as countries exchange goods and services for money through the value of currency, we all have four kinds of social currency circulating within us and ready to trade with others.

One that we've already discussed is emotional energy, resting in the mammalian brain, and the name of the currency of exchange is love. In our journey through the anatomy of friendship, we learned that giving positive emotional energy (self-esteem) to another person is the same as what we call love. Real loving is a fair deal because we already value that person, and therefore enjoy good emotions that are attached to the experience of him.

Did you ever feel a bit let down at the amount of time you've spent waiting for a man to get his act together, propose to you, or even simply show up for a date? Did you ever feel like you were in less and less control the longer you were with a man? Did you ever feel strong as a completely single woman, but weaker the longer you were with a particular guy? The other three currencies are in our higher brain, and they are *time,* the currency of idea-exchange; *freedom,* the currency of increased decision-power; and *strength,* the currency of protection and control that our Personal Boundary manufactures. If you've experienced any of the above scenarios, you probably chose men who make bad deals with women socially. You knew at some level that you were coming up on the short end of the stick with a guy, but you couldn't really measure it, or even identify what "it" was. Now you know "it" was time, energy, freedom, or strength, or some combination of them.

It takes time for us to exchange ideas, get an education, to communicate, or tell a story to connect to another person. If we want new knowledge and ideas, the price we pay is *time* to learn them. If we work for a boss who hopefully has more wisdom than we have (and therefore is given the privilege of making more decisions about the business than we are), we get a salary, and the thing we give up in exchange for that salary is some of our *freedom* to make those decisions. Freedom is what we pay in order to receive that salary, and so we start taking orders. When we protect someone else or give that person *strength,* we are "lending" that person our Personal Boundary, just as when we agree to open up our Personal Boundary to be intimate with someone else, we give up some of that strength that formerly protected us by keeping a distance from people.

Love, time, freedom, and strength are really the four universal things of value that any human being ultimately has to offer others or preserve in ourselves.

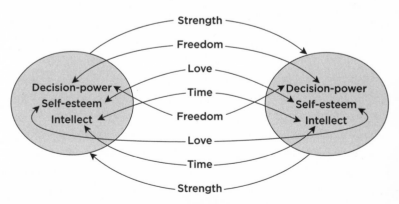

These are the "currencies" of love, time, freedom, and Personal Boundary strength.

These four forms of currency are really what lie beneath all other human transactions like finances (it takes a certain amount of personal energy and time to make money), career (it takes time, energy, and decisions to develop a career path), and, of course, relationships. Together these four form the invisible economy of relationships. If you "spend" time on your parents, they may give you love in return. If you go to a class and spend your time learning, you may receive ideas of use to you in return. If you take a job, you will spend your valuable time and energy and surrender freedom to a boss in return for money. It's all just currency. I want you to learn to spend wisely on Mr. Right and not be short-changed by all the Mr. Wrongs.

Here's how men think about this. Have you ever been with a man for a long period, known you should break up, but remained reluctant to do so? Have you ever heard yourself say, "I've invested so much"? Men definitely think about commitment this way. The way we invest in relationships is not all that different from the way we hold our money at the bank—and at times, relationships can indeed be like very bad investments. This is not to say that you ought to see relationships as only about investments, the way Suzanne did. There are nine steps to my system, and the role of investment in the currency of love only accounts for part of one of them. In fact, Suzanne (from chapter three) actually took advantage of the trades that went on with men she knew: securing a good deal for herself, often at their expense and loss. In that sense she would have failed this step as well if she had ever gotten to it.

Once you get a man to the brink of commitment, he's likely to become fearful that he is going to lose a huge amount of value if he invests his emotional, intellectual, and sexual value on the wrong woman. To men, this is as terrifying as putting our whole life savings on one number on a roulette wheel. When men take the risk of beginning to commit to you, we can at times feel as if we are gambling with our lives and our futures. The same is true for you. However, if we come to value you through friendship, this sense of risk changes. The positive energy of friendship you have superglued to our worldview makes us feel safe in our investment in you.

If you don't feel valued, it might be because your potential Mr. Right has such a negative belief system that he is prone to label everything as negative and mistakenly experience you as a source of negative energy (when in fact it is *his* negative energy he feels). He is then not being a good friend. It is also possible that you have not truly invested much in the friendship with the man by giving him sufficient positive energy in the form of self-esteem—either displaying your own or building up his. If the latter is true, then you aren't being a very good friend, either. Therefore, Mr. Right doesn't feel invested in by you, doesn't invest back in you, and doesn't hold you of high value. Now you understand why friendship bonds must take place before commitment with a man. They are the method through which we love, invest, and find true value in others. Our higher brains make us wise and mature, and a wise girl or guy never commits to a bad investment.

So now we see how beliefs and value form a bridge between the mammalian brain of Mr. Right and his higher brain cortex. They join the emotional attraction of the Bonding in Friendship Phase with the intellectual attraction of shared positive beliefs of the Commitment Phase of courtship.

Therefore, your worldview and a potential Mr. Right's need to be a match. In Phase II, you learned how to take the negative emotions of anger and anxiety and turn them into the positive emotion of self-esteem that makes up friendship. It is time to learn how in the world a person holds on to all that good energy.

Your Own Private Country with Mr. Right: The Personal Boundary

Have you ever felt out of control? Have you ever felt that your plate is too full? Have you ever felt like asking a man, "Where is this going?" Have you ever felt stressed by a man or been told that you stress a man? Have you ever felt overwhelmed? Mature, desirable, high-character men do not commit to women who are overwhelmed, don't have preferences in life or an identity they stand up for, are out of control of their own emotions, or are unpredictable when they need to be relied on. These problems always come back to the same skill of the higher brain—the Personal Boundary.

The Personal Boundary is an invisible marker of your personal space and your identity. It is a barrier against stress and an invisible psychological circle around you that marks what you control about life from what you don't. The Personal Boundary is the center of what we call strength. It functions exactly like the border of your own private country, blocking Mr. Wrongs at the passport office, and permitting Mr. Right to get in to tour your world.

When undeveloped or damaged, the Personal Boundary is the very cause of all codependence in the world, nearly all the abuse in the world, most miscommunication in the world, perfectionism, rudeness, prejudice, judgmentalism, ignorance, subjugation, imprisonment, joyless achievement, loneliness, and desperation. If this kind of boundary surrounded a nation, it would be like the Australian outback—anything can get in or out. When traumatized, cold, arrogant, isolated, or scared, it is the very cause of all self-protective loneliness and starvation for love or new ideas in the world. It is the North Korea of boundaries—nothing gets in or out.

At the same time, if you develop a strong Personal Boundary, you hold a secret, invisible vault full of psychological treasure. This is one of your most priceless skills and possessions as a human being.

The late actor Christopher Reeve (the most famous Superman of all) was paralyzed from the neck down in a horse-riding accident. Even in this condition, however, he was admired internationally for his strength. Clearly, this strength was not physical strength but personal strength. He had a very powerful Personal Boundary. The shape of one's Personal Boundary establishes one's identity, and when you think of Christopher Reeve, you have a full sense of what he stood for and who he was. The more solid the shape of a boundary, the more secure its border, the greater strength one projects.

This is a powerful concept for women to learn. Since, much more than men, women are attuned to connections to others, Personal

Boundary sophistication is not necessarily an inborn skill. Many men think that women's connectedness to others and their seemingly endless need for more of it means that they are a threat to not only our reptilian-brained territory, but our higher-brained privacy and identity as well. Men fear being overwhelmed by you. Ask any man who has been stalked by a desperate Glenn Close/*Fatal Attraction*–type girl with poor boundaries. Yet a mature woman with a mature Personal Boundary is not overwhelming. Instead, she has a balanced life in which she is both diplomatic and connected to others in her own feminine way.

Your Personal Boundary provides a way to say no to some things and yes to other things in a way that lets you budget your resources wisely. The borders to your boundary are similar to the borders of a country. When you cross the border of a country, you don't find a dotted line marking the place where one country ends and another begins. A national border is invisible yet it is still very real. If you crossed over a national border without a passport, you'd probably be stopped. If you tried to bring diamonds into a country without paying a tariff, you'd probably be stopped. The Personal Boundary acts exactly like the border of your very own country.

Have you yourself ever been stalked, abused, pestered, or harassed by a man who is at worst violent and at best a taker? It is your built-in right to use your own strong boundary to say no to him as well. We've covered the social economy going on all around us—the love, time, freedom, and strength we have for spending needs to be traded in fair deals with Mr. Right. Using your own boundary strength is just like a country blocking terrorists at the border or saying no to bad deals with other nations that tend to rip us off.

The Declaration of Independence says we are "endowed with certain *unalienable* rights." "Unalienable" means "cannot be taken away." The Declaration speaks in its own way about the Personal Boundary, about the individual citizen's rights that no other human—not even a government—can take away. There is more stored in your Personal Boundary than just legal rights, though. There are emotional energies in the form of your self-esteem, there are your ideas and beliefs, and there is your decision making, your free will. These are unalienable, so no one, not even a man you are in a relationship with, has a right to tell you how to feel or think, or what to decide to do with your actions. The same is true for you and men. You have no right to invade a man's boundary, telling him how to feel, what to think, or what to do. Nor does he have a right to invade yours. Relationships are voluntary, even if you've already had sex, been friends, or even signed a piece of paper called a marriage license. Perhaps no document more vividly describes this deep truth about being human than the Declaration. (See: http://en.wikipedia.org/wiki/inalienable-rights)

Sexual attraction, in which you have withheld the prize of sex, has kept your potential Mr. Right interested via your beauty, your elevation of his status, and your providing him with a contest to win for you. There is no commitment yet. Even in friendship, we all know that friends come and go. We need not bind them in agreements, nor force them to live by their word. We often accept friends without commitment. Emotional attraction keeps us glued together even when there is no formal agreement. When we get to commitment, however, we definitely agree to live up to a promise to join our lives while still keeping an individual identity and story.

At this point, you must check to assure yourself of your potential Mr. Right's Personal Boundary skill—and your own. Why? Because all of the other aspects of commitment—the mutual goals, decisions, communication, and sharing of beliefs cannot hold together if one does not have a solid Personal Boundary to establish preferences and identity. Realistically, how can either of you commit to the other, if the other is "unknown"?

Imagine that you went to buy a new car with all the options, were sold on its beauty, luxury, ability to raise your social status, and efficiency on gas. You signed the contract and then the dealer wheeled out an old clunker, telling you that's what you actually bought. Would you be fuming? Would you say, "The deal's off!" Would you then go see a lawyer and report it to the media? Does this sound like the process of marriage followed by divorce court? This is how many men and women feel after committing to be boyfriends, girl-friends, and spouses with someone of shaky boundary makeup. When you agree to commit to a relationship, you are, in fact, making a deal. No bait-and-switch is allowed, or the deal is off psychologically, no matter what the contract reads. A marriage contract is meaningless in the presence of an immature Personal Boundary, and this is why you have to assess his and your own before ever fully committing to a man.

When Worlds Collide

Ashley was the most intriguing woman Alex had ever met. She was tall, born and raised in London's Regent's Park district before coming to America two years earlier. She had elegantly styled brown hair and brown eyes, and she radiated confidence. At the same time, Ashley was in her mid-thirties and secretly eager to have a child "before the biological clock struck its last tick."

Alex was a couple of years older, second-generation Chinese by heritage, and, unlike some of his buddies who dated only far younger women, responded to Ashley's beauty and vibrant intellectual energy. Alex met Ashley through his former girlfriend, whose best friend had married Ashley's brother. It was a tangled knot of relationships, yet it was the perfect way to meet a potential mate, since Ashley had been "preapproved" by these friends.

Beyond her beauty, which easily met Alex's reptilian-brain needs, Ashley offered great promise for a future if a commitment ever happened. She was rolling in money from her highborn family, and she had a huge career on her own as an officer at one of the top computer firms in the world. Step Two of the Attraction Phase was complete—her high-career station certainly elevated Alex's alpha-male status. Alex was a successful public speaker and journalist. He didn't make Ashley's income, but he made six figures. Ashley's money didn't threaten him, because he already had power and status in the ranks of men.

Besides a little glitch here and there in Step Two of Attraction, the tall, stylish, athletic man got along with Ashley famously. They discussed art (she was an accomplished art historian who once worked for a major auction house as a buyer), enjoyed fine dining, conversation about world events, travel, and all the culture the world had to offer them.

The little glitch was that Ashley tended to be quite a feisty woman, used profanity profusely, and smoked like a Newcastle factory. This feistiness seemed to come naturally out of her confidence, and at first, Alex ignored it. Sometimes Ashley would invade Alex's space physically while also correcting his grammar and spouting comments such as "You really should . . . ," "People shouldn't . . . ," and "Bollocks to those peckers on CNN! Damn liberals." Alex let these pass as well. Ashley was quite gifted at giving a man a test to pass for her approval in Step Three.

There were definitely issues here, though. Alex was, in fact, one of those liberal journalists Ashley railed against—he'd once even appeared on CNN. He also wasn't particularly fond of excessive profanity. He was sure he'd mentioned both of these things to Ashley at some point. Still, she continued to spout on with her self-justified opinions on world politics, and Alex shied away from arguing with her.

There was more. Sometimes Alex spent inordinate lengths of time in the bathroom when he stayed at Ashley's mansion in the Hillsborough district of San Francisco. He was never sure why, but he liked it there, sitting on his revered and private masculine "throne." That is, until she banged on the door, decrying, "What are you doing in there, digging your way back to China?" As a man, Alex needed his territory, and on top of the invasion of his reptilian-brained territory needs of masculinity, Ashley's personality style of regular invasions of his identity, and his personal and psychological space began to wear on his sense that commitment could ever be a safe or wise investment with her.

You might chalk up some of Ashley's invasion of Alex's space to a simple misunderstanding on her part. She didn't know about the male reptilian brain even though she held her own in the business world previously dominated by men. To Alex, it was fair enough for a while. After all, she was beautiful, raised his status by virtue of her career position, was prone to challenge him to and place him in competitions to win her attention and admiration, and had demonstrated many positive shared emotions in friendship with him. She could manage anger most of the time and was fearless as far as anxiety was concerned, always willing to talk about the tough issues head-on instead of tiptoeing around them. She was much his opposite in personality style as well. In her mammalian brain, Ashley was a Warrior type, not unlike the Miranda character from *Sex and the City*. As such, she was a natural complement to the nurturing, poetic Lover type that Alex was. In fact, Alex was much like Steve, the man that Miranda eventually married on the show—the perfect house husband and man of letters. They had for the most part passed all the steps of both Phase I and Phase II.

Unfortunately for them both, the Personal Boundary thing was the deal-breaker in Phase III—Commitment. When it finally registered on Ashley that Alex was a liberal Democrat, politics became a constant argument that tore their prior friendship to shreds. Ashley was a fighter, not a lover, and Alex was a lover, not a fighter. As mature people, a fighter and a lover are perfect companions, completing each other the way a knight and a lady of medieval times did. Not for two immature Lovers and Warriors, though.

Sexual, emotional, and intellectual attraction (sex, friendship, and commitment) are the three phases and three cornerstones of any relationship. If one fails, the whole thing begins to break apart. Alex and Ashley wavered about real commitment due to their poor boundaries, then their once happy but now failing friendship disintegrated. The Personal Boundary is what makes relationships durable, and Alex and Ashley were not durable.

This was so catastrophic that it even caused their sexual attraction to unravel. As Ashley invaded more of Alex's personal and intellectual territory, he felt less inclined to have sex with her. Her beauty seemed to diminish the more she spoke the praises of George Bush (which to a journalist with good ethics would have been fine if she had not shoved her opinions down his throat).

It all came to a head on Election Day, 2004. Ashley—not even an American citizen—had the audacity to demand that Alex cast his vote for the Republican president. She even drove the point home by saying that his doing so was casting a vote "for her." When finally Alex rebelled against her and got his clothes to leave the house, Ashley let out a final burst of aggression through her poor boundary. She struck him in the chest so hard that he fell over backward. The journalist got up, dusted himself off without a word, and walked out the door never to speak to her again.

Ashley cried as if she had lost the only man in the world.

Why a Personal Boundary Should Not Resemble Swiss Cheese

Ashley was especially lacking in boundary skill, so she routinely invaded Alex's boundary like a little girl would invade her daddy's physical space. She had no sense of Alex's unalienable right to have an opinion different from her own, to have feelings that were unique, and to have the freedom to make choices that she might not agree with. Of course, you could also say that, up to the point where he walked out, Alex lacked mature Personal Boundary skill himself. You will find that as you go through dating life and courtship, you often attract those to you who have similar maturity of their Personal Boundary. Because Alex waited so long to assert his rights, he exhibited holes in his Personal Boundary that are one of the two kinds of immature anatomical parts of a boundary.

A person with holes in his Personal Boundary is overly stressed, oversensitive, immature, and weak of character. He has a bad day every time the environment is bad to him and a good day only when the conditions are just right. This is not good, because the only thing we have true control of in life is whatever is contained inside our Personal Boundary. When we have holes in our Personal Boundary,

"Thin Skin": Holes in Your Boundary

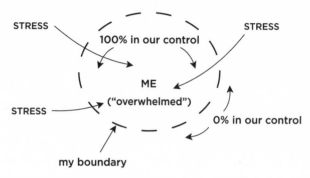

it means that the uncontrollable stresses in life seep in and gain total control of us. What does that do to your trust and security in a man? It eliminates it, and along with it, your faith in his ability to be trusted with a commitment. If he has holes in his Personal Boundary, he is said to be thin-skinned, is considered weak, and cannot defend himself psychologically—let alone defend you. Obviously, the same goes for you. Poor boundaries can ripple down, all the way from commitment to sexual attraction. If a man cannot defend you, that is sexually unattractive, and if your poor boundaries threaten his territory or cause you to not respect him, it's sexually unappealing to him in Step Two of Attraction.

You don't want to have a man who has an overabundance of these holes, because life will always be chaos and you can't gamble your life on this kind of person. A man with a weak boundary cannot be relied upon. A man without a Personal Boundary is like an adolescent at best and small child at worst. He has only the reptilian brain or a little mammalian brain to work with, no higher brain maturity. He will be a prima donna or a lazy good-for-nothing, a nightmare or a drain on your life, and a little boy on the inside.

The same is true for you, of course. If you have holes in your boundary, you will likely be a drama queen, always stressed and out of control of your own emotions. How can he count on you to be a

The Effect of Boundary "Holes" with Stress

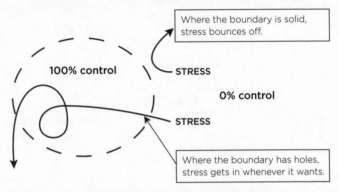

Where the boundary is solid, stress bounces off.

100% control   STRESS

0% control

STRESS

Where the boundary has holes, stress gets in whenever it wants.

You end up having a good day only because the environment is good and you always have a bad day when the environment is bad. This means the uncontrollable has total control of you. Not good.

reliable lover, friend, or committed partner if that is the case? Alex soon realized this about Ashley. If you have ever heard the phrase "You really push my buttons," this indicates that you have holes in your boundary. If you have known someone or been told you have thin skin, again, they're talking about holes in the boundary. People who have too many buttons to push or are extremely thin-skinned like Ashley are immature and send potential Mr. Rights running for their lives.

What is really going on when people have holes in their boundaries is that they find it overly easy to invade the space, opinions, feelings, and decisions of others. They get overly offended in a hypersensitive way to the autonomy, rights, and identity of others. People with holes in their Personal Boundary tend to do a great deal of suffering.

Suffering is the taking of your own emotional energy and spending it on the uncontrollable in life. Since what is inside your boundary is the only thing you can control, when you spend energy on things like bad traffic, the weather, and especially other people, you

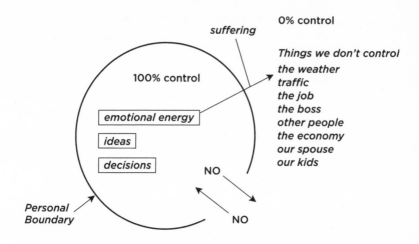

drain yourself like a gas tank with holes in it. In other words, when you suffer, you lose your self-esteem by wasting it on things you don't control.

I can't tell you how many women I have consulted with who secretly or unconsciously wish they could control a particular man. When they do this, they also feel less and less self-esteem inside. They make plans and plots to snare him, to catch him, lock him up in a commitment he did not agree to, and throw away the key, to demand he see things the way they see things, to communicate, to show emotion he doesn't have, or to change his ways. This is a horrible waste of energy. We *never* have absolute control over other human beings, and if you think you can control a particular man, you're kidding yourself. When you do this, like Ashley, you kill any possibility of getting a true commitment.

However, you *do* control what is inside your boundary, and that means your standards, your likes and dislikes, your attitude, and things you believe about yourself and about men. You *do* control going after or being open to a *general kind* of man, not a *particular* man like an ex who rejected you. One of the things I often counsel women about is grief over a lost love. Usually, the thing that gets them stuck in grief is a tendency to idealize an ex, making it impossible to find a man in the future who can measure up. The endpoint of grief is always supposed to be a happy one, where you learn what it was about the person you lost that you want to keep as a preference you have in men, versus what was distasteful to you (the most important thing being that if he didn't choose *you*, he is not too bright, and you don't like dumb men). If he didn't "get you," he didn't have enough of a sense of style and good taste, and that's not very attractive, is it? When you give up controlling particular men and realize you do control going for your type, finding a guy even better suited to your tastes (including that he chooses you!), then you're very likely to find the kind of durable magic in a romance that you've always wanted.

Intellectual attraction is the domain of the higher brain. It involves "getting" each other intellectually, being on the same page, and being able to team up to solve problems, communicate, and work toward goals that benefit you both equally. If you or your man has boundary holes, you can't be intellectually attracted to each other because your communication with each other will always be like parent to child, or child to parent—never equal-to-equal partner. The holes lead you to feel the need to protect your rights, so you stop communicating or lie to each other just to avoid minor disagreements in everyday life. We all know that when communication shuts down or lies become rampant, we can't possibly trust the word of a partner to be with us in a mature commitment.

Here's a super-secret clue to identifying when a man has poor boundaries: the word "should." When someone says "should" often, what he is really saying is that he wishes he controlled something he does not. He is suffering. When a person says, "Traffic should move faster" and beats his hands on the steering wheel, he burns a ton of emotional energy and gets nothing back. Traffic does not follow our commands. Watch out for frequent use of the word "should" from a man (and in your own speech). You won't get a solid, strong commitment if you hear this word a great deal, and neither will Mr. Right take you as a lifelong partner.

The other thing that holes in the Personal Boundary cause is a poor sense of personal identity. A Personal Boundary actually is the very thing that lets us have preferences in life. When we can't say no to things that don't feel like us, or feel too inhibited to say yes to things that do, we lack a sense of identity. Other people get an eerie discomfort about us when we're this way.

The shape of your boundary is the shape of your identity, and its gaps are the reason for every inconsistency about your genuineness that men identify.

Effects of Boundary Holes

Identity!

Identity?

Resources!

Resources?

If I were to tell you that I say yes to having dogs in my life and no to cats, yes to rock and no to country music, and yes to pizza and no to eggs, then I am a cat-hating, dog-loving, rock-loving, country-hating, egg-hating, pizza-eating shrink, which sounds unfortunately like the title of a country music song. That tells you quite a bit about my identity with very few pieces of information. Imagine how much you could learn about any man's Personal Boundary if you could elicit a wide range of his preferences on everything from the role of marriage and children to musical tastes, clothing, food, grooming, career, friends, family, and anything else that mattered to you. Discuss this with your girlfriends, and you might agree: A man with a solid identity can be trusted. Now you know why. Identity only comes with a solid Personal Boundary, which is the very container of that thing we call strength. Such a man has the strength to protect you and keep what you share secure.

Consciously or not, Mr. Right is learning the same kinds of things about you. When he asks what you would like to do tonight and you say, "Oh, anything will do," you are causing him to see commitment to you as a no-no even if it is your first date. If he asks you what movie you want to see, and you say, "I don't care," you could be setting yourself up for trouble. You're sending the message that there are holes in your boundary, that you lack a sufficient sense of identity. Men interpret this as a warning that life with you is going to be draining emotionally, financially, and spiritually.

People with holes in their boundary are prone to lie. A lie is like putting up a smokescreen over a hole in the boundary, rather than simply saying no or taking rejection gracefully.

Lies and Boundary "Holes"

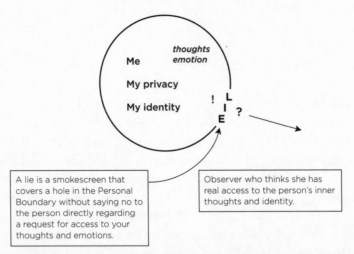

A lie is a smokescreen that covers a hole in the Personal Boundary without saying no to the person directly regarding a request for access to your thoughts and emotions.

Observer who thinks she has real access to the person's inner thoughts and identity.

If a man lies often, he also likely has many holes in his boundary. Holes in the boundary make it unlikely that the man is able to commit to you, and if he seems to, will likely lie or cheat eventually. The same goes for you, so we had better learn to fix up those holes in the sections that follow.

Locus of Control

Locus of Control is an awesome test of a man's amount of Personal Boundary weakness, or holes. What it means is that we all are being steered in our lives, whether by ourselves or by others. Someone is responsible for everything we think, say, do, or don't do. Hopefully that someone is you! When you are at the steering wheel, responsible for your own life, you have an Internal Locus of Control. When someone else is at the wheel, you are giving in to an External Locus of Control.

If you have ever known or been a woman who is easily irritable, easily stressed or overwhelmed, then this person has many holes in the boundary and likely has an External Locus of Control. If you have an External Locus of Control, you need an outside force to control your own feelings. This means that your self-control is unpredictable. People will see you as impulsive, impatient, and unlikely

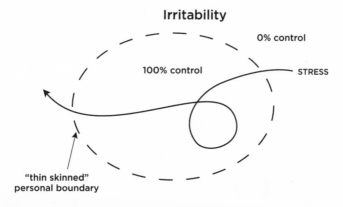

to follow through on your promises. You are what men call high-maintenance. You might turn to alcohol, drugs, or tobacco, or you might rely on people (like the men you date) to prop up your emotions.

When this happens, every stress controls you instead of the other way around. Every truly honorable action your potential Mr. Right takes has a direct line to your feelings, filtered through a swamp of negative beliefs where his intentions get misinterpreted. He senses in you that you can't even take responsibility for your own negativity and emotional management. If you display an overwillingness to let outside forces dictate your feelings—you have an up day because something nice randomly happened on the job and a down day because something irritating randomly happened—he immediately knows that you have an External Locus of Control. You are a boat with no oars, a ship with no sails. Why would Mr. Right want to take you on a honeymoon cruise in *that*? Deep in his genes, he has the unconscious intuition that you are not to be trusted with his genetic destiny. A commitment to you would be a disaster. Your weak boundary shows up on his girl-radar like the wild and random drama of a hurricane approaching. You are *The Perfect Storm*. Of course, the same is true if you see this in him.

An Internal Locus of Control is the opposite. It comes from a strong boundary that lets him know that you can resist stress. He knows that no matter what happens in the environment, you are capable of keeping your composure and grace. It lets him know that you are as strong as he is, that you won't create drama that raises his blood pressure, risks his health, his territory, his property, or his mission in life.

Strength is the currency of the Personal Boundary. It is what lets us protect others and defend ourselves in the way that the strong border of a nation does. If he is to really commit to you for life, he can't afford to merge boundaries (be intimate) with you if you are going to be like a sieve that drains his energy by sharing your worry, complaints, rage, victimization, and suffering all the time. A

committed relationship is meant to give you both a shoulder to oc-
casionally lean on, not a Dumpster for either of your negativity or
suffering.

Further, if you diminish his territory by wasting the resources
that build and maintain that territory (calling him all the time at
work, fighting with him or complaining to him that he doesn't listen
enough while he is trying to study for an exam, spending his money
when he has just begun a career transition, and so on), he will leave
you in the dust. These displays of weak boundary skills make him
feel as though he is losing dominion over his future.

Likewise, as a woman with some two hundred to three hundred
total eggs to use for procreating in your lifetime, you cannot afford
a man who is not strong in his own right. He will need to withstand
your little tests of him, your assessments of his strength and ability
to hold his own even during stressful times.

In giving him sex too early, before a true commitment, you have
far more to lose than a man does. Yet in giving up the single life to
enter a commitment to you before you have proven to be a best
friend and master seductress, a man also has a great deal to lose. If
you have an External Locus of Control that lets everyone else influence you (and therefore hassle him, via your intimate connection),
he is going to run away from you or cheat on you. He will never
commit to a potential partner who is such a clear liability and threat
to your joint survival.

How do you use the boundary to fix this? I once heard it said that
in medieval times, one could fight an attacker with a sword or a
shield, but that the shield was much better to use than the sword. A
sword burns up all your energy. Yet if you simply hold up your
shield, your boundary against stress, you use much less energy than
in a direct confrontation. Your boundary is a shield, and its most
practical use is in the simple ability to say no to time or energy
drains that hurt you both, and to take no gracefully, to tolerate rejection without creating drama (in other words, to refuse to suffer
away all your positive emotional energy). This is the value of having

an unshakable Internal Locus of Control. Let's learn how through a real-life example of the kind I see nearly every day.

Addicted to Love: Mature Growth Through Patching Boundary Holes

In psychiatry, the term "addiction" is often mentioned in the same sentence as "codependence" and "being in denial." In any addiction you or a potential Mr. Right face, there are just two negative ingredients. Whether you deal with smoking, overeating, drugs, alcohol, porn, gambling, shopping sprees, workaholism, or being a neat-freak, the two simple, sneaky causes are holes in the boundary, and impulsiveness (the down-arrow option we learned on the Anxiety Map).

Addiction equals boundary holes plus impulsive anxiety management. Therefore, the cure for any addiction is saying no and gracefully hearing no in order to fix boundary holes, and having the courage to transform impulsive anxiety into confidence instead. This might make great sense to you if you have ever heard the Serenity Prayer used in 12-step programs:

"*God grant me the serenity to accept the things I cannot change* [outside the boundary], *the courage to change the things I can* [inside the boundary], *and the wisdom to know the difference* [which is the boundary itself]."

I once saw a man as a patient who had a live-in girlfriend and came to me to ask for Valium for his anxiety. When I asked him what he was anxious about, he said, "She lives with me and does drugs. When she is around, I'm anxious—especially when the cops come. When she isn't home, I am less anxious."

I told him that an addictive medication like Valium couldn't solve this problem. We use valium in ERs for physical problems that cause anxiety, like alcohol withdrawal or seizures. The cause of his dismay was that this guy had a hole in his boundary for the woman. She was dumping her anxiety into his boundary through her immaturity and thoughtlessness. No pharmaceutical drug would ever fix the kind of poor boundary situation these two were in.

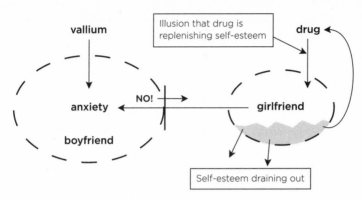

Of course, he said, "I guess you're going to tell me the only cure is to ask her to move out." I admitted that was true. The problem was not a medical one. The problem was caused by the holes in their boundaries. The cure for boundary holes is tolerating rejection or disagreement with poise and grace—patching the holes by using or hearing the word no and getting comfortable hearing the word no from others.

When the man finally asked his girlfriend to move out, he found a sense of relief. His anxiety went away, but not for long, because he

Repairing Boundaries

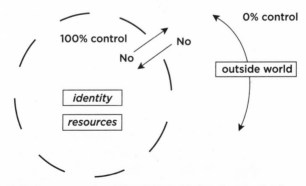

had an incredible sense of guilt. Did you ever feel this way when you had to tell a man no for his or your own good? Of course. You were using what they call tough love to patch up a hole in both of your boundaries by saying no for both of your own good.

The reason the man still felt guilty was that his girlfriend found another hole through which to manipulate him. She called him regularly to tell him how hard it was being out on her own. He patched one hole with her, but she simply found another hole in his boundary. I told him he needed to patch that hole as well by using his Personal Boundary to shut out her further attempts to make him feel guilty.

I also explained to him that he was actually helping her by patching her boundary holes. When we say no to others for their own good, we can give them an experience that may help them patch up their own boundary and stop suffering so much. I thought it was possible that if he held the line, she would seek drug treatment.

He returned to me again saying he still felt guilty because he felt protective of her, and he couldn't stand thinking that she might be out in the street without anyone to help her. He thought he might be the only person capable of helping her. While a primal sense of protection by a man for a woman is one of the core traits of our gender differences, the degree to which this man's boundary was impaired was pathological and codependent, not merely an act of being a man. He was taking responsibility for what ought to be his girlfriend's routine higher-brained duties at good self-care.

This was a very persistent problem with ongoing holes in his boundary. He was looking at her through one of these holes and feeling as if she belonged to him like a possession, that he somehow owned and controlled her decisions and the quality of life her decisions produced. That's her responsibility, and he was in what we call denial, failing to see the limits of what he owned and controlled.

The man didn't see that assistance could come to her not only from him but also from the police, the drug-treatment centers, a therapist, her family, her friends, and every other public or private relationship. Through the hole in his *own* boundary for her, he

Denial = Not seeing the limits of our control

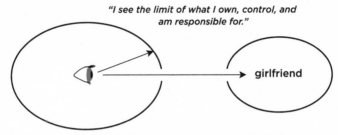

"I see the limit of what I own, control, and am responsible for."

girlfriend

"This belongs to me, too. It 'should' be this way or that, I 'should' get what I want."

"Why is this not going the way I want? The way it should go?" (we suffer)

looked out under the illusion that everything he saw belonged to him like his own arms and legs belong to him. It was as if he thought he was the whole world to her and had just kicked her right off the planet. Their boundary holes played them into perfect, dysfunctional roles with each other, with the boyfriend acting the parent, which he is not, and the girlfriend acting a child, which she also is most certainly not.

Going back to Ashley and Alex, Ashley also had a serious problem with denial. She felt she had the right and power to dictate Alex's opinions, beliefs, emotions, and even his voting decisions. She felt she owned him, was the only source of ideas, energy, and sustenance for him, and even went so far as to feel she was responsible and right in taking over his decisions for him, most notably the decision in a presidential election. This is a process called codependence.

Codependence Versus a True, Mature Commitment

Codependence is the bane of modern relationships. It is invisible and sneaky. It creeps in on you and slowly causes you to regress to ever deepening immaturity.

When two people first meet, they are in a state of independence. People who have just met have unique emotions, ideas, beliefs, and preferences in their decisions for themselves. Sometimes, when they start to relate to each other, they never get beyond a kind of formal connection that is merely cordial. These people might be said to have walls in their boundaries. In other words, no matter what happens, they tend to maintain a deep privacy and always say no to each other's request for intimacy, never deeply connecting. If they were nations, they would both be isolated countries, with no openness of cultural sharing, trade, or connection to others.

"Thick Skin": Walls in the Boundary

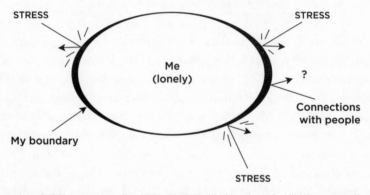

People like this may have been hurt in the past and chose to cut off from deep connections to others out of self-protection. You might even say that the walls in their Personal Boundaries are caused by emotional scar tissue caused by past romantic hurts or other psychological traumas. People with this kind of boundary are just as immature as people with many holes in their boundaries are. They can't truly connect, communicate, or commit to others in a mature fashion. They are as weak internally for lack of connections to the energy, ideas, and social teamwork with others as a person with many holes is weak externally against stress.

Someone who is childish in his higher brain might jump back and forth between saying yes to all the demands of others (through holes in his boundary) and saying no to all requests of others wanting to connect to him (having walls to intimacy). None of these anatomical parts of a boundary need be exclusive. We can have holes for some things in life (like people who are bad for us) and walls for other things (like being frugal with our money). If you ever meet an aggressively difficult man who disagrees with everything, you are probably looking at a guy who has many walls in his boundary. He is likely to stay in a state of independence from you. If you meet a passively difficult man who goes along with everything you say and then sabotages what he's agreed to, you are looking at a guy with holes in his boundary. He is likely on the other hand to get into a state of codependence with you.

When a couple first meets, they might notice a sexual attraction. Then a friendship (emotional attraction) buds because they share positive emotion consistently and their emotional energies are opposite but complementary. They make each other feel good, and that is the beginning of love. Soon they begin communicating, and their two Personal Boundaries begin to open up. They exchange opinions and compare beliefs, finding common ground. They begin to have an intellectual attraction with the higher brain. Soon they start making joint decisions. They go on the same date at the same place, get married in the same church hand in hand, and have the same children. This illustrates the progression through the three phases of courtship.

The diagram on the following page shows you everything you need to know about commitment and its connection to falling in love. If you have ever known a man who seems afraid to commit, he has walls in his boundary. He is being run only by his reptilian brain, which cherishes the territoriality underneath his independence and enjoyment of male freedom. This man has not developed a more mature boundary capable of both retaining a masculine sense of territory and finding intimacy with a woman at the same time.

When a couple goes from having the walls of independence to a spark of sexual attraction to opening their boundaries and joining in

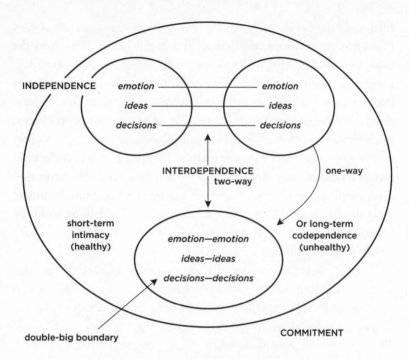

positive emotional energy (friendship's emotional attraction), they can finally join similar ideas, decisions, and beliefs (intellectual attraction). In sharing joint decisions, they have begun to commit in small ways. Even if they commit to one date, two dates, or to being boyfriend and girlfriend, they have invested time and energy. They have reached a temporary state called intimacy, a willing opening of the boundary to each other, to share everything in there.

Notice that the size of their collective boundary is double the size they were as individuals. This is why falling in love feels so great. Reptiles cannot fall in love, or have a commitment. Lower mammals cannot have a commitment. While love itself is a property of the mammalian brain, the act of falling in love and guiding it slowly to commitment is the exclusive domain of the human higher brain, the most complex, sophisticated cerebral cortex in the animal kingdom. For no new effort, the two people who have fallen in love have doubled the size of what they control about the world (their boundary size), doubled their positive emotional energy, their ideas, and the collective wisdom of their decisions.

The problem arises when this sweet state of two people acting as one starts feeling as if it can be maintained just like that permanently. We don't *actually* double the size of our identity, our energy, our ideas, or wisdom. We only team up with someone else to join forces. Someone childish will be tempted to imagine the whole relationship belongs only to him or her. This is what codependence is— a persistent state of intimacy where one person begins to dominate and control the whole relationship, using the other person to his or her own gain.

Eventually, something very bad happens:

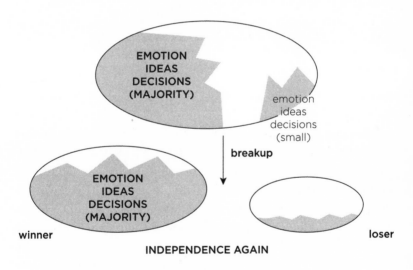

Codependence is a struggle between a winner and a loser.

The bigger bully begins taking all the energy, ideas, time, and decision making for his or herself, leaving the other person to feel depleted and afraid to break up or terrified of being broken up with. The result of codependence is always a breakup, eventually. Sure, some people stay together in a whiny, combative, essentially loveless roommate-type situation, even for years. But isn't that a *psychological* breakup without the finishing touch of *physically* walking out the door? A breakup of what once might have been *real*?

The state of codependence is always caused by holes in the boundary, and now you know why someone with holes in their boundary is not capable of a true commitment. He is doomed to codependence because he doesn't know any more mature way of being.

There is a way to grow, though, and you can assess a man's ability to do this along with your own. Interdependence is the only mature Personal Boundary quality capable of making a commitment. It happens through using doors in the boundary instead of holes of codependence or walls of overindependence.

Boundary Doors and Interdependence

The ability to use doors in your boundary instead of holes or walls is one of the ultimate goals of maturity, personal growth, and truly workable, satisfying adult relationships. When you build doors in your boundary, you find a way to live successfully in the world, paired as a couple and partner to another. All people have different tastes and preferences, emotional styles, ideas, and beliefs. We can never be an identical twin to another, nor do we want to be—after all, as teammates we need to share complementary skills to be better together than apart.

Doors enable us to work together, teaming up only when we are in agreement and feeling full good-energy friendship, and not teaming up in times when we disagree or feel bad. In this way, we can still be committed, even though we aren't perfect mirror images of each other. Not even Mr. Right is ever going to be perfectly in tune with you or on the mark of what you need at every moment of every day. The mature doors of a mature Personal Boundary open up to

A mature boundary with doors, not holes or walls

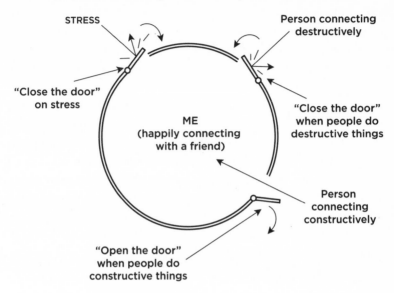

win/win deals, things that are good for both of you, and close to win/lose deals, things that aren't good for both of you. This property makes doors much like the customs and immigration service at a national border.

How many people do you know who have one disagreement and then decide never to be friends again? People have "shit lists" for the friends they lose by the dozens over small hurts, infractions, or miscommunications. If you yourself are in these shoes or dating a man who cuts off people in this way, you are in trouble. Ashley was certainly this way. It will lead to losing any realistic chance of getting along in the world, let alone getting along with the man who might be your Mr. Right. Mature people find a way to say no temporarily to what doesn't work for them at the time, but to forgive and forget when there is a future opportunity to get along just fine. All the while, they can stay true to their promises and be committed even when there is temporary disagreement or two people need to go off to do hobbies and recharge their batteries.

Interdependence is the ability to have doors in the boundary. Co-dependence is a one-way travel from normal, healthy independence to a weird kind of permanent intimacy with boundary holes. Social isolation is a kind of overindependence in which a person uses only walls that never let a person get intimate in the first place. Interdependence, on the other hand, is the ability to open doors in the boundary when things go well, and close the doors in times when they don't. It is a two-way ability to bounce back and forth in balance between independence and intimacy. When you find the ability to agree to disagree the way doors in the boundary allow, you have found one of the highest markers of relationship maturity and the ability to truly commit for life.

I think the great rampage of codependence in modern relationships is due to a lack of some sort of societal protection of commitment around the whole system you see above. A lack of the very process this book helps you with—*courtship*. Commitment is an idea, a higher-brained agreement, a kind of contract, a promise to keep your word no matter how difficult things temporarily get emotionally. With a lack of respect for commitment today and such ease of getting out of commitments, people tend to think that if they disagree with their partner just once, or someone goes a little independent for a while, it will mean the end of the relationship. What kind of state of fear is that to live in? This is why whatever your spiritual, religious, or political beliefs, I want you to know you are also protected by something else in your courtship, and any relationship meant to last. You are protected by a story that you share with Mr. Right.

If you learned to use your Cool Eye to watch the plot of your life unfold with his, then you are well aware that a story is something neither of you can escape, nor would want to escape. It is a good story, a protective story—a happy ending is waiting—and you will "just know" Mr. Right when you see him. If you can convince yourself to go independent when you disagree with your man, and let him disagree with you, if you can both sometimes go off to do your own thing for a while and not suspect each other of wrongdoing or cheating, then you are testing your relationship in the best possible way.

The Tests

Here are the tests of whether your potential Mr. Right can ever begin to be able to commit in this phase:

- If he says "should" often, he has holes in his boundary through which he suffers, will cause you to suffer, and he cannot commit.

- If he tells you often how to feel, think, and act, he doesn't respect your boundary due to holes in his own and cannot commit like an adult and a real man.

- If he has an External Locus of Control, rather than an Internal Locus of Control, he will rely on you to tell him who he is and should be, as if you were his mother rather than partner. He will not be able to commit.

- If he lacks identity and does not have an opinion on matters that are important to you both, he has many holes in his boundary and cannot commit.

- On the flip side, if he is so private that he won't tell you anything about himself, he is overly independent, has walls in his boundary, and cannot commit.

- If he goes off to do his own thing almost all the time and never opens up to you, he has walls, is independent only, and cannot commit.

- If he thinks that for him to be right, you have to be wrong, then he has holes in his boundary and cannot commit.

- If he thinks that in admitting you are right, he must be wrong, then he also has holes in his boundary and cannot commit.

- If he surrenders his worldview to yours most of the time, then he has holes in his boundary and cannot commit.

- If he can't agree to disagree, be independent sometimes and intimate sometimes as the situation calls for, he does not have doors in his boundary. He can't be interdependent, and so cannot commit like a mature, real man.

- If he can't compromise, see how both of you are right in your own way, then he does not have doors and cannot be interdependent and commit like a mature real man.

- If he always agrees with you, he has holes in his boundary and cannot commit.

- If he always disagrees with you, he has walls in his boundary and cannot commit.

- If he can't sometimes challenge your thinking, he lacks doors in his boundary and cannot commit as an interdependent, mature, real man.

- If he lies often, then he is trying to hide the holes in his boundary and cannot commit.

- If he is often in denial and feels that your feelings are his, your opinions are his, and your decisions to be made are his, rather than yours alone, then he has holes in his boundary and cannot commit.

- If he feels responsible for all of your feelings, thoughts, or decisions, as if you were his daughter rather than partner, he has holes and cannot commit.

- If he can't budget or manage his money, his time, or his health, then he also cannot commit.

These are just a few ground rules. I couldn't possibly give you as comprehensive a list in these pages as I do in my seminars for women and men, but using these, you'll be able to sense the rest.

When people have matching and opposite temperaments in friendship, everything is easy. When they have good boundaries as well, the relationship becomes easier still. These people rarely need to go outside the relationship to keep it afloat. Collectively, they have all the skills, ideas, and fun they could need together.

You are submitting to a story. Either this is "the One," or he is not. The only way to find out is to go through the Commitment Phase of building solid boundaries first, then exercising independence when it is called for. You grow interdependent on a kind of faith in your story together. It will be okay to agree to disagree sometimes, and to go do your own thing sometimes. If you really do have a shared story, the relationship will last no matter what happens around you. It will work itself out as long as you use the doors of a mature Personal Boundary, or else it never really was your true story together. The sooner you know that, the better.

You know you have a man who can truly commit for the long term if:

- He has a strong sense of identity with specific tastes and preferences.

- He is accountable for his own tastes and preferences, but does not force them on others.

- He does not suffer much over things he does not control (including you). Instead, he works with what he does control to solve problems, accept himself and his limitations, and accept the limitations of people around him.

- He doesn't let anyone—including you—tell him how to feel, what to believe, or what he should or should not do.

- He doesn't tell others what to do, be, think, or feel. He accepts people for what they are.

- He keeps his privacy to himself, honors it, and respects that of others.

- In his privacy, he keeps some masculine secrets to himself, decides what he does and doesn't want to share, and he doesn't feel defensive about that decision. However, he doesn't lie often. He would rather tell you "That's private" than lie.

- He tells the truth when others need help in facing their own bad behavior but doesn't invade the privacy of others if help is not asked for. He is not your daddy, your therapist, your financial adviser, or your banker. He does want to be your partner, though.

- He doesn't take on responsibility for the normal self-care of others, nor does he dump his own responsibilities on others. Yet he is empathic, caring toward others when they need a shoulder to lean on.

- He doesn't dump anger, anxiety, or any other unpleasant emotion on others, and he doesn't accept dumping from others.

- He is not a perfectionist, but he is ambitious. He wants to grow and see you grow.

- He takes credit for his own victories in life and doesn't take credit for your victories. Nevertheless, he fully celebrates both of these with you.

- He has separate qualities of relationship with various people and keeps the nature of those relationships straight in his mind. He doesn't play one person against another, but honors each as a unique, separate relationship.

- He doesn't let himself be forced to choose between the people in his life he has agreements with and commitments to. He strives for harmony and balance among them, yet in a committed romance to you, he places that first and of highest value.

- He keeps his word, or doesn't promise in the first place, no matter how convincing you are.

- He is on time but honors his own limitations.

- He is good at budgeting time, energy, and money, and makes fair deals with others for these.

- He is independent, with a masculine sense of territory, but is able to open up to intimacy.

- He is open to intimacy but does not let himself get permanently stuck there in a condition of codependence.

- He respects your opinions and his own, and is able to agree to disagree and still live by agreements and commitments.

- In any argument, he is able to see both of you as being right in your own ways. Then he looks for common ground of understanding.

- He is able to leave intimacy for a time, to go be his own person, have his own friends, hobbies, territory, and activities.

- He tolerates your leaving intimacy for a time, to go be your own person, have your own friends, hobbies, connections, and activities.

- He doesn't use the most hurtful facts about you to fight. He uses the facts of the moment's situation.

- He doesn't beat you over the head with the past, nor does he tolerate that from you.

- He doesn't worry you about future events that haven't happened yet and doesn't tolerate that from you.

- He doesn't try to be right. He tries to be masculine, fair, and seek teamwork.

- He is able to tolerate disagreement from you and speaks up when you don't seem to tolerate disagreement from him. He asserts his personal identity anyway, even if you threaten to break up with him.

- He doesn't threaten to break up with you unless there is an absolute impasse between you that will kill the relationship.

- He is not afraid of breaking up with you or your breaking up with him if that's necessary.

- He loves you respectfully, not unconditionally. Unconditional love is what there is from a parent to a child. It is Agape Love, not Amour (Mature Romantic Love). You are not his child and he is not yours.

Once you have a good sense of your Personal Boundary and that of Mr. Right, you need to continue to do maintenance on your boundary preferences and intimacy. This can only happen through having a great deal of beliefs in common, lots of communication, and setting goals that actually make the shared boundary of intimacy grow. (This is our next step of courtship.) You must learn to grow as a couple, not only as sexually attracted lovers and emotionally attracted friends, but as intellectually attracted partners.

Your Story and the Sacred Nature of Boundaries

There are specific reasons I use so many diagrams and symbols that have an appealing shape. For one, they give you automatic practice at the Cool Eye. If you look at a diagram of your own psychology, then you are looking at you, which is the definition of having a Cool Eye. Your Cool Eye is the higher-brained skill that lets you follow your own story through life, with you at the steering wheel. It is the only human skill that allows change or growth, and using symbols to help you cultivate it is a great way to accelerate your progress. Secondly, given that a picture is worth a thousand words, I can then write you this couple-hundred-page book that has the equivalent of more than a million words in meaning.

The value of symbols is similar to the value of stories and myths in understanding the behavior of men and women. They have special meanings and uses not unlike the kind of deep wisdom and detective work we've all seen in the likes of *The Da Vinci Code* phenomenon or the works of master artists like Leonardo himself.

When I designed the symbols of KWML™, many people asked me why I used a circle to represent all the possible personality styles and skills people have. After all, there are four types—the King/Queen, Warrior, Magician, and Lover—and that would lend itself to using squares to represent how we think and feel. Well, when it comes right down to it, much of what I teach you is a model of perfection in your skills, character, and the ability to judge the character of Mr. Right, but who can be absolutely perfect? Nobody. Since ancient times, the symbol of the circle has represented many things that do have a close relationship to one another.

For one, the circle represents the concept of unity, which most of you eventually want to find with a Mr. Right of your own. At the same time, the circle has always been a symbol of the divine, considered the perfect shape like no other. All human beings have a sense of spirituality regardless of what their native culture or religion is, and a circle represents a target to shoot for in your personal growth. As far as KWML™ is concerned, that target is the center of the circle, which is a perfect balance of intellectual and emotional skill. None of us, of course, can reach that exact point, or we *would be* divine ourselves. We can only aim for that.

At the same time, through much of recorded history, the symbol of the square has always represented man- and womankind's pleasing but imperfect shape, the shape of the terrestrial, or worldly rather than the divine. And so you can actually see the very human characteristics of intellectual and emotional skills on spectrums able to be plotted within that circle, as if on a square graph. In total, the KWML™ diagrams then show both the imperfect and human (square measurement) aiming for the goal of divine perfection (the circle and its center) in the process of coming together in love and friendship. Going from the edge of the circle in all kinds of interesting paths toward the center (psychological integration) really is the story of your life.

The Personal Boundary itself is a circle. As such it is a perfect thing, symbolically. And yet nobody has a Perfect Boundary. That would just be an ideal to aim for as we grow our boundary ability as individuals. We all have at least some holes and walls, as well as doors in us.

What about two boundaries that interact with each other? I'd like to tell you about an extra-special symbol from history, literature, and myth. That symbol is called the mandorla, as seen on the next page. When I draw boundaries for people, they take the form of a circle, too, which you might say is another example of trying for perfection, since none of us has a Perfect Boundary without any holes at all. We all have more of a dotted-line-circle for the shape of our psyches, which you might find to be an interesting, symbolic way to see human beings as created in God's image (dotted circle versus full solid circle). Few would scoff at the nature of intimacy, commitment, and marriage itself being anything less than divine, two boundaries coming together as sacred partners in a durable love. Symbolically, the mandorla helps us literally see how this is so.

What happened for Ashley and Alex, and what you may have at times seen in your life is something more like the diagram on page 204.

What this has to do with your own personal story of growth toward balance and happiness in a relationship is that you have likely felt this process before, or seen it happen to those you know. What was

The Mandorla

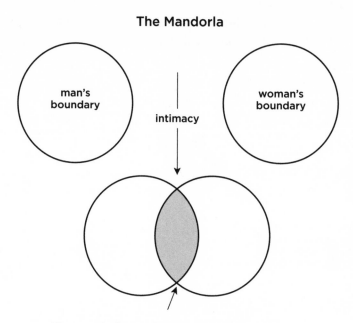

The mandorla, or almond shape of the intimacy
shared between two people

a mandorla of perfect intimacy and shared resources—and one that also maintains each person's sense of identity—was shattered for Alex and Ashley (and many divorced or divorcing people you know) by the poor boundaries at work.

On the other hand, when you have worked on your Personal Boundary by learning to say no to what you don't want, yes to things you do want, developing preferences, identity, an ability to budget, be fair, diplomatic, and respectful of both yourself and others, you will find that the story of your life naturally begins to weed out all the Mr. Wrongs who bring bad deals to your life and naturally begins to open up to potential Mr. Rights who bring just the right good deals and worldviews into your life.

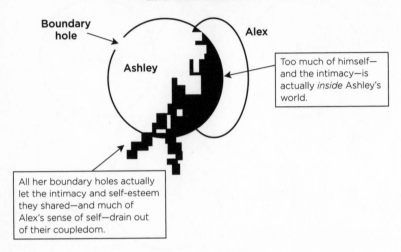

Codependence "Drainage" of Intimacy and Self-Esteem

Boundary hole

Alex

Ashley

Too much of himself—and the intimacy—is actually *inside* Ashley's world.

All her boundary holes actually let the intimacy and self-esteem they shared—and much of Alex's sense of self—drain out of their coupledom.

Your Action Plan

To bring this lofty stuff down to earth, I have a simple suggestion for new couples who want to avoid the boundary problems of codependence and losing one's self in bad relationships. When you are with someone, there is an identity (and story) that is all your own, one that is all his or her own, and one that is shared between you. They are like three different countries. When you suspect something doesn't feel right or natural about your story with a candidate for Mr. Right, simply imagine a circle around you that is your reality, a circle around him that is his reality, and a mandorla shape in the middle. You need to enter the other person's world of experience, but it is good to do so with only one foot (on the mandorla), keeping the second foot firmly planted in your own circle—your boundary.

You want your relationship, and your story, to have the ring of something deeply spiritual, a timeless beauty that not only satisfies the requirements of practical living, but a feeling of what is easy and natural. Your Personal Boundary makes everything in life just that—real, genuine, natural, and, most of all, easy. Once you get a lock on what makes for a solid boundary, your action plans and story can safely, securely, happily become a *joint* action plan, and a *joint* story for two.

The Commitment Phase (Intellectual Attraction)

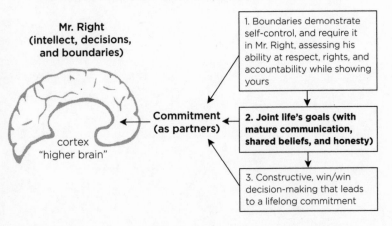

Mr. Right
(intellect, decisions,
and boundaries)

cortex
"higher brain"

Commitment
(as partners)

1. Boundaries demonstrate self-control, and require it in Mr. Right, assessing his ability at respect, rights, and accountability while showing yours

2. Joint life's goals (with mature communication, shared beliefs, and honesty)

3. Constructive, win/win decision-making that leads to a lifelong commitment

Chapter Nine

~~~

Like Attracts Like

Phase III: The Commitment Phase
*Step Two: Achieving Joint Life Goals Through
Communication, Beliefs, and Actions*

> *The difference between an optimist and a pessimist?
> An optimist laughs to forget, but a pessimist forgets
> to laugh.* —TOM BODETT

$\mathcal{M}$ANY PEOPLE ASK ME what I think might constitute the perfect
personal ad. I'm often amused and concerned about this at the same
time. Love is so obviously more than a checklist of interests or clinical psychological surveys. Love is a story with fire and passion, unexpected challenges and joys, predictable seasons, and improbable or
even magical first encounters. Online dating for the most part does
not sound very magical or even romantic to me. Still, I can see how
someone might come to believe that a comparison of lists of things
you prefer in a mate, things you believe in or value, and expectations
for the future might lead to Mr. Right. This approach does, in fact, get
a woman a head start on what a commitment to a man might be like
but only within Step Two of the Commitment Phase. Beware: This online dating approach done alone leaves out the other eight steps.

Often you see such entries as this:

Wanted: SWM, late 20s to mid-30s, for fun, friendship, and,
possibly, commitment. Must be kind, generous, thoughtful, and

attentive, like movies, TV, theater, sports, mystery novels, coffee, romantic walks, cats, and children. No smokers, heavy drinkers, or players.

Why are personal ads so vague? Why do they use such generalized terms to screen the opposite sex for appropriateness? Why are so many people dissatisfied with Internet dating? Woman after woman tells me the guy who seemed so great on paper was not at all what he promised—he was boring, a hundred pounds heavier than advertised, and he cheated on his last three girlfriends. Like all dating, Internet dating begins with the Sexual Attraction stage of courtship. Yet these lists of personality traits are higher-brained. They address only the Commitment Phase of relationships, and they are so general as to leave the real person's nature totally up in the air. When we use phrases like "I'm athletic," that could mean a 90-pound woman with an eating disorder or a 350-pound man who goes snowshoeing once a year.

Maybe a personal ad could read this way:

Wanted: SWM, exactly 28 in age, no kids, smoking, heavy drinking. You must be a former player, proving to me that you have mastered adolescent sexual-attraction skills, have a sense of territory, rank among other men, and power. You ought to be ready to be put to the test by me (showing willingness, for instance, to shop for clothes for more than six hours each weekend), are okay with being challenged, and yet open to my support. In addition, you must have control of your own anger and anxiety, and not be afraid to make a good impression on me. Be yourself. But you better look like your picture, be honest, and do all of the impressive things you say you do. You need to be fun and give me pleasant emotions when I am around you, and if we make for attracted friends for a few months, you must have solid boundaries before I will consider committing to you. I will spend my valuable time on you if I am exactly what you want in life and you find yourself willing to give up being a player forever. If, however, we don't get swept up in the story of our love, I reserve the right to end things without finding you standing on my lawn, wearing a trench coat, and holding a boom box over your head playing the song you think was "ours."

That would certainly be refreshing. Having read this far into this book, you already know why.

Now that we have journeyed into the higher brain, we are at a place in relationships (maybe some months into joining stories with a man) where "birds of a feather flock together." We need the security of sameness, mutual goals, beliefs, and values. Now that we have reasonable assurance that we both have good Personal Boundaries, we know it is possible to commit.

Do we want to, though?

The answer is dependent on how much sameness we have in our intellectual higher brain, our cerebral cortex. We need a partner who is similar to us in intelligence and in general core values such as politics, religion, children, family, lifestyle, habits, health, finances, and the meaning of life.

Men and women both have higher-brained preferences in a partner. As we've discussed, the unique shape of your Personal Boundary determines these.

I once came across a list of typical preferences that men and women have for each other:

HOW TO MAKE A WOMAN HAPPY

IT'S NOT DIFFICULT. TO MAKE A WOMAN HAPPY,
A MAN ONLY NEEDS TO BE:

1. a friend
2. a companion
3. a lover
4. a brother
5. a father

6. a master
7. a chef
8. an electrician
9. a carpenter
10. a plumber
11. a mechanic
12. a decorator
13. a stylist
14. a sexologist
15. a gynecologist
16. a psychologist
17. a pest exterminator
18. a psychiatrist
19. a healer
20. a good listener
21. an organizer
22. a good father
23. very clean
24. sympathetic
25. athletic
26. warm
27. attentive
28. gallant
29. intelligent
30. funny
31. creative
32. tender
33. strong
34. understanding
35. tolerant
36. prudent
37. ambitious
38. capable
39. courageous

40. determined
41. true
42. dependable
43. passionate

WITHOUT FORGETTING TO:
44. give her compliments regularly
45. love shopping
46. be honest
47. be very rich
48. not stress her out
49. not look at other girls

AND AT THE SAME TIME, YOU MUST ALSO:
50. give her lots of attention, but expect little yourself
51. give her lots of time, especially time for herself
52. give her lots of space, never worrying about where she goes

IT IS VERY IMPORTANT TO NEVER FORGET:
• birthdays
• anniversaries
• arrangements she makes

HOW TO MAKE A MAN HAPPY

1. Feed him
2. Have sex with him
3. Shut up

It seems that there is a bit of a difference in these two lists. On one level, it's comical to compare the expectations men and women have for each other. Yet this list underscores the differences in priorities. Remember, the reptilian brains of men tell us it is advantageous to us to go for as many women as possible, due to the trillions of sperm we create over our lifetimes. Women, however, find it advantageous to look to the higher brain needs that make for a commitment. They have the several hundred eggs to preserve via a man with means, character, and reliability in a commitment.

What would it be like to go through a lifetime with someone with whom you have exact opposite views? You are a Democrat and he is a Republican. You are Christian and he is atheist. You are a party animal and he is a couch potato. You want to go to law school and he wants to start a family right away. How are you going to make it work even if you are wildly attracted and have amazing friendship chemistry? You need to talk about these things early on, but not before you have already found a great sexual attraction and friendship potential in emotional attraction. Otherwise, you might find that the man meets many of your higher-brained requirements (such as the items in the personal ad), but that he doesn't excite you sexually. Your closest thing to friendship might be that you both enjoy Italian food (only when other couples are there to entertain you).

You won't find lasting love with Mr. Right unless you learn the skills of this step of commitment: the ability to master communication and find shared life's goals, beliefs, and values.

What You Don't Say Matters

Karla was a secretary in her late twenties. She wasn't particularly intelligent, but she had Nordic good looks and a heart of absolute gold. She had a strong social conscience, and her many friends considered her motherly. She was close to her family and lived very near them in Iowa.

Nico, also in his late twenties, was a Greek immigrant living in Philadelphia, where Karla was visiting her aunt for a weekend. He was there to finish grad school in political science, after which he hoped to join a well-connected Washington think tank. They met at a church festival in her neighborhood. Karla was blonde, which Nico found alluring, since he rarely encountered blondes in Greece. Nico had an old-world masculinity that Karla rarely saw in metro-

sexual America. He was also taller than most men she had encountered.

She had him at hello with her looks and bright smile. Their chatter
was simple but full of passion from the first moment. It didn't bother
Nico much that she wasn't an attorney, doctor, or some other American measure of career success, though this fact bothered Karla im-
mensely. She couldn't talk about the nuances of politics, but she knew
that she was a Democrat and was glad to hear that Nico shared her
views. As they talked, Karla told Nico about all of the dreams she had
for her life. She wanted to be a poet, an animal rights activist, work
for the ACLU, and even become an actress. She talked about these
things with such passion that Nico believed she could become any one
of them.

Son to a wealthy shipping magnate, Nico had been raised in the
proper ways of European aristocracy. Like many middle sons, though,
he was a rebel—culturally, politically, and spiritually. Though most
Greeks were Orthodox Christians, he became a Buddhist after travel-
ing to China and the Near East. Karla knew very little about Bud-
dhism, but despite their differences in education, the two found they
had great similarity in spirit.

Karla had one little bad habit, though. She tended to leave out information about herself and how she felt about certain things if she
thought these might worry a man about her ability to be a good
partner. These things included her fears about her job and her career
future, about her inability to support herself adequately without
help from friends or family, and about feeling lonely when friends
weren't around. She was a bit of a liar by omission. In her head, she
wanted to be all kinds of accomplished things. She wanted to reach
all of her dreams. Yet in reality, she never seemed to make any true
effort at them.

Nico couldn't notice this when they met, but he did notice how
all the men at the festival eyed Karla's height and fine figure. He displayed a quiet, confident patience in moving near and around her in
ways that were neither threatening nor timid. He deftly blocked access to her from all the other would-be suitors.

She had passed Step Two of the Attraction Phase. There was "something about her." She raised his status with her exotic beauty, and her admiration of his background, accomplishments, and ambitious dreams made him feel important deep inside.

They'd exchanged numbers early on, but when Karla inexplicably sauntered for the door at the end of the night, Nico was flabbergasted that he'd made no plans for a date.

"Why leave so soon?" he said. "When can I see you again?"

Karla replied that the party was over and that she needed to return to her family for some chat and to turn in early for Thanksgiving preparations in the morning.

"Oh, yes," he said. "Your custom." Nico was not at all familiar with women resisting his charms.

She kissed him on the cheek, gave him her mailing address to send a letter if he'd like, and fully guaranteed her passage through Step Three of the Attraction Phase: putting the man to a contest to win the woman. She didn't do this on purpose, just naturally. She wasn't aware that she was so wildly attracting him.

Back in Des Moines weeks later, Karla was quite surprised when Nico showed up at her door. He told her he was on winter break for a month and had set aside some time to work on his thesis. Since this could be done anywhere in the world, he rented a corporate apartment nearby. Karla got the very clear impression that Nico chose Iowa to be with her during this time.

The simple life in Middle America stripped them both of any cultural cues except those of the local people. Karla and Nico spent many starry nights bundled up and sitting on a rise in the fields behind her family's modest ranch home. They grew a friendship of positive emotions in those weeks, rarely fighting for more than a few minutes, and confident in their future.

On Christmas Eve with her family present, Nico popped the question. Well, not *that* question. Nico asked Karla to move in with him in Washington, D.C., where he would soon start his new job with the think tank. He told her she could find dozens of secretarial jobs there and, in the rich, deep voice she had come to hear in her dreams, he told her he couldn't imagine life without her.

They seemed meant to be. While she was feminine and fragile in her own ways, he was solid in a rugged masculine way. While he was logical and businesslike, she had a flair for the artistic, even though she had no formal education. When he would start a serious sentence, she would finish it with the innate intuition of a poet, even though she hadn't written a line of poetry in her life.

Yet four months after she moved in with Nico, the hustle and bustle of the city had taken its toll on them both. Their spirits had not changed, but everything around them did, and when that happens, so does the unfolding story between people.

Nico found his job far more difficult than school. He worked long hours at an office hard to find in the Beltway and the financial rewards of the job were less than 25 percent what he'd been promised. As Nico was estranged from his father, he couldn't turn to him for money.

Meanwhile, Karla felt like a fish out of water, stuck in an apartment in the middle of a lonely city of more than a half million people. She couldn't find a good job, her hours (and her paycheck) were light, and she had none of the comforts of the many friends she used to have, nothing familiar, nothing connected to a sense of belonging that women need. Nothing felt safe and comfortable to her anymore.

One day Nico came home, found Karla crying, and it enraged him. Both of their dreams were dying through no fault of their own. It was just life. Their story was turning out differently from what they expected, but neither had the Cool Eye to notice.

As the weeks passed, Karla became resentful that Nico was never home and didn't seem to like spending any of the free time he did have on her. Nico was resentful that she seemed to lose interest in sex. They were living in the same home yet entirely alone with the stresses of life in a new city.

Above all, Nico resented that though Karla's meager salary was not all that much less than his own, she never offered to contribute even a nominal sum to the rent. He paid that, the bills, bought her clothing when she cried that she couldn't afford any, and paid for her dry cleaning. By the time he was finished, he had far less disposable income than even she did. Meanwhile, Karla exhibited no intention of either chasing her career dreams or doing the kind of work necessary to make paying bills easier.

Nico felt his territory as a man diminish, shrink, and die away. Karla was always home, always in his space doing nothing that could further their lot. She always wanted more of his time, more of his energy, and more of his money. She had a good enough boundary to let him do what he wanted but would passive-aggressively guilt him if he did just that. She wouldn't take a stand, leave, or be truly in the relationship as a mature woman who had her own thing going on outside the relationship.

In short, she wasn't good at Step One of the Commitment Phase (boundaries), and utterly failed Step Two—the mastery of joining life's goals, communicating maturely, sharing beliefs and values, and making an effort to coordinate those goals. Part of the problem was that Karla didn't actually have any goals. Her habit of lying by omission had given them both false expectations.

Their story would not be with each other, but one full of much pain in a breakup, her struggle to start a new life on little income, and his loneliness and loss of faith in the romance of love. It would take each of them years to find the right partner.

Communication, Lies, and Living Together

Let me get something on the table right now. Living with a man before going through the last two steps of my system could be a *huge* mistake. The absolute must—if you do this—is to be mutually solid with your Personal Boundaries first. At least then you won't end up losing the house you share, your job, and your sanity (all of which may be at risk if you allow someone with Swiss cheese holes in his boundary to move in to your *physical* boundary).

When you merely live together without first finding that you have similar beliefs, good communication, and at least a survivable level of mutual life's goals, you are agreeing to a partial commitment that can carry a lot of pain. What if you want to be a corporate lawyer who absolutely needs both a quiet home study for career and the big city life for personal tastes, but he wants to be a cowboy who has a hobby singing country music? You may have the greatest sex in the world, the most valued friendship, and even mature, respectful boundaries, yet when you have such divergent goals, even your most honest, earnest strivings to be yourselves together are going to tear down each other's dreams.

When you join boundaries *physically*, living with a person as opposed to living in your own places, you're bound to have far greater difficulty keeping boundaries *psychologically* up if your life's goals are opposed. He can't physically live in the city and be a cowboy, and you can't live on a ranch, planning the merger of two companies while he's howling away to those infernal songs. I know some of you will say that marriage and commitment demand sacrifice, and we should just accept that and swallow our medicine. Well, I say that we don't have to swallow any medicine and shouldn't have to do anything that kills our dreams. Not when we could be doing the steps of courtship up front before we ever get so deep in the quicksand that overwhelmed Karla and Nico.

Karla failed to fully disclose who she was with Nico. They made a partial commitment based on only some of the information necessary to make a lifelong commitment. That gave them too much wiggle room to back out of the commitment and too much wiggle room to lie outright (or by omission, as Karla was prone to do). When you lie within a commitment, you put the other person at risk of failing to achieve their life's goals. Why? Because once a commitment begins, you are not only a team of friends; you have made a promise, no matter how limited so far, to be *partners*.

This means that you are either *with* Mr. Right, honestly assisting him toward a mutual dream, or *against* him, a dishonest kind of baggage around his neck that is silently leading both of you to fail at your individual purpose in life. Living together too soon makes this even worse for you both, because not only are you sharing emotional resources, time, and decisions, you are sharing all of your physical resources as well, including the roof over your head. This increases the odds that you'll not only wind up brokenhearted, but that you'll break the bank, too.

To understand the role of lies in harming your mutual goals with Mr. Right, we need to bring back some Personal Boundary ideas on the subject of dishonesty.

A tendency to lie is closely related to the quality of your Personal

"Thin Skin": Holes in Your Boundary

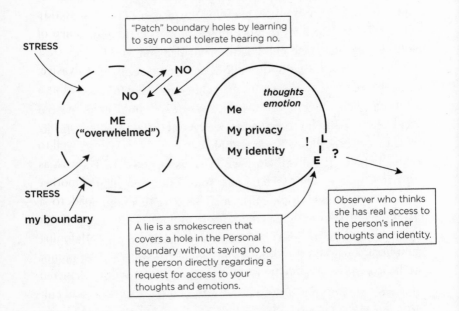

STRESS

"Patch" boundary holes by learning to say no and tolerate hearing no.

NO

NO

ME
("overwhelmed")

STRESS

my boundary

Me

My privacy

My identity

thoughts
emotion

! L
I ?
E

A lie is a smokescreen that covers a hole in the Personal Boundary without saying no to the person directly regarding a request for access to your thoughts and emotions.

Observer who thinks she has real access to the person's inner thoughts and identity.

Boundary. It is nothing more than a smokescreen covering what is really a hole in the Personal Boundary. If you lie, a man believes he has true access to you intimately when he really does not. This is, of course, true of Mr. Right as well. Many men use lies as an immature method of protecting an already weakened, hole-filled Personal Boundary. They take the path of least resistance in retaining their territory and protecting their resources, all without doing the hard work of building a true set of boundary doors.

Why do people lie? For one, lack of Cool Eye skill causes people not to notice their own identity, needs, wants, and realistic relationship skills. In addition, over a lifetime of experience, people come to develop beliefs about themselves, others, and the world they live in. If a man has encountered a large number of experiences where women rode roughshod over him and invaded his boundary, he may have come to believe that "women want to take over my life," or that "women just want to change me," or "women just want to trap me." A lie is the easiest way to defend against invading women of poor boundaries while still having some connection to them.

In addition, if a man's mother was harsh, judgmental, invasive, and lacked good boundaries of her own, he may have learned at a very core level that one can't escape females invading his space. At some point, he learned he could lie to his mother to keep her at bay and still be himself in his own private space. It can serve you well to take notice of how mature your potential Mr. Right's mother is, as this can help you understand how he sees women. A good mother teaches a son that it is okay for him to speak his mind to a woman and that although she may disagree with him, she won't harm him for it. She won't withhold love or connection, abandoning him because of his opinions, feelings, or actions. Some men are not so lucky, and in a postfeminist world where men are often depicted as silly, foolish Homer Simpsons and Al Bundys, the media and culture has a tendency to drive men's true, honest, masculine feelings, opinions, and identity underground. Still, a man who lies frequently reveals to you a priceless (and hopefully early) clue: He is not capable of truly committing to you due to the holes in his boundary.

With holes instead of doors, he cannot be truly interdependent, an absolute requirement of a true commitment.

The same is, of course, true of a woman. If you lie frequently, this will catch up to you eventually. Lying outright isn't okay and neither is lying by omission nor telling "little white lies." If a man notices this tendency, he will know that he can't have a commitment to you for life. He can't afford to merge boundaries with you in intimacy, only to find out that what he sees is not what he gets. A woman who lacked a good father may find herself stuck in a perpetual habit of trying to please all men at any cost, while remaining helpless enough that she is always dependent on men. It is as if she is waiting for a good father to come along and give her an endorsement. Of course, if this never happens, she is one day shocked that the man who seemed so masculine and caring is now resentful and impatient with her progress in life.

Without good boundaries and the ability to be honest, Step Two of the Commitment Phase is impossible. A solid boundary with doors is the very thing that lets you know what your identity and preferences are. Without a boundary that strong, you can't honestly figure out what your personal life's goals even are. Karla's lack of honesty by omission led to the eventual destruction of her relationship with Nico. Better communication might have provided them with a better fate. If they had a better understanding of their personal life's goals and expectations of each other, or considered ahead of time how very different their purposes in life were likely to be, Nico and Karla may not have moved in together, saving each other a financially and personally disastrous situation.

"Birds of a Feather Flock Together": *Beliefs and Communication*

We have already discussed quite a bit about good communication. In the Bonding in Friendship Phase, we saw that if communication is part ideas and part emotional energy, then beliefs are nothing more than opinions of reality based on gut feeling as much as or more than reason. Beliefs are not scientific facts. If you ever have a disagreement with a potential Mr. Right, remember all communication is just an opinion, the sharing of our beliefs with others. Opinions can never be absolute truth because of this.

Since friendship is consistent shared positive emotion, our communications in friendship need to send good energy to those we call friends. Sometimes, of course, friends lie to one another, even in an effort to send good energy. A friend is overweight and you tell him he isn't. You haven't fully prepared for your job interview, and he tells you that he believes in you, that it will go fine. This kind of thing can generate good energy in a lesser friend or acquaintance, but if someone is a best friend on the verge of commitment with you, even a white lie like that can throw off your mutual health, your mutual finances, and make you both fail as a committed team.

In the Commitment Phase, it is time to get more honest than ever with your potential partner even if it temporarily feels bad to do so. There is much more at stake than there was in friendship alone. Imagine you are partners on a mountain-climbing expedition with your friend. You aren't "just friends" in this scenario. You're in a precarious situation a thousand feet above ground, strung together by nylon ropes and steel hooks that can mean the difference between life and death. Communication is critical in mountain climbing and it is critical in a true committed relationship. At this higher brain level where you become intellectually attracted to each other, honesty is a critical attraction factor, as is budgeting, balance, and patience—just as they would be attractive in a climbing partner in the Himalayas.

The doors in your boundary make this possible. Interdependence on a mountain climb will succeed, while independence or codependence (weakness in a partnered climber) will make an expedition fail, risking the lives of the whole team. Karla was oblivious to the fact that her lack of honesty with Nico led to him accept a challenge to do a difficult joint climb in life with a woman who was ill equipped. He didn't know she borrowed money from her family and couldn't pay her own bills. He didn't know that she not only did not share life's goals with him, but that she didn't really have solid goals at all. Joining her on a mountainside was like joining a novice climber on Mount Everest—a deadly agreement to commit.

Along the climb to true and durable commitment in a relationship, communication isn't just data and energy, it is ideas and emotion spent wisely using boundary doors. The maturity of boundary doors then gives us sophisticated *diplomacy,* or what we all call good politics.

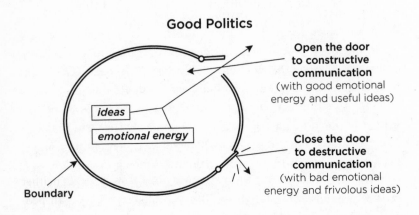

Good Politics

Open the door to constructive communication (with good emotional energy and useful ideas)

Close the door to destructive communication (with bad emotional energy and frivolous ideas)

ideas

emotional energy

Boundary

When a man communicates to you with constructive ideas or good energy, open up your doors to him. Yet when he slips and uses destructive ideas or energy, yelling at you cruelly when he has a bad day, or when you go to him for inspiration, planting the idea in you that you might just not be cut out to reach your personal dreams, temporarily close the doors of your boundary. You deserve to have as much good emotion as you can fill yourself with and to chase your dreams as foolishly as an equal amount of persistence allows. Since all men are imperfect, you need to do this without giving up totally on the commitment or you'll never find a good man. Find the same level of compassion in a man that you have in yourself, because you are imperfect too and will have bad days when you are destructive with your language or emotional energy.

In good communication, you are patient and tolerant of the other person, knowing that he has a right to his opinions, that his beliefs help create his opinions, and that there is always a way to reach an understanding if you have a true commitment in the works. Remember, the highest mark of maturity in communication is the ability to agree to disagree and still have a commitment. Your story together will protect you and get you through any misunderstanding.

When I do seminars for women or men, I teach an amazingly simple skill at maturity in communication. I draw this diagram:

The Communication of Opinions and the Teamwork of Commitment

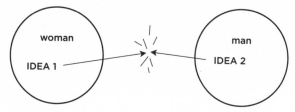

I then ask, "Which one is more right?" The answer is that neither is absolutely right, since they are just opinions based on both people's subjective and emotional beliefs. At the same time, the answer is also both, in the sense that within your own Personal Boundary, you have every right to your opinions, perception of reality, and your worldview.

Whenever someone you are considering committing to tells you that you are absolutely wrong, that person is, in fact, wrong. There is no absolute right or wrong when it comes to beliefs. They're just emotion-based opinions. This person is immature and an unfit judge of your ideas. If you ever get the feeling that a man thinks that for you to be right, he must be wrong, or for him to be right, you must be wrong, then he is thinking childishly—he is being a win/lose person—and you don't want to commit to him. Avoid judgmental people like this, because they cannot make good partners in dealing with all of life's challenges.

If you are going to be true committed partners, climbing the expected relationship challenges of Marriage Mountain, you have to communicate maturely. You can't afford to stake your whole lives on faulty information, sulking, manipulation, passive-aggressiveness, or any other kind of subtle dishonesty that destroys your friendship. In a true, mature, committed relationship, whenever there is a conflict, *both people are right in their own way.* The trick to coming to terms with each other is in finding an Idea 3.

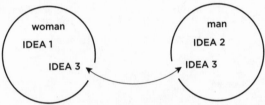

A successful communication, the all-important "connection," is made between a man and a woman through Idea 3.

The boundaries open up to true intimacy, yet with "agreement to disagree" on Idea 1 and Idea 2. This is true interdependence, the ability to close the door to things disagreed with, while simultaneously opening the door to things agreed with.

What happens when you find Idea 3? You set aside Idea 1 and Idea 2 as things to agree to disagree on, and finally get your man to open up, get intimate, and really connect on what joint goals and beliefs you really do share in common. The couple with the woman working the day shift and the man working the evening shift find that they both value all the weekend time together they can handle. The couple who disagrees on how many children to have finds that however many they have, they most certainly are going to learn piano and go to college someday. These are all examples of finding Idea 3. This is how mature people communicate.

Once you can do this, with good, interdependent boundary doors instead of holes, you are well equipped to face life's challenges as a coupled, partnered team that sets goals and reaches them. To do this, though, you will need to budget your joint resources.

The Effect of Good and Bad Time Management on Goals

When I do seminars on the secret economics of psychology, I often say, "Your budget is only as good as your boundary." Remember that. When you have a boundary like a sieve, everything leaks out, including time, energy, and money. If a man has ever lied to you about why he is late or why he is out of money, it is once again because of holes in his boundary.

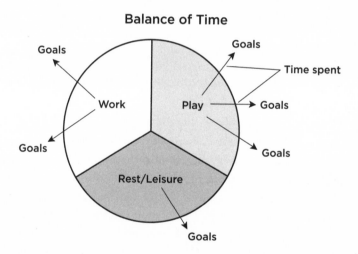

Balance of Time

In *Poor Richard's Almanack*, Benjamin Franklin wrote that a "perfect day is eight hours of work, eight hours of play, and eight hours of rest." This speaks to the ability of the boundary to budget your resources.

The very concept of a person budgeting anything happens because of the ability to use boundary doors instead of holes. If you can open the doors to allocate time, energy, or money on what is important to you and your life's goals, and close the doors to what is not, you are always going to spend your resources on what counts.

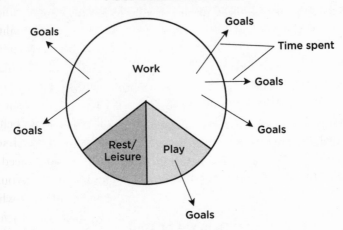

Poor Balance of Time

Many of your goals grow out of your longstanding needs in life, and your needs grow naturally out of your identity. We learned in the last chapter what your identity is—it naturally springs from a solid boundary with very few holes in it.

We reach a second golden clue to men's ability to commit to you, a secret you ought to have learned way back in step three of sexual attraction: if a man is horrible at budgeting time or money, he will likely be horrible at committing. He may lie more often than other men, may be a poor communicator, and may be unable to work with you on reaching joint goals. If your man cannot find balance in his life alone, then what effect will it have on *your* life's balance when you share a joint boundary? How will you find a balance to set goals that you both desire and ones that make you grow?

Not only did Karla not tell the truth about her skills to Nico, she didn't ever think through the goals for her own life. She knew what she wanted in a man and thought often about what love was. She was creative and was a good friend to most. But she didn't ever think long term about what she wanted her life to be. These must be considerations in a commitment or your lives together are sure to diminish in quality.

When you have a good, solid boundary, you can set aside what you don't prefer around you and set goals for the things you do prefer. You want a career that grows, you want children when the time is right, and you want to do this with a man who has all the qualities that will make these preferences easy rather than hard. At this point, your intellect kicks in and you narrow down your specific details of preferences and chart a course to them. You are willing to set goals based on these details and take action toward them before your future Mr. Right even arrives on the scene. You'll buy a house before you first set eyes on him. You'll build a career before you even know his name. You are real, not just a dreamer, and you don't need to wait for Mr. Right to come along to make things possible for you. It seems to be one of those hidden forces in a woman's life that when you have begun a path to your own life's goals, that's when you'll find a Mr. Right who is able to commit.

You can't be in the middle of striving toward something that originated at the center of your identity (life's goals) and suddenly stop. Deciding on joint life's goals with Mr. Right has a way of locking you in with the teammate you have chosen. This person is your true partner now, and his health and happiness has become inextricably intertwined with your own destiny. You cannot afford to lose him, because he is the one teammate in the world that you are completely dependent on for reaching those goals. Hopefully, you have chosen well in the first place. Otherwise, you may be with a teammate on a mountain climb to the pinnacle of your potential carrying a frustrating slab of lead on your back.

Getting to a Goal

At this stage of commitment you will need to set aside the time to sit down together and talk about what you both want for the long term of your life—career, kids, family, location, finances, friends, creative life, spiritual life, political life, and all the most important beliefs, values, and goals you have. So many couples make the error of just winging this, or letting life sweep them up in the romance of moving in together or marrying too soon.

Remember that there is a seductive effect to codependence where you join boundaries in a way that feels like you doubled your size, doubled your resources, and doubled your control over the world around you with no real effort. This, of course, is an illusion. The way mature adults get a relationship to grow in size is to grow their shared boundary by setting goals together and working on them as a team.

Reaching Goals and Growing the Boundary Size

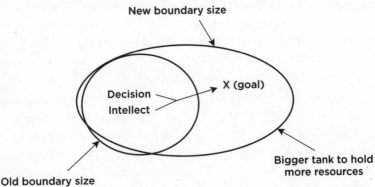

New boundary size

Decision
Intellect

X (goal)

Bigger tank to hold
more resources

Old boundary size

I once had a goal of graduating medical school. Once I got there, I didn't call my medical school diploma a goal anymore. I already owned it, and you might say controlled it. My education cannot evaporate or be taken away. It is unalienable, just as the Founding Fathers described our Personal Boundary function in the Declaration of Independence. You might say that once I got to my goal of completing my medical education, I had grown.

Setting and reaching goals is the only way to expand the size of your Personal Boundary. Shooting for joint life's goals with a partner expands the size of the territory you control in life together. If you have successfully reached a goal, you now own the goal and control it. It is a part of you. This is how mature people extend their control in the world—by patiently, carefully, teaming together to achieve goals. If you have mastered communication in the ability to get to a mutual Idea 3, if you have good boundaries and ability to budget together, and if you have positive beliefs in the future, then you're ready to climb the highest mountain of relationship challenges to whatever you both dream of together.

I often tell people that reaching goals requires intellect in your left and right brains, as well as a budget of time for you to spend efficiently. Rather than speaking about mountain climbing, let's switch to piloting a plane to examine this. Pretend that one of you is more gifted at the left-brained planning of goals, organization, timekeeping, detail work (a King/Queen or Warrior style of temperament), and making the most of education. Let's also pretend the other person is more gifted at the right-brained, creative work of flexibility, spontaneous ideas, and learning from experience (a Magician or Lover style of temperament). If you have this kind of intellectual attraction in your team, you make perfect copilots. With what you know about KWML™ now, you'll see why opposite temperaments not only make you best friends with an endless supply of good emotions together. Opposites are also the best teammates to reach joint goals efficiently.

This is how in matters of love and commitment, the old maxims "opposites attract" and "birds of a feather flock together" are *both* true. Having opposite intellectual *styles* makes you a more durable, flexible team together, but having a majority of joint life's goals, beliefs, and things you value gives you a common *content,* or *purpose,* for your intellectual efforts together. Committed partners need *both* opposite styles and common goals to be most effective.

Imagine you are flying as copilots from your current success level, Denver, to your *goal,* Los Angeles, California.

This underlines how difficult it is to try for goals in life alone. Those of us who are too left-brained tend to fly into obstacles. A plane locked into a particular route to get to a particular destination might fly through lightning storms that could otherwise be avoided. We are overeducated and not experienced enough to work creatively around problems. We cause ourselves creative failures. As a couple, if you ever try to reach a goal and feel you are bumping up against

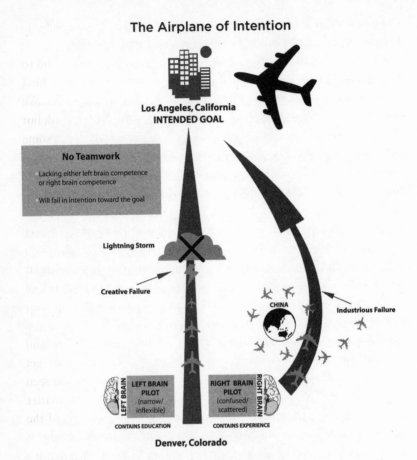

The Airplane of Intention

the same blockage to your outcome repeatedly, you are too left-brained together and need to get more creative, more right-brained, or more experienced.

This often happens when a Queen pairs up with a King or Warrior, all left-brained people by temperament. Fix your ability to find success together by going to a comedy improv acting class together, more parties, concerts, any artistic performances, art classes, or other environments that favor creative expression. You'll find creative, right-brained solutions will become easier to reach. The right brain makes us flexible and innovative at getting around obstacles.

On the other hand, those of us who are too right-brained tend to lose track of our original goal, and get lost—flying halfway to China before remembering that our original intention was to get to L.A. We are great at trying new approaches around obstacles to our goal, but those new approaches tend to take us off course and send us in some other direction entirely. This is a signal that you need more organization, planning, book smarts, or education in order to reach your joint goal. The left brain keeps our eyes on the prize when we try for goals.

Getting lost on your way to a goal happens often when a Lover pairs up with another Lover, a Magician pairs with a Magician, or a Lover pairs with a Magician. All of these temperaments are right-brained, gifted at new experiences but not at the disciplined work of planning and education. These folks need book smarts to keep their eyes on the target and still get to their goals.

Notice that the right brain helps us get more imaginative and flexible, finding many ways to solve a problem. It helps us get around obstacles, and even to find solutions for never-before-seen problems. The left brain gets us targeted on our goals no matter what difficult route we need to take to reach it. This is one of the greatest challenges women face in finding a committed Mr. Right. It is easy for a woman to find a guy who wants to sleep with her. It's easy to make friends and stay that way. Yet to find commitment, we need to have good boundaries and shared goals. To do this, we need detail, detail, detail, about exactly what it is we want. I have known countless people who go through a string of steamy love affairs that fizzle, always wondering why they never seem to strike gold. The most common reason is that they never decide what they really want *in detail*. This is a problem of lacking boundary definition and lacking left-brained intellectual skill. If you don't know what you want, how in the world are you going to get what you want?

Luckily, all human beings have both a left brain and a right brain, and we can train the part of this higher brain that we lack by practicing new skills. Couples in this overly lost situation need to plan better by using calendars and organizers, clocks, flowcharts, and perhaps even go back to school.

When a left-brained person teams with a right-brained partner, they form a powerful, whole-brained success team, capable of both keeping their eyes on a goal through detail work and being flexible and creative enough to fly around obstacles. Since Kings/Queens and Magicians are natural intellectual opposites, and Lovers and Warriors

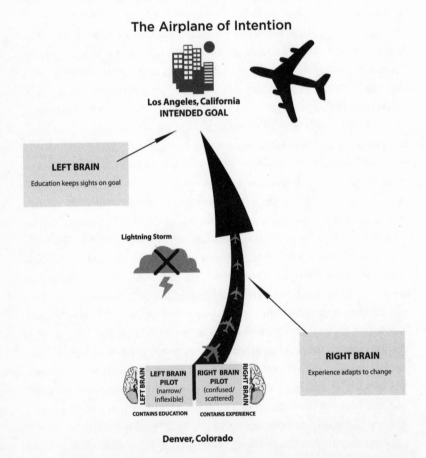

The Airplane of Intention

Los Angeles, California
INTENDED GOAL

LEFT BRAIN
Education keeps sights on goal

Lightning Storm

RIGHT BRAIN
Experience adapts to change

LEFT BRAIN PILOT (narrow/inflexible)   RIGHT BRAIN PILOT (confused/scattered)

LEFT BRAIN   RIGHT BRAIN

CONTAINS EDUCATION   CONTAINS EXPERIENCE

Denver, Colorado

are natural intellectual opposites, these two pairings make a perfect goal-seeking couple. They complement each other's intellectual skills.

Have you ever teamed up with a man to go on vacation and everything ended up a mess? You missed half your flights, got the reservations wrong, lost your passports, found out one of your credit cards was cancelled due to a forgotten payment, and all around got more stressed by your own vacation than you would have been staying at work? Chances are that both you and your man are right-brained— both Lovers, Magicians, or one of each.

Have you ever gone on a date with a man and found that neither of you knew a single joke, were both somewhat bored, and neither of you had had very imaginative ideas of what to do on the date in the first place? Chances are that both you and your man are left-brained—both Warriors, one a King and the other a Queen, or one a Warrior and the other a King or a Queen.

When you and your man are opposite in brained-ness, when things are too serious, one of you injects humor (right-brained), when things get too silly, one of you brings it down to earth (left-brained). When you are lost, one of you sets your course straight again (left-brained), and when you crash into a challenge, one of you suggests a great innovative solution no one has ever thought of before (right-brained).

One of the most beautiful things in a true mature commitment is to see a couple teaming up in this way to strive for goals together. They see their love grow along with their careers, families, and wealth. Their shared intimacy grows along with their joint boundary size. All the while, they encounter challenges like childbirth, job transitions, physical health problems and losses in the family, economic downturns, bad weather, disappointments, and all other troubles "for better or worse" as they say at marriage ceremonies.

When you are trying to determine if a man has true Mr. Right status, do you really want to find out that you can't be successful together, that your relationship will not grow, but rather fail every time you try to reach a goal? Of course not. Therefore, if one or both of you lack left-brained book smarts or right-brained street smarts, get to work fixing this. You'll find in the end that you have one shared higher brain, equally balanced in both left-brained education and right-brained experience that weathers any challenge and makes you grow.

All the communication skills you've learned, the success skills you've learned, and the budgeting skills built into the boundary have successfully moved you through Step Two of the Commitment Phase. All that remains is the very last step of courtship—the ability to make constructive decisions, a marker of all maturity and full ability to commit to a soul mate for life.

Your final decision and that of Mr. Right will be to decide together to grow your two stories into one masterpiece. To grow in an ongoing way for the rest of your lives together.

You're a total team now, an unbeatable force, a couple that is more than you could ever be apart, and one with a whole brain made of both great left-brained ability *and* right-brained ability. You are truly two copilots in life who can fly through any storm together as sexually attracted lovers, friends, and partners on the journey of life, the story of love.

Your Joint Action Plan

Sit down once a week with Mr. Right to do a check-in with him on areas of conflict you have had in the past or have now. Find the Idea 1 and Idea 2 where you differ from each other. Open up your boundary to each other and use that right brain you both have to envision an Idea 3 that you both share about the former conflict. If you think you'd like to go on vacation to the beach (Idea 1), and he thinks you should go to the mountains (Idea 2), then you might both be pleasantly surprised to find by sitting together nonjudgmentally, that you both have always loved London. Go there. It's neither a beach nor the mountains. London is Idea 3.

Combine goals, communication, and budgeting. Take an hour every week and make a list of your goals, comparing them to the list made by your potential Mr. Right. Find the goals that you disagree on or that interfere with each other. These are like Idea 1 and Idea 2. Drop them for now. Find the ones that you *share*. These are Idea 3 goals.

Now decide on a budget together. Create a pie chart that includes all of the expenditures of energy, time, and money you have, and see how closely they match your goals. See if there are ways you can redirect your resources to bolster and back up a team effort at those several joint goals you have found. Then take action.

If you follow your progress weekly in this way, you'll likely see an improvement in both of your abilities to have a secure Step Two of Commitment together.

Your Joint Story

As you cultivate your Cool Eye in every step of courtship so far, you might find that it can get somewhat lonely. However, once you find another person who's mature enough in his higher brain to understand the concept, whole worlds of teamwork open up. You might discover that helping each other with the Cool Eye is one of the most enjoyable parts of the story of your Step Two of Commitment together. That Cool Eye is the very thing that lets you read your own life story as it is happening, but by now, you are really in a *shared* story and have *two* Cool Eyes to use.

When he is tired or inattentive, your Cool Eye can save the day. When you are frazzled from all the appointments you have, his can kick in and steer you both right. As you both fly the plane toward your goals, storms come up, hidden dangers in the clouds of career, finance, and child rearing will challenge you, and at times you may feel lost. Yet your Cool Eyes together are like a plane's avionics systems that monitor altitude, wind speed, direction, and weather. When he's the tired pilot and needs a nap at the wheel, you take over. When you're in need of a rest, your trusty copilot Mr. Right takes command. You're safe and secure as long as you're together and communicate openly and honestly.

I found the 2004 film *Wicker Park* touching, dramatic, and full of lessons in psychology. It starred Josh Hartnett, Diane Kruger, and Rose Byrne, and it was an amazing study of Step Two of Commitment and the effect of dishonesty on it.

Hartnett's character, Matthew, is haunted by the memory of his ex-girlfriend (Kruger's character, Lisa), who cruelly disappeared from his life two years ago in Chicago. Since that time, he's been to New York, found a new career, and met a new girlfriend he is debating taking that last step with—engagement. Little does he know that the very reason he has been apart from Lisa is the deceptive tricks played on them both by Lisa's roommate—Rose Byrne's character, Alex. She has seen Matthew from afar and fell in lust—not love—with him. Through a web of lies, Alex intended to keep Matthew and Lisa confused and apart for life.

Lisa is a Warrior, Matthew is a Lover, and they match in every crucial way. They go through sexual attraction, friendship, and commitment, even so far as having complementary life's goals as artists who want to live in Chicago.

When Alex manages to lie her way into sleeping with Matthew, his error in judgment leads him to further justify his own dishonesty with his current girlfriend and soon-to-be fiancée. She, too, is a Warrior with a good Personal Boundary but lacks any hint of shared life's goals with Matthew. She loves New York and wants Matthew to move back there with her from Chicago. She wants him to work in a stuffy but lucrative corporate job in the company her brother owns, while he is a simple artist and photographer who is happy with less.

Separated through the entire film, and their shared story told to us only through flashback, it is amazing to see Lisa and Matthew's Cool Eyes slowly awaken to the fact that there is still a meant-to-be love between them. Matthew struggles with the step of realizing that his urban girl will never be the one he can commit to, not only because of the flame he keeps lit for Lisa, but because they lack joint goals together. Eventually those Cool Eyes manage to help him and Lisa find each other again, revealing the web of lies that Alex has spun all along. When the expectations for each other are all revealed, and dishonesty eliminated, real boundaries can be set for the first time, and those truly meant for each other can literally see how interwoven their future dreams are. When Matthew reunites with his lost love at the airport, it is as if they had never parted.

This is the way your story will run with Mr. Right as well. When you stay true to yourself and to others about exactly who you are, what you need, and therefore what you must seek out in life, you need do no work at all. Your own path will find the path of Mr. Right, because your goals will have led you not just toward your personal dreams, but into each other's arms in the process. Your life stories will join each other naturally—at the right place, the right time, and with the right person if you keep your Cool Eye turned on to notice that opportunity at a love that lasts.

The Commitment Phase (Intellectual Attraction)

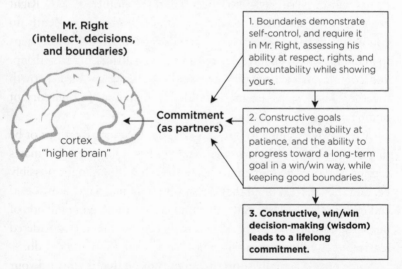

**Mr. Right
(intellect, decisions,
and boundaries)**

cortex
"higher brain"

**Commitment
(as partners)**

1. Boundaries demonstrate self-control, and require it in Mr. Right, assessing his ability at respect, rights, and accountability while showing yours.

2. Constructive goals demonstrate the ability at patience, and the ability to progress toward a long-term goal in a win/win way, while keeping good boundaries.

3. **Constructive, win/win decision-making (wisdom) leads to a lifelong commitment.**

Chapter Ten

Do Unto Others Before "I Do"

Phase III: The Commitment Phase
*Step Three: Deciding to Make Commitment
Long-term by Constructiveness*

*Love itself is what is left over when being in love has
burned away, and this is both an art and a fortunate accident. Those who truly love have roots that grow towards
each other underground, and when all the pretty blossoms
have fallen from the branches, they find that they are one
tree and not two.*
—LOUIS DE BERNIÈRES, *CAPTAIN CORELLI'S MANDOLIN*

THIS PROCESS OF WINNING over all three brains of Mr. Right
doesn't end at marriage. It continues right through "'til death do
you part." Even in a marriage, you will need all nine of these steps
to maintain what you have, fix areas of sexual attraction, friendship,
and commitment where they are weak, and measure your growth
together. These steps are markers of where you are in the story of
finding a soul mate.

A soul is not a thing to buy, sell, or own. It cannot wear out or be
thrown away as you throw away old clothes. Likewise, soul mates
cannot be forced to come into being, be what they cannot possibly
be, and they share a bond that doesn't begin at marriage, nor does it
end even at death. The soul mate bond is something quite outside of
our sense of time in the very same way that stories that are considered
masterpieces will last many lifetimes longer than their authors do.

Some people actually subscribe to the notion that if you and your
partner say "I love you" or sign a document saying you are married,

some magical force will cause you both to be good for each other forever, belong to each other always, and perpetually remain honest, reliable, and true. Sadly, the ever-climbing divorce rate suggests otherwise.

The only real security and protection of committed relationships comes from raising your understanding of instinct and character to the highest level you can reach and choosing well before you even begin to enter a commitment. This has always been the most valuable role of courtship. It comes from getting real about your own personal growth and being open to men entering your life who display the same skill at sexual instinct and character that you do. This requires work and patience, but you'll find that as an adult woman you are solely responsible for parenting yourself to a level of maturity that naturally brings all of your dreams in career, romance, and life into reality. As Freud (and Heraclitus millennia before him) said, "Character is destiny." One can find any number of mere mates through the instinct of sexual attraction, but to find a true soul mate, you must live your way to a match of character with someone else that feels right, natural, and perfect.

We've learned that the Personal Boundary parallels maturity as it goes from being full of holes and walls to doors that budget our resources, establish our preferences, and keep bad things out while keeping good things in. The doors we build in our boundary also make us quite versatile in a changing world. The very psychological skill that opens and closes those doors is our decision-making power called wisdom, a marker of character maturity whose quality gives even greater accuracy about our level of maturity.

Biologists have a universal definition of life that applies to all organisms, including humans. They say, "Life is irritable." What this means is not that life is annoying or irritating, but that the environment does things to an organism, and the organism does things back on purpose. This implies a *decision*. When you look at life this way, you can see that all of our lives—each with a unique story—are actually a long string of decisions that we make out of our own free will. Whether you decided to move out of state to be with him or to stay to be with your family, to leave him because something's not right or not leave him because enough is right, to go to a particular school or not, to become dedicated to taking care of your body or to remain a long-term smoker, your decisions led to the next plot point of your life, with a whole set of options unique to that plot point. Based on this definition of life, a human being is alive because she responds in all sorts of complex ways *on purpose*. After all, in this last step of human courtship, you are actually making a decision to live a life together, so your purpose together—your mission in life—must be compelling enough to shape the meaning of your whole existence. It must compel you toward the role of partnership with him.

Life-threatening psychological diseases such as depression and drug addiction happen in large part because we become passive and wait for someone else or something else to make decisions for us. Passiveness can lead to the death of your career, your relationships, and your sense of ownership of your life. Don't be passive. Of course, as we've discussed earlier, you need to accept passively the things you can't control, but ought to make decisions whenever you have the opportunity. You'll find yourself feeling more alive even if you choose poorly.

Wisdom: Are You a "Win/Win" Person or a "Win/Lose" Person?

An interesting thing about decisions, and therefore life, is that every decision we make is a destructive (or win/lose) decision or a constructive (or win/win) decision. Every decision you have ever made has been one or the other of these, or it wasn't really a decision at all. One of the core sciences I build into my systems for women comes from a theory of economics called the Nash Equilibrium. This concept from the general field called Game Theory was popularized by the Oscar-winning film *A Beautiful Mind*, about its inventor, John Nash. This Nobel Prize–winning economist taught us that in a world where our very financial, emotional, and, at times, physical survival depend on an interconnection to others, our decisions

242 The Secret Psychology of How We Fall in Love

always affect either us or someone else, or both. In the case of a committed relationship, if you are using your Cool Eye, you'll see that nearly every decision you make is going to affect your potential Mr. Right. Therefore, we'd be smart before taking that last step walking down the aisle to check ourselves and the groom for wisdom, the ultimate measure of decision-making quality.

All we have been learning about in the mammalian brain and higher brain has been for rising in higher and higher maturity with Mr. Right. There is perhaps no better measure of maturity—not even a solid boundary—than the ability to make wise and, therefore, constructive decisions, the kind that benefit both you and someone else.

Every now and then, we get a gift from the universe, a moment shared with a special other person. In that moment, we can remain passive, or we can take the one required action that the universe is begging us to take. We can go for it and see what comes of it. Have you ever been a procrastinator? Have you ever been ambivalent about a job, a friend, or even a spouse? Have you ever said "I just don't know what to do" because you were waiting for the perfect conditions at the perfect time and hoped that wisdom would just drop out of the sky to advise you? Keeping passive on these is like living your life in quicksand. Decisive action is the cure, the ladder out of that quicksand.

I illustrate this concept with the idea that passiveness pulls us down in our life's momentum and action lifts us up. A decision makes us grow wiser and more skilled each time we make one, and momentum is a force that comes out of such actions. It is hard to get started on new behaviors or directions in life in much the same way as a diet or exercise regimen can be, but like those weight-loss methods, it gets easier over time, and with less constant effort. Still, every decision we make in life has a destructive or constructive effect on others and ourselves, or it wasn't a decision at all.

What the diagram on the following page shows us is that at any point in the serendipity of our joint story, we have choices to make, plot points that give us the opportunity to go this way or that. The upward direction is positive momentum for us, and the lower direction is decay of our mission in life. We can decide to move forward with a decision, creating momentum that makes our lives easier, or just sit and see what happens, falling into negative momentum that feels like we weigh four hundred pounds. Mature couples are *proactive*, not *reactive*. They are not procrastinators, but are the initiators and designers of a life together. They don't let passiveness be a force that grows mental illness or immaturity in their lives and kills the friendship they share.

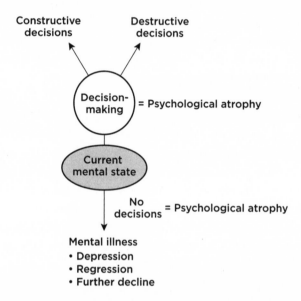

There are only two ways of looking at the world. You can have a constructive view, where you see the world as an *abundant* place and where we treat one another in a win/win way. Alternatively, you can choose to have a destructive view, where you see the world as a place of *scarcity*. In this latter view, we tend to treat one another in a win/lose way. When you have a partner with this latter view, every decision he makes will have an impact on your momentum. In a very real way, his sense of scarcity becomes your own sense of scarcity. This is an immature, unwise force that can someday bring down the life you've built so far.

Nothing is more intellectually attractive than someone who is constructive, someone whose every choice benefits not just himself, but others as well. In a very real way, this person's abundant world-view leads to your own abundance, too. You can trust for life and commit for life to someone who cares well for himself even as he takes on the responsibility of being your partner and taking care of you. Any form of win/win behavior based in abundance is a wise force that grows momentum for you both. Win/win means "mature" in a psychological sense, and, therefore, is the absolute and final must-do in taking the plunge of durable commitment with Mr. Right.

Who's "More Right" and Who's "Going Places"?

Have you ever been with a man who often gives you a feeling that you're wrong? So many people have trouble getting along with others unless they have a sense of absolute certainty and control over the opinions of those people. We've already learned that we never control other people due to boundaries, but the myth persists that there can be ideas that are more right than others. Someone who can't feel good about himself unless he is more right than you has a maturity problem, and someone who feels wrong simply because you are right has one as well. People who think and act this way are being win/lose communicators.

Win/lose thoughts and actions regard the world as a place of scarcity, where there isn't enough of anything to go around. It is a punishing, competitive, eye-for-an-eye mode of dealing with others in conflict, agreements, and in love. Win/lose behavior is destructive in that for one person to feel happy or be right, another person *must* lose or be wrong. It is a childish way of dealing with the stresses and problems of compromise and relationship, and is a deal-killer as far as making a foray into commitment permanent.

Say that you and your potential Mr. Right had identical skills and the exact same job title at the same company. He gets a promotion and you don't. A woman with a win/lose attitude would see the world as a place of scarcity and feel down on herself when her man gets his happy news. She interprets the promotion as meaning that she is less-than and will never be promoted herself. She can't genuinely be happy for her man, and this ironically begins to kill the friendship, because at first they don't share positive emotion about the promotion, and later this may expand to a competitive, negative emotion about everything else that ought to be enjoyed as a team accomplishment. If the woman takes a win/win stance instead, she sees the world as a place of abundance. Her potential Mr. Right's promotion not only benefits her via her shared finances with him, but it also serves as a sign that she could be promoted as well. After all, they both have the same skills. She simply needs to wait for the next opportunity to come along, even if that opportunity arises at another company. In the end, she can truly be happy for her partner, and the friendship flourishes.

In the adult world, there really are plenty of opportunities for adults to prosper. For competent, mature adults, abundance in the world is a reality, and scarcity is an illusion. Win/win behavior and wise decisions then are the only way to prosper, in life and in any quality relationship. Don't settle for less in yourself or others.

As you look at the chart that follows, you'll see many of the features of commitment we have covered. What you are really after as a woman is not only a life that has all the animal passion of the reptilian brain, or the comfortable feelings of the mammalian brain, but also the civility of a higher-brained intellect. The same is true of your one, real Mr. Right. He will be the one who can keep his word, see your evolving story together, respect your boundary and his own, be self-respecting, not selfish like a boy, be patient, not impatient, a striver, not a victim nor mere survivor. He will protect you with his strength and find solace in your nurturing. Above all, he will gladly forego the genetic animal destiny that makes him want to get sex without commitment in favor of that commitment *you* want before sex.

None of this is possible without joint understanding, compromise, openness, and communication. The climax of your love story will come through constructive decisions that benefit you both.

Mature and Constructive vs. Immature and Destructive Commitment

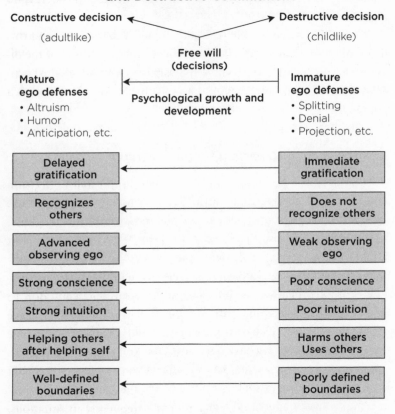

Constructive decision ◄━━━━━━━━━━━━━━━► Destructive decision
   (adultlike)   (childlike)

                          Free will
                          (decisions)

Mature   Immature
ego defenses   ego defenses
• Altruism   Psychological growth and   • Splitting
• Humor   development   • Denial
• Anticipation, etc.   • Projection, etc.

Delayed gratification	◄━━━	Immediate gratification
Recognizes others	◄━━━	Does not recognize others
Advanced observing ego	◄━━━	Weak observing ego
Strong conscience	◄━━━	Poor conscience
Strong intuition	◄━━━	Poor intuition
Helping others after helping self	◄━━━	Harms others Uses others
Well-defined boundaries	◄━━━	Poorly defined boundaries

Notice how the childish destructive side weakens your sexual attraction to him and from him by disrespecting you and others. Notice how the destructive side destroys friendship by encouraging negative emotion. Notice how it tears down intellectual attraction with poor boundaries, conscience, disrespect, and impatience in immediate gratification. One who is destructive literally cannot commit or be committed to by nature of their poor Personal Boundary. The right side of the diagram carries all the traits of immaturity for men and women, as if there were nothing going on in the person's head except reptilian brain activity and some rudimentary mammalian brain activity. There is no maturity of the cerebral cortex, no higher brain.

We are all charged in life with moving from the right side of this diagram in the scarcity of win/lose behavior to the left side of the diagram in the abundance of win/win behavior. These are the last general features to mark off on your checklist for Mr. Right. Then it's a go, for life.

Habits (Styles of Decisions) and Momentum

A habit is a series of behaviors based on a certain style of decision about a particular type of problem. Let's use an example that starts with your leaving your makeup in his bathroom. In this example, you might be living with a potential Mr. Right and thinking about marriage. You display a habit of leaving your makeup in his bathroom simply because you tend to run late for work and wind up getting ready in his bathroom, which is the closest to the front door. To you, it makes perfect, logical higher-brained sense for you to leave the makeup there. You tend to make the same decision each time you are running late. It is a style of decision you make in that circumstance. The only problem is that he doesn't like your habit. It "habitually" bothers him.

People have styles of decisions they use frequently in situations, some of which are healthy (taking a time-out, working out, eating well, and so on), and other styles that are not so healthy (smoking, drinking, yelling, evading discussion, falling silent, slamming the door, among others). Think about momentum. To stop a drifting car with the emergency brake off takes great effort at first but gets easier with ongoing attention and force. To stop a growing, twenty-pound weight gain in its tracks takes a heroic effort at diet and exercise at first. Negative momentum slowly decreases with ongoing effort.

Building positive momentum takes time and patience (delayed gratification seen on the left side of the diagram). In the previous example, if he assertively tells you that using his bathroom has got to change, and maybe he can help you strategize making that happen, you might both discover that a new habit of planning to be on time for work fixes his annoyance at your bathroom use but also ripples over into countless other parts of life. You soon find you get fewer speeding tickets, get kudos from colleagues from projects turned in on time, your friends appreciate you more for the quality time you spend with them, and your health improves because you don't need to stay up as late at night playing catch-up on your frantic day. Healthy styles of habit are constructive, win/win decisions that one uses repeatedly. They benefit both you and the man in question. They also bring positive momentum to your personal and relationship growth.

Destructive habits, like addiction to cigarettes, benefit only one or neither of you. These latter habits bring negative momentum to your growth together. What you've already learned about addictions and a weak Personal Boundary confirms that you two are in trouble in the commitment department if destructive habits have a significant place in your lives. Get rid of those bad habits if you want to have a future with a real Mr. Right.

Since your higher brain is very logical at times, and the left-brained part of it is about listing the details of things, it can make sense to review all of the habits you tend to have with the potential Mr. Right. If some of them seem to benefit only you to his detriment, they are destructive and need to be removed in order to give your relationship a lift. Likewise, do your best to create any habits that benefit you both constructively, as this will generate more momentum for growth of your intellectual attraction and therefore your commitment. You could stop leaving your makeup case in his bathroom and set the alarm a little earlier, which may benefit you both. He could stop smoking and start exercising with you, which benefits you both. By identifying these specific habits, you actually discover things about each other you may never have known and find ways to boost your momentum into growth of the commitment.

Ego Defenses: General Habits or Styles of Solving Social Problems

The lists in the previous diagram illustrate immature ego defenses and mature ego defenses. These are collections of decisions (or habits) that are not about small details like failing to flush the toilet or smoking, but rather are broad, pervasive styles of solving social dilemmas. People use ego defenses in varied situations to survive socially, and they affect your whole life, not just one little area of it.

We tend to learn these styles over time from an early age. Unfortunately, what worked as a style in our youth seldom has any value when we are adults. A man you have been dating might habitually turn inward and stop talking when you say something that offends him. He might wait weeks or even months, using an ego defense habit called passive-aggressiveness, until so much anger has built up about it that he blows his top. This is a destructive, or immature, ego defense.

Immature ego defenses are things like passive-aggressiveness, denial (of what our limits of control are in life), projection (of our bad traits onto another person, such as angrily accusing *you* of being the one with the anger problem), black/white thinking (labeling everything in the world as all good, or all bad, when everything is in reality gray), splitting (getting someone else involved in your disagreements to get them to take action on it instead of you), and intellectualization (ignoring tough emotions that need to be dealt with by turning them into intellectual terms that don't directly confront a problem). There is a whole host of these general habits in any book on psychoanalysis if you are interested in exploring this further.

Mature ego defenses are fewer in number, but more useful in a widespread way. They consist of styles or strategies such as humor, altruism (doing something kind for someone else when we feel bad), sublimation (taking our uncomfortable feelings about something we don't control and putting them to work on an effort at something we do control), suppression (putting a problem that is not solvable now on the back burner until it can be solved sometime later), anticipation (planning for future trouble before it affects us), and several others.

To stop the negative momentum of immature ego defenses takes time and patient effort even when there is no immediate reward. Consider getting a relationship journal and beginning to work away on these in yourself and identifying them in your potential Mr. Right.

Let's look at the diagram on page 246 again to examine the other differences between a childish person (lacking higher brain activity) and a complete and mature adult.

Strong Versus Weak Personal Boundaries.   You've already learned a great deal about these. Here you can see that weak boundaries are immature and bring down relationship momentum. This not only prevents commitment, but also reverses it once it has begun.

Patience Versus Impatience.   Children are impatient. So are Mr. Wrongs. Mature Mr. Rights are patient. Patience leads to the ability to generate positive momentum, gives time for the things we don't control about life to change and possibly become more controllable, and ultimately gives time to use your Cool Eye.

Recognizing and Helping Others.   When we recognize the value and autonomy of others, we not only exhibit good Personal Boundaries, we also allow ourselves to receive a gift of new life for our joint story together. We get new ideas, feelings, and actions that move us forward. Children ignore the rights, needs, and feelings of others. Mature Ms. and Mr. Rights do not. Children cannot really help others in the way that adults can. The territoriality of Mr. Right's reptilian brain may seem to make him selfish, but be more sophisticated than that. If you have reached the Commitment Phase, you still need to make sure he employs the reptilian brain activity of using his alpha-ness to be helpful to you.

Weak Versus Strong Observing Ego.   When a man has a weak ability to use the Cool Eye (what psychoanalysts call Observing Ego), he cannot grow. Momentum and everything else dies. Children do not have a Cool Eye. Only you and Mr. Right do as mature adults.

Conscience and Intuition.   Every decision you ever make involves some conscience or ethics and some intuition or shrewdness. Men who are too goody-goody or naive are poor partners in Intellectual Attraction because those around them will always take advantage of them. If you commit to these guys, you will also be taken advantage of by association. On the other hand, men who are shrewd, fast-talking, and conniving con artists are full of intuition about being in the right place at the right time to manipulate or capitalize on a situation. They will be poor partners because they will ultimately turn this behavior on you. The former guy is the wimp and the latter is the player. An equal balance of both conscience and intuition equals wisdom, the ultimate last checkbox of high character to look for in Mr. Right before turning a commitment permanent in life.

Have you ever known a guy who was brilliant, made a lot of money, then lost it, had the brightest smile, the most sparkling personality, and yet seemed to lose friends all the time? He lacked wisdom. The momentum of his life was in fits and starts, like the ignition of an old junker car that has a beautiful paint job. Many women look for intelligence in a man, but intelligence is different from wisdom. When you are merely intelligent, you get to goals with ease, but when you make wise decisions, the habits you build lend upward momentum that assures you never lose those goals you achieve. The ultimate character trait that wraps up all our high character resources, from the boundary to a good self-esteem to the Cool Eye itself, is the wisdom of how to use them.

The greatest thing about wisdom is that it never goes away. It will be with you and Mr. Right always. The toughest decision you ever ought to make is whether to complete the last step of courtship with a man and make it for life. If he is the wisest man you've gotten this far with, and you have cultivated your own wisdom, then walking down the aisle is not a decision at all; it's a self-assured destiny you can always count on.

Your Action Plan

If you want to be wise enough to weed out Mr. Wrongs in the final stage of courtship before making a commitment permanent, review and act on this list of destructive, childish, win/lose decisions and the list of constructive, mature, win/win decisions that follows it.

Mr. Wrongs:

- Have immature ego defenses. His way of dealing with social situations involves childlike strategies such as being passive-aggressive, denial, projection, and the other attributes I described earlier in this chapter.

- Have Personal Boundaries with holes or walls in them, leading to either independence or codependence, but not interdependence.

- Are impatient and try to find immediate gratification in everything.

- Don't value others' opinions, feelings, actions, commitments, or decisions. It's "all about me" with them.

- Have poor ethics of conscience.

- Have poor worldly wisdom. They lack the shrewd, intuitive ability to read environments for the best conditions for both of you.

- Lack a Cool Eye, the self-monitoring ability to see their behavior for what it is.

- Use or harm others. They might not do this to you personally, but if you see them doing it to their friends, coworkers, employees, family, or others, it's just a matter of time before they turn this behavior on you.

- Make win/lose decisions, or have destructive habits.

- See the world as a pessimistic place of scarcity.

On the other hand, Mr. Rights:

- Have mature ego defenses. They enter social situations using adult strategies such as being altruistic, humorous, anticipatory, and other things we discussed earlier in this chapter.

- Have Personal Boundaries with doors in them, leading to interdependence. These people have a high degree of preferences that create a substantial personal identity.

- Are patient and comfortable with delayed gratification.

- Value others' opinions, feelings, actions, commitments, or decisions. It's "all about we" with them.

- Have good ethics of conscience.

- Have a high level of worldly wisdom. They have the shrewd, intuitive ability to read environments for the best conditions for both of you.

- Utilize a Cool Eye, the self-monitoring ability to see their behavior for what it is, and help police the relationship for places where you falter.

- Don't use or harm others, and help others when they have more than enough to give.

- Make win/win decisions, or have constructive habits.

- See the world as an optimistic place of abundance.

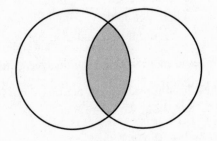

Chapter Eleven

∽

The Mysterious Story of Mr. Right and You

*In the arithmetic of love, one plus one equals everything,
and two minus one equals nothing.*
—MIGNON MCLAUGHLIN

I'VE WANTED YOU to keep your Cool Eye turned on through this whole process for a reason. I believe deeply in something that guides us and protects us through all of these dating and relationship stages. It is a natural miracle like the one that Stacy and Michael, whom we'll meet later, found. It will never let you down and it is in perfect alignment with your spiritual and religious beliefs. It is the power of "story"—the story of your life and that of Mr. Right. Your Cool Eye is simply a light that you shine on that story that allows you to be the narrator in that story. You've learned much about the three brains in this book. You know at this point that we are much more than animals with brain stems. We have emotions in the mammalian brain and the even more sophisticated intellect and boundary in the higher brain. It is out of this rich, complex circuitry of brain cells that the very nature of creativity, story, and choices in that story of your life and love emerge.

What could be deeper than understanding the core drives for survival, power, and sexual union in us? What could be deeper than the symphony of emotions we experience in a lifetime? What could be deeper than the ideas we create, innovations we make, beliefs, rules, and laws we live by, or the whispers of poetry we communicate in the words of romance? The answer is our story.

Imagine that at all times you literally stand at the center of your Personal Boundary. As the first book of your love story goes (Attraction), you have been enjoying the tale of flirting with a man, finding him mysterious, strong, and dominant in his own way, and able to win you over repeatedly. Part of that mystery about him, that spark that started this boy-crazy state of yours, was that you imagined what he might be like to know personally, even intimately. You haven't yet crossed his boundary with yours but think you might like to.

Sexual Attraction and Boundaries

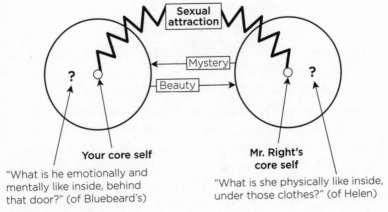

Your core self

"What is he emotionally and mentally like inside, behind that door?" (of Bluebeard's)

Mr. Right's core self

"What is she physically like inside, under those clothes?" (of Helen)

In the next book of your story (Friendship) you share fun times, even raising each other's self-esteem, which is what love is. You teach each other about places you've been, experiences you've had—you've communicated—and join each other in ways that complete you both, becoming friends. You two have actually done far more than admire each other from afar. You've shared just a little view of the total territory of each other's personal world. You have connected through love and communication by opening the edges of your Personal Boundaries.

Finally, in the third book of your story together (Commitment),

Friendship and Boundaries

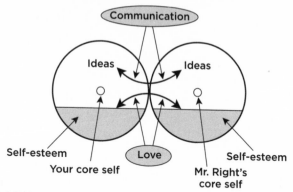

Whether through a hole or a door, and therefore regardless of maturity level, love and communication happen at the edge of two people's adjoining Personal Boundaries.

you are standing in your circle, at the very edge of his boundary, considering literally entering his world with your whole self—all the way to your core as an individual. You do so where you discover shared beliefs and you embark on joint goals together. You are going to let him know your whole self and even give up some of your former world to join with his if the conditions are right. It is your win/win behavior and his win/win behavior that secure a constructive partnership together.

You now have a real commitment, a joining of worlds, and you may find yourself fully ready to be sexual without risk of it feeling cheap, being used, or feeling a shred of guilt over the matter. You might even say that the symbol or shape of what you share in a mature commitment is not only right in how it *feels*—it is naturally and even *mathematically* perfect. The mandorla.

When two people barely let the other person know who they are and what they are all about, there is not much of a sharing of their worlds or their individual realities. If two characters in a love story did this, you would never suggest the novel or film to anyone you know. It is cold and stilted and, in the end, it doesn't feel natural.

Boundaries in Full, Mature Commitment

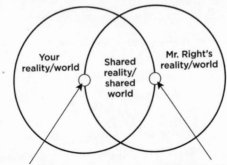

Your core self   Mr. Right's core self

When two people share too much too quickly, they tend to cross into each other's world so deeply that they can tend to lose all sense of their original, individual stories. Their connection loses its mystery, and they no longer feel like their former selves. This love story wouldn't pluck at your heartstrings; it would leave you feeling uncomfortable.

But when a couple takes it not too slowly, not too fast, and surrenders wishes for control and instant gratification of what they desire in the relationship, they find that they don't have to work that hard at all. They share more and more of their lives, joining some of their individual worlds until they reach a comfortable familiarity with the sexual core of the other person—and do so without losing a solid, individual sense of self. The relationship is easy because a story develops around them, bringing them together naturally.

Serendipity

There is a whole world of people out there who do not know us personally, have lives and stories of their own, and will never meet us unless fate and serendipity offer a chance crossing of our stories. The story of your life is composed of all the decisions you have ever made and the structure of your character. However, the places where your story crosses that of others is not entirely up to you. There is a story bigger than yours, and that is the story of all people everywhere. You can be a part of this Grand Story simply by recognizing that it exists and that it sends you little opportunities to join in, connect with someone else's story, and begin a whole new path in life that you never thought possible. The skill inside of you that allows this is none other than your Cool Eye, and the force outside of you is the serendipity your Cool Eye reads.

While the film *Serendipity* is a sugary-sweet love story that was widely panned, it does in fact contain several crucial lessons about life and love that apply to us all. It actually teaches you to read the story of your own romance for clues and signs of the right way to go next.

In my own life, I have often made choices based solely on fact, on what is logical and statistically supported. I would take a job because it looked good on paper and date a woman because she had a certain list of right things about her that I had to have in a relationship I value. Yet even with the best educated guesses at these kinds of life-changing decisions, I would often begin a new phase of life and end up quite unhappy. The job that looked so good on paper was a bait-and-switch offer from a hospital that was about to go bankrupt. The woman who seemed so perfect on paper—mature, kind, intelligent, and self-sufficient—was in fact high-maintenance, immature, selfish, lacked curiosity about learning or growing, and was void of a purpose for her life.

When I spent years in the rigors of medical training, I learned that without purposely *thinking about* and *planning for* what we want in life or love, we end up with nothing. The film *Serendipity* showed me that, without *feeling* for exactly what we want, we have nothing in life, either. It never occurred to me until seeing that film that people sometimes look perfect on paper for us, and might still not be the one we were meant to be with if there is not a story we have found ourselves wrapped up in and protected by. It never occurred to me that it is okay to break up with somebody "just because." Just because I am worth it. You are worth it, too—worth discovering that there are no more important things than your feelings and the story that they guide. In learning the skills of serendipity, you will take all we've learned and find that the secret of all those happy couples who "just knew" comes down to their knowing how to feel in the right way.

In the film, Jonathan Trager, a character played by John Cusack, meets Sara Thomas, a character played by Kate Beckinsale. In what begins as a moment of opportunity to enjoy a brief shared story and impromptu date, the two reach simultaneously for the last pair of black gloves in Bloomingdale's in Midtown Manhattan. Each of them keeps one glove of the pair, and they stop time for a few hours to enjoy playing games of chance and fate with each other. They both have enough Cool Eye going to recognize this rare opportunity to assess a potential future with each other for all nine steps of courtship. They also find themselves captured by a joined story, a shared "mythology." Their brief interlude ends in the confusion of trying to pick the same floor to get off separate elevators in the Waldorf-Astoria Hotel. Before that interlude is over, though, they've experienced an indelible chemistry of sexual, emotional, and intellectual attraction that has locked them in a shared story.

Years later, both Jon and Sara find themselves in perfect relationships with other partners that seem destined to end in marriage. They've both accepted the reality that love is an illusion best addressed by finding a suitable partner and friend with whom sex is good. However, something has been nagging at both of them for years. This nagging isn't exclusively logical, emotional, or sexual. It is a kind of spiritual feeling that something is amiss in the thought of moving into permanent commitment to people with whom they have no compelling story to share.

Driven by this nagging, they each set off on an illogical, chaotic adventure to try to find the other, undirected except by the force of serendipity. The one impossible problem is that neither has any idea *how* to find the other. All they shared with each other was that moment. Everything they try to force during this search is stymied.

Yet when each temporarily gives up the search for the other, some mysterious event happens to move them closer together.

Through this all, they learn the four basic skills of serendipity, the skills to follow when one's life story joins that of another. These are play, clues, signs, and letting go (there's also the matter of destiny itself, but we'll get to that in a little while).

Play

Playing is a right-brained notion. The right brain is also the source of creativity in us, the very ability to read and tell stories, submit to the spiritual notions of faith, hope for the future, and guidance from a power that is higher than we are. One could easily argue that it is impossible to be romantic, have faith in the story of your life, and in the guidance of a higher power that protects it, without the ability to play. The ability to play is the very ability to participate in a story, to feel a story, and be moved by it, to read it with your Cool Eye, and be guided by it.

When Jon and Sara exhibited willingness to play with each other, they exhibited a willingness to play in the story the universe was creating around them. They were not in the overlapping loss of self called codependence—both were willing to walk away from the relationship since neither was free of romantic entanglements to others. They were also not so clinical and old as to have no shared world at all (total independence)—both were willing to entertain the strange few hours together that fate had sent them. It was only through tolerating the chaos and uncertainty of play that they were able to see what their future could be together and listen to that nagging feeling that something wasn't right when they weren't with each other. Jon and Sara had firm individual identities but were willing to play in the mandorla between them, the area of magic in relationships where all worthwhile stories take place.

In your own life, you need to be willing to play along when your Cool Eye tells you that your story is joining with someone else's story in an intriguing way. If you're too timid to play, you might let the most meaningful plot point in your life slip away.

Clues

In the story of *Serendipity*, clues arise at unexpected (and therefore serendipitous) moments to help Jon and Sara reunite. This reminds me of the story of the romance between Barbra Streisand and James Brolin. Each was in between relationships when they independently chanced upon a Manhattan apartment that stole their hearts. It "felt right," it perfectly suited their identities, and each independently "just knew" it was the one to buy. When finding out through their respective agents that these two stars were bidding against each other, they insisted on meeting—and their romance has not ended since. Serendipity's "clues" were at work with them. The clues were there that there was more to this apartment search than just finding a place to live—that their similar passion for the place meant they should meet and share a powerful story together.

With your Cool Eye turned on, you can read the clues when you see your date mistreat a waiter in uncalled-for anger, or the very different clues you would get if you saw him (when he didn't know you were watching him) give a homeless man the leftover bag from your dinner together. These clues give you an intuitive sense of not just the future with this particular man, but also to the specific fit of his character and experience to your own. He yells at the waiter about having brought mustard for the fries when you happen to love mustard with fries. He hums the song you've always loved as he gives the food to the homeless man. Clues are inextricably linked in both a shared story and the specific courtship steps you must assess in Mr. Right. The story and its plot points are inseparable.

For Jon and Sara of our film, clues arise that indicate the shared preferences they don't consciously know they have. When her fiancé ignores her, Sara runs from the scene and finds herself standing in front of an antique movie poster in Chinatown for a movie Jon told her he loved. Jon mindlessly reads a letter of consolation from his best friend after both giving up his search for Sara and breaking up with his fiancée. When he looks up from the letter, he is standing at Wollman Rink in Manhattan, where he had shared that one and only date with Sara ten years prior.

These actions were unconscious instinct on the part of the characters, yet their Cool Eyes told them there was greater significance to them. You might say that the reading of clues involves an inspiration of our entire selves—the instincts of the reptilian brain, the feelings of the mammalian brain, and the intellect of the higher brain. The serendipity of stories in our lives requires all three of our brains to come to life. Once we have collected clues to our joined story, it is time to be open to signs that direct us.

Signs

Just as some stories require us to collect enough clues or evidence of what is happening to us, some stories also require us to take action on what we find. This is the role of signs in following your serendipitous love story.

Sharing a moment with a man hardly creates an entire romance. What starts as a seductive wink from a gentleman may turn into the lewd groping of a jerk. What starts as an offer of assistance in picking up your dropped wallet may end up with that wallet racing down the sidewalk in the hand of a pickpocket who didn't even need to pick your pocket to get his prize.

Signs in your love story are like traffic signals. They tell your intuition that it is time to act or not act. Reading them requires a Cool Eye and the intuitive sense to know whether they are leading you toward the real Mr. Right or away from him into the hands of a boring, inappropriate, or even emotionally dangerous stranger.

Here's an example: As a man is about to drive you home from your first date, you see that he has a pile of traffic tickets on his passenger seat. He nervously moves to hide them under the backseat in hopes you didn't see them. You get a strange twinge. Your Cool Eye is turned on. You have a feeling that you should get out of the car, thank him, and walk the eight blocks home instead. Months later, you hear from a friend of a friend that he has been jailed for fraud. By following this sign, you saved yourself not only heartache, but the possible risk to your person at the hand of a man with no respect for the law.

Here's another: You are about to leave a restaurant when you notice the glimmer of a man's ring as he happily waves at his friends. He is tall, handsome, and genuine in his smile. You think the ring is on his left ring finger, maybe he's married, and that you aren't interested in being a home-wrecker. Yet something stops you. Your Cool Eye is turned on. You wheel around and grasp his hand. It is not a wedding band, but the family crest of neighbors you played with as a girl—the exotic family who'd moved to New Jersey from Spain, then moved on to parts unknown almost as suddenly as they'd arrived. He was the long-ago little boy whose name you can't remember but who'd already won your heart at age seven. This was a sign whose time to act was now.

In the *Serendipity* story, when Sara forgets her jacket at the very same ice rink of her first date with Jon, she receives a sign from her best friend who notes how cold it is outside and that she ought to put on a jacket—the one she had forgotten at that very magical spot in her story. Does she simply step into a store to buy a new one? Should she wait until morning to see if her jacket is still in Central Park? No. She immediately follows the sign to fetch it, unaware that Jon has already found it, and carries it around with him for no particular reason other than it feels right to do so.

When Jon is preparing for his wedding rehearsal dinner, his stylist calls in sick to be replaced by a woman named Sara. He acts, leaving abruptly, only to find that riding to the dinner in his cab, the radio is playing a song called "Sara." When he arrives, his fiancée gives him a gift that was actually once owned and inscribed by *his* Sara. Jon later calls off the wedding based on nothing other than these signs that his story is pleading with him to follow.

Ridiculous? Maybe. Yet virtually everyone can tell you of some moment when he or she followed a sign and benefited from it. They have avoided disasters, muggings, and financial ruin, and found riches, friends, and lifelong love just by reading serendipitous signs in life.

Letting Go

After years of fruitless searches for each other, Jon and Sara independently surrender to the sheer improbability of forcing a reunion with loves of unknown identity. In the very moment of this surrender, however, they each receive the last clues and signs to the exact identity and whereabouts of the other.

I was once invited to a wedding in Cabo San Lucas. A friend named Natalie had lost her mom to cancer only a month before, but her mom's last wishes were going to come true—Natalie's marriage to Matt, her love of two years. When asked, neither Matt nor Nat could explain why we had all flown two thousand miles to see their happy day, except that it "felt right." It was their favorite place to vacation, out far on the peninsula that is Baja Mexico.

As Matt and Nat exchanged vows on the beach at sunset, Johann Pachelbel's famous canon was played by a string quartet in the still air. There to witness the ceremony, I thought back on all of the failed romances of my life. As I did, I pondered what I would say on the mike when I toasted them at the reception.

As I listened to the music, I thought about how beautiful a canon is, a work structured as a simple melody played repeatedly in countless variations until it reaches a simple climax at the end. I thought it was the most beautiful sound I had ever heard, on the most beautiful beach, nearly surrounded by the warm waters of the Pacific. If only Natalie's mom had been there, everything would have been perfect.

After the vows and before the reception, I walked the beach alone for a while to find my words to them both. Slowly, like the crescendo of the canon, it came to me—the advice of a professor from long ago. This professor once told me that he had only seen one universal symbol in people's dreams: the symbol of water signifying "mother," the symbol of birth, femininity, creativity, and soothing, nurturing health. Matt and Nat had chosen to be married in a place nearly *surrounded* by water. I realized that in spirit, symbol, and story, Natalie's mom *had* been there as silent witness to her love and her joy. We had all unwittingly come to her, the water that surrounded us.

I wept at the unexpected story I had unwittingly joined, one of love triumphing over tragedy, of death and renewal, and peace that comes from acceptance of the stories of our lives. We all have lives that one day must end, and the stories of our relationships with them. Yet even in death, our stories go on through the children that naturally spring from our loves.

I had been through many relationships and dreaded the end of every one of them. I usually held on longer than was right for me, either because I wished that I could salvage something or simply out of guilt. Now, in finding a meaning for Natalie and Matt, I also had found a healing inspiration for myself.

When I heard the melody of Pachelbel's Canon in my mind, I realized one last thing about letting go of the story lines we do not control in life. Why was this canon—a baroque piece without a direct connection to matrimony—so loved and universally performed at weddings? Because it symbolized our stories in love. In our character, our identity, we play the same simple melody in everything we do in life. Yet because of the uniqueness of each new person we love, that melody sounds a bit different, a bit richer, louder, and clearer as we grow spiritually. It may be played ten times, twenty, thirty, or forty, and each time is the same and yet somehow new. Each relationship that ends begins the possibility of a new, richer, more mature one, just as each measure of a canon's music ends and begins with a new variation.

Our growth in love builds, person by person, only if we are willing to let go of the prior measure, the prior play of our same old melody in favor of the newer, richer one. If we let go, the music of our single lives ends on the right simple notes, at the right time, right place, and climax of the right story.

Destiny

Freud said, "Character is destiny." Our character carries with it a destiny that will no doubt result if we don't take conscious action to change. The criminal mind who doesn't change and grow will someday find himself in increasingly greater trouble. The passive woman who sits around and waits for her prince to come will wait until the day she dies. Yet the moment we begin a new way of life, a new decision, a move, a breakup, a new start, we give ourselves a new potential destiny. The simple act of courage leads to a new life. The simple act of assertiveness leads to everything we have ever wanted. Both lead to countless friendships that are the absolute requirement for the best sex of your life and the most reliable partnerships you will ever know. They are all rooted in that personal psychological style that psychoanalysts call character.

Stories also have a built-in destiny. In the story of *Serendipity*, we learn that love is not something that can be rigidly planned, ambitiously pursued, or logically directed. It can only be recognized, accepted, and acted upon when the time is right.

For all the futile struggles that Jon and Sara endured in their search for each other, they found that destiny calls to you every day and night. Only the Cool Eye turned on can see it, and only your imagination, intuition, and gut can hear it. Only your spirit can know it, and its rewards are yours for the taking. Jon and Sara found that active surrender is the only way to love.

In the director's commentary of *Serendipity*, Peter Chelsom says that in the scene before he finds his lost love, Jon has "laid himself completely open" to the universe. He has tried everything to find his lost love, failed, and now there is "nothing left to do." When in the pivotal scene, I heard Chelsom describe Jon as having a "terrific sense of abandon," the word "abandon" struck me deeply. It is a word of dual meanings. On the one hand, when one is abandoned, it is a sad and lonely experience. However, when one lives life *with abandon*, one feels freedom, joy, and openness to whatever comes next.

You must have both senses of abandon in order to find destiny. You must find yourself alone or leave someone alone with each ended relationship and yet be open to the next just as the measures of Pachelbel's Canon lead to marriage vows for countless couples.

Destiny is neither passive nor controlling. It is something that asks you to listen and to act when the time and feeling is right. There is a great deal of active waiting involved, and I hope the nine steps I have given you offer you the inspiration to continue to act intelligently even when it takes you longer to find Mr. Right than you'd like. You can't control your destiny, but you can make sure you are ready when destiny calls.

These steps are a way for you to recognize what is right for you and what is not, a way to see your destiny and steer yourself toward it more quickly and efficiently, not against the tides of the universe around you. These steps will give you the chance to join the story lived by every great lover since the beginning of time—from Cupid and Psyche to Jon and Sara—to someday tell your grandchildren how you "just knew."

Choose reckless abandon, and find yourself in a love story that has been always destined.

The Love Story You Have Been Waiting For

A perfect story is rarely perfectly smooth, easy, or uncomplicated, but it is perfect in its spirit, its lessons, and its satisfying climax nevertheless. Such was the love of Stacy and Michael.

Stacy was a student of life, addicted to learning about world cultures, fashion, and the beauty of great literature. She was a self-described "book snob," and yet one of the most courteous, gracious women of the world a man could be blessed with meeting. She had short brown hair, with bangs so meticulously shorn that she looked like the CEO of a cosmetics company, though much younger. Her eyes were blue and had the most unusual and exotic feature—large as pools of water, but tapered at the corners as if she had some Asian heritage. She looked like a mysterious, seductive cat when she smiled. She was Scottish by bloodline through her father and Welsh through her mother, the latter of which accounted for her high forehead, straight eyebrows, and dainty nose, all of which gave an ethereal beauty to the symmetry of her face.

Stacy also worked hard to maintain a good figure. She was five-eight, with the modest bustline and perfect hips of a Hollywood starlet. To Michael, she was "sex on a stick," and he wanted her the very moment he saw her breathe deeply, in between hanging new clothes on the window racks of the high-fashion boutique she worked in near his urban loft. He left his home to take a walk on a sunny Denver day, and on glancing in the store window, suddenly stopped in his place, surprising them both. Stacy did not look away, however, but rather smiled slightly. She was not afraid, but rather taken aback. Brief moments passed before Michael smiled back brightly and walked on.

Weeks later, Michael was enjoying the company of two male friends in a local Irish pub. As they caroused in the place that had become a Friday ritual, he glanced out to a series of thick wood columns that supported the ceiling and were arranged a bit like an indoor forest. There he saw drifting in and out of view the partial silhouette of a woman's arched back. When her hair partially peeked out at Michael's view, he rose from his seat slowly, walked around the columns like a lost traveler in the woods, until, circling the last pillar, he found himself, once again face-to-face with Stacy. This time there was no glass between them.

He asked her if she was a tourist or visitor to the town, even though he knew that didn't make sense. Stacy laughed it off and they started to speak.

Stacy had studied the classics and French literature at college and had lived in Paris afterward for an internship in fashion. Perhaps the City of Light seeped into her, giving her such an alluring spirit. Her father was a captain of business in Washington, and while Michael was a physician, he always dreamed of becoming an entrepreneur, making strides toward doing just that in the coming year. The tales Stacy told of how adventurous her dad had been in his youth and how accomplished he had become having risen from such limited means endeared her to Michael. He felt he had much to learn from her, and it didn't hurt that Michael noticed men constantly staring at Stacy. Stacy was a natural master of Steps One and Two of the Attraction Phase—displaying beauty and demonstrating the ability to raise the man's alpha-male status.

Stacy masterfully set Michael to a contest to win her sexually. She was beautiful, showed admiring interest in his ideas, and had quite the sarcastic wit to shake him off her trail when he lay the flirting on too thick. She talked on with him until it was very late and Michael's friends abandoned hope of capturing his attention. They simply waved their good-byes, acknowledging that Michael was wild with desire for Stacy.

Michael, too, had his share of culture, having sailed the world on the Semester-at-Sea program in college, which turned him into a travel addict. He regaled Stacy with stories of being lost in the Himalayas, chased by bandits in an Egyptian bazaar, and weathering a typhoon in the middle of the Indian Ocean. Her gaze was so fixed and determined that at times he could not tell if she had started to fancy him, or had held on to a lingering fear of him from his innocent, albeit clumsy dumbstruck appearance at her store. He was not the one to keep secrets, but rather prone to blurt out the most entertaining jokes and stories any of his friends had heard, and you might say that although Stacy likely knew every posture he took was an obvious overture to his growing lust for her, she actually liked this interesting, funny, accomplished man. They were opposites by temperament— Michael a balanced Lover, the storyteller of any group, the romantic to the bone, yet masculine, action-ready, and outgoing, too. Stacy was a mysterious territory to conquer, and a balanced Queen, Warrior, and Magician in one single delectable woman.

Outside it had snowed at midnight. The blanket of it so shrouded the streetlamps that it softened their walk home with an intimate, private light. In one evening Michael and Stacy had become friends, demonstrating unwitting and natural skill at Steps One through Six.

Stacy needed a cab when there was none to be found. The winter storms of Denver were not gentle on those who chose to carouse in a bar until closing time. Michael offered to let her wait in the warmth of his loft, just a block or two away, and she took him up on the offer after placing her call.

It was utterly silent.

Back in Michael's place, they stood there gazing in each other's eyes, waiting for the cab. There was an unexplainable force that moved them into each other's arms, like water spirals down a drain, or sand spills through the center of an hourglass. The distance between them narrowed naturally until their bodies pressed together. They whispered of things they'd planned for their lives in the future, and when one would begin a thought, the other would finish the sentence.

"I'd always thought I'd spend a—" she said.

"A few more years in Paris," he said. "It would be a dream."

"What are your dreams?" she said.

Michael thought a moment, then said, "Someday I'll stop seeing individual clients—"

"And teach huge audiences," she said.

"Yes," he said.

"What else do you want to know about me?" she said.

"Hmm. I love learning," he said. "I'm wondering what you like to read."

Stacy leaned to her purse, pulled out a book, and said, "This is my favorite book of all time. Gabriel García Márquez. *Love in the Time of Cholera.*"

"Never heard of it," he said.

She dropped it to the couch to hug him closer. "You can have my copy. I nearly know it by heart. It's about the pains of love that make the heights even higher. And it's the funniest story you've ever heard, too."

Michael and Stacy were sexually, emotionally, and intellectually attracted to each other, a story that had begun over weeks, but from moment one were each given that feeling of "just knowing," a rightness about the other. Like any red-blooded man in the arms of an irresistible woman, he wanted to have sex with her right there and then. The warm confines of a comfortable home that with the howling wind of the blizzard outside made it seem as if they were the only two people on earth. He whispered innuendoes, and she leaned in as if yes, she would like to. They were a sexual, emotional, and intellectual match.

Michael stroked the small of her back, gazed once more in her eyes, and kissed her.

When their eyes opened again, something was different. It was as though they could speak with their eyes, as if they could in a moment know the entire life story of the other.

Michael could not bring himself to seduce her (or be seduced by her). He did the gentlemanly thing and held her as they looked out the frosted window to see a silent yellow cab creep to a stop. Michael's whirling desire stopped, too. His Cool Eye turned on. He respected her, and didn't want to give in to sexual urges thoughtlessly. They had superb boundaries. They obviously shared some mutual life's goals and beliefs.

It was then that Michael's wisdom turned on. He realized that if he pressed for sex, Stacy would likely give in. They were as hot for each other in the moment as two soul mates snowed in on a magical late night could be. But they had only been together a short time. There had been no month or more of friendship and no chance for a slow exploration of stories to interweave and develop. Somehow, in his heart, he "just knew" that she was the one for whom he should set aside the chance for one night of lustful passion.

When they heard a distant honk, Stacy glanced up at him once more, looking for a clue to whether she should stay or go. He let her go and watched the street for a very long time after her cab disappeared in the city lights, sparkling in the relentless ongoing snowfall.

He settled into bed, pulled a paper and pen from the drawer, and memorialized the feeling he had never known before. After dating dozens of women, he had never felt this way.

Her eyes held fast on me—like no others, speckled green and blue, with a shape and soul all their own, passageways to anywhere in time that I have been or want to go in the future. It is a time in my life when nothing is established, and nothing permanent. I couldn't know as I looked in these eyes whether I would ever see her again, or whether this was something to last. But one thing is for certain—this was one of those kisses that would exist forever, if only in my memory.

Only then did Michael realize that, in the magic of their "moment," he'd made a horrible blunder: He didn't know how to contact Stacy. He knew her first name, but he had no number, and although he walked past her store many times, he would never see her there hanging new clothes again.

Michael moved on and had many satisfying dates, but he never lost the lingering nagging of his spirit, nor the strange and beautiful feeling in that kiss, those eyes, the ones that inexplicably held him back from wolfishly undressing her in a seductive night of passion. Somehow he knew that that one night would have been their only night together if he had.

What seemed like an eternity went by with no more chance encounters. When New Year's Eve came around, Michael wondered whether he ought to have made love to Stacy while he had the chance. Michael joined some friends at a party of hundreds, though he didn't have a date. He looked across the ballroom . . . and there she was. Forsaking his friends once again, he stealthily angled through the crowd, still with time before the stroke of midnight. When he reached her near the railing where she waited demurely, their eyes met again—a split second before another man came between them and kissed her deeply on the lips. The man then whisked her away. As she departed, Michael saw the diamond on the hand her fiancé held. Her eyes glanced at him once more, bearing a look of both longing and pity.

Not the type to lose it in public, Michael held back tears until he could dash outside. He let them burst out on the long walk home— a walk similar to the one he'd taken with her that night he came to know her as only soul mates can.

Many years would pass, and many adequate relationships would begin and end for Michael. He began to wonder whether wisdom had let him down. At first, he compared the women he dated to Stacy, but eventually he was able to go an entire season without thinking about her at all.

Then he saw the film *Serendipity* and it made him remember her. It didn't seem like a very good film at first, but the more he followed the characters, the more they so precisely resembled his night of a lifetime, the eyes, and the kiss.

A full-grown man doesn't yearn for a woman this way, he said to himself. *He just goes and gets another one.*

After all, he had become quite an accomplished lover and seducer. He'd read and reread Stacy's favorite book, stricken by the irony of the main character, a man who, in unrequited love, spends the next fifty years sleeping with every woman in sight to drown the pain of the one lost. Michael, too, had resolved to reverse the effect of his one mistake with Stacy, his failure to go for the sex in that short window when it was available.

He got to the part in the film where the two characters decide to test the fates, to send clues out into the world to see if they would lead them together again. John Cusack's Jon wrote his name and number on a five-dollar bill and put it into circulation. Kate Beckinsale's Sara wrote her number in the cover of a book in her purse to sell it the next morning to a used-book store. If either of them found the clues again, they would be able to call each other and consider themselves meant to be together.

The name of that book in the film was *Love in the Time of Cholera*.

It had been years since Michael had cried, but at this point, he did so as deeply as he had on that New Year's Eve so many years ago. It was late afternoon as he left the theater alone, walking in yet another winter toward his home. This time, though, he turned down the street where that old store was, where he first saw her. He rarely went near there anymore, but today he wanted to remember, to honor that feeling again. Michael had found satisfaction with everything in his life—rich friendships, many loves, a great career as a physician and amateur speaker. He loved himself just as he was. His tears were in quiet honor of a long-ago and beautiful moment, of being as alive as he could be.

He approached the window of the store and peered in—jumping in shock to find Stacy standing there once again. She was newly divorced, returned to the city, and the proud new owner of her very own high-fashion clothing store—that very same one where she was once an employee.

Stacy's eyes were the same, barely aged but for tiny crow's-feet of wisdom at the corners. Michael's hair had only a strand or two of gray.

He rushed in to see her.

They have not been apart since.

Stacy and Michael were, above all, constructive with each other, able to make a true commitment for life. Constructive behavior and a belief in the world as a place of abundance are natural outgrowths of mature, adult wisdom, the gifts of patience. They "just knew" all along, from the very first meeting, sensing all of the sexual attraction, friendship that would follow, and intellectual connection and chemistry.

Whatever may come in to confuse and make timing wrong does not matter when you are open to soul mates. In the end, your instincts of the reptilian brain and your character of the mammalian and higher brains determine the story of your life. This story leads you, feeds you, emboldens you, and protects you, until the time you are meant to find your life with Mr. Right. He is looking for you right now, just as the Michaels of the world are looking for their Stacys.

A story like this can be yours. In the end, Mr. Right cannot help but find you, and you find him, when you learn to read your story in the clues of life and dare to act on the moments of the plot that are calling you—for once and for all—to true love.